SECRETS TO
GOD

and

STRENGTHEN YOURSELF
IN THE LORD

Bill Johnson

Authentic

Secrets to Imitating God
First published in U.S.A. 2006 by Destiny Image Publishers, Inc.
P.O. Box 310, Shippensburg, PA 17257-0310
Strengthen Yourself in the Lord
First published in U.S.A. 2007 by Destiny Image Publishers, Inc.
P.O. Box 310, Shippensburg, PA 17257-0310

17 16 15 14 13 12 11   7 6 5 4 3 2 1

This edition first published 2011 by Authentic Media Limited
Presley Way, Crownhill, Milton Keynes, MK8 0ES
www.authenticmedia.co.uk

British Library Cataloguing in Publication Data

A catalogue record for this book is available from the
British Library

ISBN 978-1-85078-953-6

Cover design by David Smart
Printed and bound in the UK by Bell and Bain, Glasgow

Secrets to Imitating God

Secrets to Imitating God

How to Redesign Your World

BILL JOHNSON

Dedication

I dedicate this book to the "fathers" in my life. They lived unselfishly, seeing the best in me when I could see little of anything. They weren't always much older than me, but were always more mature and stable. I am forever indebted to them.

To my own dad, M. Earl Johnson. He lived at home as he did in the pulpit—honest, humble, visionary, devoted to his family, a man of character, great compassion, and lived life as a worshiper. He has gone home to be with Jesus, the lover of his soul. Thank you, dad! I am forever thankful for you.

To Chip Worthington. You taught me the value of the life of prayer and trained me to hunger for revival.

To Mario Murillo. You helped me to see that miracles are normal, revival is possible, and that being sold out to Jesus is the only acceptable way to live.

To Darol Blunt. You illustrated the life of grace, and helped me to discover the pleasure of the Lord over my life.

To Dick Joyce. Your commitment to me as a pastor of a small church in a small town established a standard of kingdom principles that I hope to never loose. You illustrated that the normal Christian life is a supernatural life.

To all of you, thank you. A million times, thank you.

Acknowledgments

My special thanks to Dann Farrelly, Carol Reginato, and Allison Armerding for your labor of love in editing my manuscript. This would have been near impossible without you.

To the whole Bethel Church family—you amaze me. Your tireless passion for God and your lifestyle of risk has helped to create the context for the greatest move of God I have ever witnessed. Together may we go to the next level!

Endorsements

Bill Johnson has an appetite for friendship with God, and all the mystery, revelation, power, and glory that comes with it. He can't bear to miss out. He contends for breakthrough, for the impossible, for all that only God can do. And in passion and worship he calls on God to allow us to experience what we thought was reserved only for the future. Bill is living in revival now, and it is a rare joy in this book to let him lead us to higher ground and increasingly taste the powers of the age to come.

Rolland Baker, Ph.D.
Heidi G. Baker, Ph.D.
Directors & Founders of Iris Ministries
Authors, *There's Always Enough*

Bill Johnson is a wonderful friend, a covenant brother, and a revivalist who is moving in extraordinary signs and wonders. He is also a mentor to me through his books and his revelatory teachings concerning the Kingdom of Heaven. I have no doubt that *Secrets to Imitating God* will change your life as his teachings have impacted countless thousands.

Dr. Che Ahn
Senior Pastor Harvest Rock, Pasadena, CA
Founder and President of Harvest International Ministries
Author, *Into the Fire* and *Faith that Heals*

If you have ever wondered what God's ultimate intention and purpose is all about, you'll clearly discover the answer in Bill Johnson's newest book, *Secrets to Imitating God*. When I read it I felt as if Bill was reading my thoughts and my yearnings. I felt like somebody finally had the guts to put these truths in printed form.

While Bill shares about the "tools" of the Kingdom trade as heirs of the Father, I believe this book is perhaps one of the greatest "tools" for accessing the riches of God's grace in the new millennium. When I think about Bill Johnson's life and ministry, one word emerges clear as crystal: Congruence. He embodies the quality and state of being in harmony both within and without. If you have ever heard any of his teachings, there is an ease of flow that is indicative of a life lived in harmony with the One who delights in intimacy with him. Take your time with each chapter and discover the secrets and the hidden mysteries of the indwelling Christ, apply your heart to wisdom, and dream big with God.

Mark J. Chironna, Ph.D.
Mark Chironna Ministries
The Master's Touch International Church
Orlando, Florida

Bill Johnson's latest book, *Secrets to Imitating God*, is written for Christian believers who are being "held in abeyance." It's not obeyance, it's abeyance. This is a military term describing the hand-picked soldiers a general trains for specialized activity, to win the war. The general keeps them on the sidelines and they are given special training that helps them achieve a readiness for the last battle. When the conflict reaches a certain stage that only the general recognizes, they are sent in fully prepared to win the war and carry it to finality.

While reading Bill's book I was impressed over and over again of his battle plan and how appropriate his explanations are for the final conflict between spiritual darkness and spiritual light. I believe this book is especially written for those of us now being held in abeyance. We're just waiting for our marching orders to get in and help wrap things up. You'll be spiritually challenged knowing you've been prepared for such a time as this.

Dick Mills
International Evangelist and Conference Speaker
Author, *The Spirit-Filled Believer's Daily Devotional*
and *Marriage Bliss*

Bill Johnson has made a major contribution in his latest book, *Secrets to Imitating God*. It is a brilliant sequel to his previous two books.

The history of this era will record the awesome impact of Bill's thinking and writing. He has given us a report on the Kingdom of God, but that is not all. It is a report that is credible, balanced, authoritative, and laboratory proved. What is happening in Bethel Church in particular and Redding, California, in general, is confirming indeed. Add to this the fact that Bill is found dashing around the planet simply sharing the story and seeing the results of Kingdom preaching, and you have irrefutable evidence of the value of the message.

I asked Bill a few months ago, "What has the fact that you have been preaching the Kingdom message for 18 years have to do with what is happening right now in Bethel Church and Redding, California?" His immediate and terse answer was, simply, "Everything!"

Jack Taylor
Founder of Dimensions Ministries
Author of *The Word of God With Power*

For the seeker, this book is a discovery of truths that will challenge the way you think and affect the way you live. It will require several readings to contain and apply the revelation found on every page. For me personally, it brought clarity to unspoken questions, practical understanding of my own desires and purpose, and passionate increase of love for my Father.

Karen Wheaton
Founder, The Ramp Youth Ministries
Recording Artist and TBN TV Host

Once again my friend, Bill Johnson, demonstrates a clarion call to bring Heaven down to earth. The content of this book is thought-provoking, inspiring, and most of all a clear challenge for Christians desiring to recapture their inheritance in God. Be advised: once you have read this book you will no longer be satisfied with the ordinary. Bill's passion to see the Kingdom of God established in our lives is highly contagious and will stir your appetite for extraordinary encounters with a supernatural God. Refreshing and real, this book will revolutionize your thinking.

Larry Randolph
International Conference Speaker
Author, *User Friendly Prophecy* and *Spirit Talk*

Writer Victor Hugo said, "There is nothing more powerful than an idea whose time has come." The truth is there is one thing more powerful, a God idea whose time has come. *Secrets to Imitating God* is that idea.

Do you wish to live large in Christ in the greatest revival in history? Did you know you could be purpose-driven, talent-laden, and Spirit-powered? Did you know that the Church's destiny is not to impress the world by imitating the world? God has called us to overwhelm the world with original music, inventions, art, and miracles! Not only can we know God and worship God, we can *dream* with Him. This book shows you how to make those dreams a reality.

Original expression is virtually unlimited and as unique as every person God has created. Bill exposes the traditions that have limited

God and devastated our progress. Now we know why there have been so many casualties in spiritual warfare. We sent in only the preachers and told the rest of God's army to cheer us on from the sidelines as tithers.

This book hands out weapons to all the Christians. The arts, business, science, education, politics, and even the media are no longer a safe haven against a new breed of believer.

The common Christian can morph into a fountainhead of excellence, originality, and skills that will overwhelm this present darkness.

Mario Murillo, Evangelist
Founder, Mario Murillo Ministries
Author, *Critical Mass* and *I'm the Christian the Devil Warned You About*

Bill Johnson has captured one of the most important concepts in human development—how to dream the will of God. His inspiring and insightful presentation of the concept of "desire" and its role in human activity, creativity, wisdom, and personal fulfillment is guaranteed to provide answers to the deep questions of the human heart. I highly recommend this book and hope everyone will read it.

Dr. Myles Munroe
MMI - International
Nassau, Bahamas

Bill Johnson extends to us vital keys that will unlock the latent creativity residing in everyone who is willing to open their hands and take hold of the Kingdom purpose. Every chapter will take you through new thresholds leading you to greater appreciation of the uniqueness of your gifting.

Randall Worley
Founder, Headwaters Ministries
Apostolic Consultant and Conference Speaker

Bill Johnson's newest book, *Secrets to Imitating God*, is great. Great because he has said things others were afraid to say because the statements were so contrary to traditional ways of interpreting Scripture or the traditional opinions of evangelical scholars.

Bill has written a book that is based in grace not law. It is about enjoying God as He enjoys us—not about performing for God. The author gets us to look at earth from Heaven's perspective, and to look at the Bible from a first-century perspective, instead of a 16th-century perspective. I doubt if anyone can read this without having to stop and think through the implications of its statements. *Secrets to Imitating God* does not look at difficulties, challenges, or problems from earth's limitations, but from Heaven's unlimited power. This is not a book for the timid, the doubters, or those who want Christianity to be reduced to a mere moral philosophy. It is a book for those who desire the supernatural aspect of their Christian faith that is consistent with the Christianity of the Bible and the Christianity of the history of the Church that is full of the supernatural exploits of those who believe in Christ.

Randy Clark
Global Awakening Ministries
Author, *God Can Use Little ol' Me* and *There's More*

The *passion-driven worshiper* will always accomplish more than the *purpose-driven worker*. The first is motivated through friendship and intimacy, the latter through fear and responsibility. The Ephesian church was filled with those who persevered and toiled but had left their first love. Paul, on the other hand, commends those in Thessalonica for their labor of love.

Bill Johnson challenges us to rethink our priorities, thereby becoming *passionate partners* rather than *persevering producers*. After all it is those who *know* their God who will be strong and do exploits.

David Ravenhill
Author, *The Jesus Letters*
Lindale, Texas

I always cry when I read Bill Johnson's books. I cry because I am provoked to desire that has no language but tears. It's as if I am on the threshold of a kingdom that my spirit longs for and there is suddenly language and definition to concepts that have hitherto only rattled around in my spirit. As I read *Secrets to Imitating God*, my spirit echoed the final words of the book: "The thought of missing something that could have been the experience of my generation is pure torture. I can't possibly sleep in this atmosphere, because if I do, I know I'll miss the reason for which I was born." *Secrets to Imitating God* inspires me to live with God more deeply.

Stacey Campbell
Cofounder, Be A Hero
Coproducer and Coauthor, *Praying the Bible*

In Bill Johnson's book, *Secrets to Imitating God*, Bill outdoes himself—as usual. In this new brilliant work, we're told that David, of the Bible, set a new "high water mark." But then, so does Bill Johnson. He tells us God is saying to each of us, "The Temple wasn't my idea. David was my idea." If you are, as this work states, one of those who feel "discouraged because their dreams have failed...," please know that Bill has written this book for *you*—because *you are God's idea*! And if that isn't good news, as they say, "it'll do until good news comes along!"

Steve Shultz
THE ELIJAH LIST
Founder, *The Voice of the Prophetic* magazine

The inspired Psalmist said, "the path of the just shines brighter till the perfect day." When the Church breaks through to new revelation, the whole world gets enlightened. The Reformation produced the Renaissance, and 90 percent of the world's inventions have been created since Azuza Street broke loose in 1906. As the Prophetic movement gathered momentum in the 1980s, another power surge occurred and knowledge began to double every seven years! Apostles are now bringing us into a rendezvous with "the perfect day" as men like Bill Johnson forge a path of revelation that is brighter with each book. As the world creeps into deeper darkness, torchbearers like Bill Johnson open portals to release the knowledge of the glory in language so tangible and accessible it can't help but inspire end-time exploits. It certainly inspires me!

Lance Wallnau
President, Lancelearning Group
International Conference Speaker

Contents

Foreword 19

Introduction. 21

Chapter 1   Co-laboring With God. 23

Chapter 2   The Creative Edge 37

Chapter 3   The Value of Mystery. 55

Chapter 4   The Language of the Spirit. 67

Chapter 5   Invading Babylon. 87

Chapter 6   The Practical Side of Things 111

Chapter 7   The Spirit of Revelation. 125

Chapter 8   Celebrating the Living Word 139

Chapter 9   Redesigning Our World. 157

Chapter 10   Pulling Tomorrow Into Today 169

Resources. 185

Foreword

Did you know that the stars speak?

They did in Abraham's day! The Creator of the universe gave a direct and amazing word to one of His friends. He told him to go out and count the number of stars that lit up the sky at night. Imagine, counting the stars at night!

So what did Abraham do? He went out and started counting the stars! I suppose it was something like this. Abraham goes out in the evening air after telling his wife, Sarah, good night and goes on a long walk pondering and peering into the heavens. He begins in obedience to count the stars while talking to himself and God. "One, two, four, twenty-seven, forty-five, one hundred fifty-five, two thousand sixty-two, ugh, ugh, ugh…Wow, count the stars?! What do you mean, I cannot count the number of stars—they seem so limitless."

The Lord replied, "Abraham—count the stars." Perplexed a bit as he attempts to mentally perceive what the man upstairs could mean by this strange command, Abraham continues in his quest to follow the direction of the unseen voice. "Three thousand seven hundred and…oh, I forgot—where was I?"

The voice is heard again, but this time offering some inside explanation. "The number of the stars will be the number of your descendants." "What, huh? Did you know that Sarah and I have been married for a long time and we don't have any fruit, let alone…?" But the voice of the Master persisted, "Count the stars. How many are there?"

Yes, the stars spoke to Abraham. Perhaps for a while, the voice of the stars haunted him as he would go out night after night staring into the realm of the impossible. But somewhere along the way, something changed. Did the circumstances change? No, well, not yet at least. What changed then? Abraham, like the rest of us, went from mentally assessing to heart believing.

Somehow God's dream seeped into Abraham's heart. After many trials and tests and errors, Abraham reached a point when he went out at night and he rejoiced when he looked up! "Yes, there's a promise! Yes, that one is for me! That star is declaring that God's Word will come true! In fact, that glimmering light right there is saying to me, the promises of God are 'Yes and Amen'!"

Yes, the stars do speak.

You know the rest of the story. It is a true-to-life piece of history that has effected us all. You see, God is a dreamer and He is looking for people who will dream His dreams with Him.

In every generation, dreamers arise. They think outside of man-made boxes and dare to forge ahead. But today a new breed of dreamers is arising. They not only talk of things to come—they call it into being in the here and now. They live their dreams.

Thus, I have the great pleasure and honor of introducing you to a man and a message. The man is Bill Johnson. His message is a dream for sure! It is with utmost esteem that I present to you an example of when a man and his message are one.

Behold, here comes another dreamer! Will you join the growing throng?

Yes, the stars continue to speak!

Wasted On Jesus,
James W. Goll
Cofounder of Encounters Network
Author, *The Lost Art of Intercession*, *The Seer*, and *Dream Language*

Introduction

I write that His Church would rise to her potential and change the course of world history. We do not have an inferior message. It is the only one that can be demonstrated through the transformation of a life, family, and city. *Secrets to Imitating God* is written in response to the cries of the devoted, but unfulfilled. It is to give true believers permission to dream, knowing that God longs for us to partner with Him in manifesting the divine plan.

Dreaming With God was the title of a chapter in my book, *The Supernatural Power of a Transformed Mind*. Don Milam, of Destiny Image Publishing, felt it deserved more attention than I was able to give it in one chapter. I agree, and have attempted to expand it in the following pages. Thank you, Don, for the encouragement.

Chapter 1

Co-laboring With God

*God has made Himself vulnerable
to the desires of His people.*

The disciples lived in awe of this One who called them to leave everything and follow. It was an easy choice. When He spoke, something came alive in them that they never knew existed. There was something in His voice that was worth living for—worth giving one's life for.

Everyday with Jesus was filled with a constant barrage of things they could not understand; whether it was a demoniac falling at Jesus' feet in worship, or the overbearing, religious leaders becoming silent in His presence; it was all overwhelming. Their lives had taken on a meaning and purpose that made everything else disappointing at best. Oh, they had their personal issues, for sure, but they had been apprehended by God and now nothing else mattered.

The momentum of the lifestyle they experienced would be hard for us to comprehend. Every word, every action seemed to have eternal significance. It must have occurred to them that to serve in the courts of this King would be far better than living in their own palaces. They were experiencing firsthand what David felt when he lived with God's presence as his priority.

THE ULTIMATE TRANSITION

Toward the end of His earthly life, Jesus gave His disciples the ultimate promotion. He told the twelve that He no longer called them servants, but friends. To be in the same room with Him, or even to admire Him from a distance, was more than they could have asked for. But Jesus brought them into His life. They had proven themselves worthy of the greatest promotion ever experienced by humanity—from servants to intimates. Perhaps only Esther of old could really understand what that exaltation felt like, as she, a servant girl who descended from captives, was promoted to queen. *"No longer do I call you servants, for a servant does not know what his master is doing; but I have called you friends, for all things that I heard from My Father I have made known to you"* (John 15:15). With this promotion, the disciples' attention would now shift from the task at hand to the One within reach. They were given access to the secrets in the heart of God.

When Jesus gave His disciples this promotion, He did so by describing the difference between the two positions. Servants don't know what their master is doing. They don't have access to the personal, intimate realm of their master. They are task-oriented. Obedience is their primary focus—and rightly so, for their lives depend on success in that area. But friends have a different focus. It almost sounds blasphemous to say that obedience is not the top concern for the friend, but it is true. Obedience will always be important, as the previous verse highlights, *"You are my friends if you do whatever I command you"* (John 15:14). But friends are less concerned about disobeying than they are about disappointing. The disciples' focus shifted from the commandments to the presence, from the assignment to the relationship, from "what I do for Him" to "how my choices affect Him." This bestowal of friendship made the revolution we continue to experience possible.

TRANSFORMED THROUGH PROMOTION

Several paradigm shifts take place in our hearts as we embrace this promotion. First, *what we know* changes, as we gain access to the heart of the Father. His heart is the greatest resource of information we need to function successfully in all of life. Jesus paid the price of our access to the Father, thereby granting us the *freedom* that comes from the truth we gain through that unlimited knowledge of His heart. Liberty is found in this phase of the promotion.

Second, our *experience* changes. Encounters with God as an intimate are quite different from those of a servant. His heartbeat becomes our heartbeat as we celebrate the shift in our own desires. The realm of His presence becomes our greatest inheritance, and divine encounters our greatest memories. Personal transformation is the only possible result from these supernatural experiences.

Third, our *function* in life radically changes. Instead of working *for* Him, we work *with* Him. We work not *for* His favor but *from* His favor. In this position He entrusts us with more of His power, and we are naturally changed into His likeness more and more.

Fourth, our *identity* is radically transformed. Our identity sets the tone for all we do and become. Christians who live out of who they really are cannot be crippled by the opinions of others. They don't work to fit into other people's expectations, but burn with the realization of who the Father says they are.

A SHIFT IN FOCUS

The classic example of the difference between servants and friends is found in the story of Mary and Martha. Mary chose to sit at Jesus' feet while Martha chose to work in the kitchen (see Luke 10:38-42).

Mary sought to please Him by being with Him while Martha tried to please Him through service. When Martha became jealous, she asked Jesus to tell Mary to help in the kitchen. Most servants want to degrade the role of the friend to feel justified in their works-oriented approach to God. Jesus' response is important to remember: "*Mary has chosen the better part.*" Martha was making sandwiches that Jesus never ordered. Doing more for God is the method servants use to increase in favor. A friend has a different focus entirely. They enjoy the favor they have and use it to spend time with their friend.

To say we need both Marys and Marthas is to miss the point entirely. And it simply isn't true. I've heard it said that nothing would ever get done if we didn't have Marthas. That, too, is a lie. That teaching comes mostly from servants who are intimidated by the lifestyle of friends. Mary wasn't a non-worker; she just learned to serve from His presence, only making the sandwiches that Jesus ordered. Working *from* His presence is better than working *for* His presence. Pastor Mike Bickle put it best when he said that *there are lovers and there are workers. And lovers get more work done than do workers!* A passionate lover will always outperform a good servant in pleasing Him.

THE WILL OF GOD

We usually think of the will of God as something static—fixed and unchangeable. We primarily associate it with specific events at certain times. The element missing in our understanding of this subject is our role in the unfolding of His will.

When God was going to destroy Israel, He told Moses to get out of the way, because He was going to kill the people that Moses had led out of Egypt into the wilderness. Moses then reminded God that they weren't his people—they were God's, and not only that, he didn't lead them out of Egypt, God did! God responded by basically acknowledging he was right, and then promised not to kill them.

The astonishing thing isn't so much that God changed His mind and spared Israel; rather, it was that He expected Moses to come into the counsel of His will, and Moses knew it. Abraham was another who understood this. These covenant friends throughout history all seemed to have a common awareness of God's expectation that they be involved in the demonstration of His will, influencing the outcome of a matter. They understood that the responsibility rested on their shoulders, and they must act before God to get what people needed. The priestly role of an intercessor was never more clearly illustrated. The primary focus of His will wasn't whether or not to destroy Israel; it was to bring Moses in on the process. His will is not always focused on events; it is focused on His friends drawing near into His presence, standing in their roles as delegated ones. The will of God is as much process as it is outcome—often fluid, not static.

THE BLANK CHECK

As kids, many of us dreamed about being granted one wish. Solomon got the "one wish." When God appeared to Solomon and gave him that opportunity, it forever raised the bar of our expectations in prayer. The disciples were given the same "wish," only better. Instead of one blank check, they were given an unlimited supply of blank checks. And this gift was specifically granted in the context of their friendship with God.

Surrounding their promotion to friendship, Jesus gave His disciples this amazing list of promises. Each promise was a blank check they were to live by and use throughout their lives for the expansion of the Kingdom. They are as follows:

> *If you abide in Me, and My words abide in you, you will **ask what you desire**, and it shall be done for you* (John 15:7).

> *You did not choose Me, but I chose you and appointed you that you should go and bear fruit, and that your fruit should*

*remain, that **whatever you ask** the Father in My name He may give you* (John 15:16).

*If **you ask anything** in My name, I will do it* (John 14:14).

*And in that day you will ask Me nothing. Most assuredly, I say to you, **whatever you ask the Father** in My name He will give you. Until now you have asked nothing in My name. **Ask, and you will receive**, that your joy may be full* (John 16:23-24).

For us to properly receive what Jesus has offered us in these verses, any robotic understanding of what it means to be a follower of God has to change. God never intended that the believer be a puppet on a string. God actually makes Himself vulnerable to the desires of His people. In fact, it can be said, "if it matters to you, it matters to Him."

While much of the Church is waiting for the next word from God, He is waiting to hear the dream of His people. He longs for us to take our role, not because He needs us, but because He loves us.

Family Reunion

My mother's side of the family had a family reunion in the early '90s. Around 160 people came from all over the world to the campground we rented in northern California. Astonishingly, they represented 48 different pastors and missionaries.

It had to be one of the most highly unusual reunions on record because of the extraordinary number of ministers involved. But it was even more unique because it was so much like a formal conference. There were meetings, panel discussions, and the like. I was even asked to write a song for the event, taken from the Old Testament Book of Zephaniah. It was a great time of celebrating the grace of God upon our family.

On one of the evenings, someone had scheduled a square dance as a recreational activity. Now, I don't dance, except in worship. It doesn't matter to me if it's square dancing, or if it's on some night-club dance floor, I simply don't dance. I find it to be an embarrass-ing activity. In junior high, I got out of square dancing by telling the teacher that my church didn't believe in it (which was partially true). And here at this reunion, this embarrassing behavior was scheduled as a family activity. Wonderful!

When Beni, my wife, asked what I was going to do, I told her emphatically: "I don't dance!" She already knew my thoughts and wisely chose to not attempt the impossible, which was to talk me out of such an idea so that I could join in the family fun. (One of the strengths of my personal makeup is that I don't change my mind eas-ily. It doesn't matter who is challenging my position. I just don't move. One of the weaknesses of my personal makeup is that I don't change my mind easily.)

We went to the hall where the party was in full swing, as entire families were attempting to dance together. It was fun to watch. It was also obvious which families actually knew what they were doing, and which ones didn't. We laughed and watched as people stepped on each other's feet, awkwardly attempting to learn such difficult moves so quickly. Then the unexpected happened. My daughter, Leah, then about 10 years old, asked me if I would dance with her.

I am known for being unmovable. Some family members call it stubborn; I call it commitment. Yet in that moment I felt like I had been ambushed. My feet were solid, my resolve firm, and my argu-ment was steadfast. But daughters, especially 10-year-old daughters, have a way of getting in under the radar. To my horror, I found myself without a will saying, "Yes." Where was my toughness? What about my resolve? Where did my gift of stubbornness go when I needed it most? To this day I don't know. I had been "brought to my knees" by a little girl. Moments later I was on the dance floor, attempting what I knew better than to attempt. But the look in my little girl's eyes told me all was well. Her pleasure more than made up for my embarrassment. And I understood again how fathers willingly make themselves vulnerable to the desires of their children—and how God joyfully makes Himself vulnerable to the desires of His people.

God's Sovereignty

There is no question that spending time with God changes our desires. We always become like the one we worship. But it's not because we've been programmed to wish for the things He wants us to wish for; it's because in friendship we discover the things that please Him—the secret things of His heart. It is the instinct of the true believer to search for and find that which brings pleasure to the Father. Our nature actually changes at conversion. It is our new nature to seek to know God and to please Him with our thoughts, ambitions, and desires.

Those who have the greatest difficulty with this line of thinking are those who consider this to be an assault on the doctrine of the sovereignty of God. There is no question; God is sovereign. But His position of rulership is not denied by our assignment to co-labor with Christ. One of my favorite quotes on this subject comes from my dear friend Jack Taylor. He says, *"God is so secure in His sovereignty that He is not afraid to appear un-sovereign."*

All Desire Has a Father

A good way to remember the intent of the word *desire*[1] is to break it down by syllables. "De" means "of." And "sire" means "father." All desire is "of the father." The question should not be, "are my desires from God?" The question should be, "With what, or with whom have I been in communion?"[2] I can commune with God or with the enemy. If I take time to ponder an offense I experienced some years ago, and I begin to wonder if God ever judged that person, the desires of vindication and retaliation will stir up in my heart.

Why? Because I have been fellowshipping with the *father* of bitterness, and those desires are the *children* formed in my heart.

If fellowshipping with evil can produce evil desires in us, how much more should it be said that time with God forms desires in us that have eternity in mind and ultimately bring Him glory? The thing to note is this: these desires are not there by command; they are in our hearts because of our fellowship with God. They are the offspring of our relationship with Him.

The main purpose of this book is to teach and encourage believers to live from the desires that are born in them through their intimate fellowship with the Lord. Many believers discount their desires, automatically trying to get rid of everything they want in order to prove their surrender to God. Their selfless approach overshoots the will of God and actually denies the fact that God is the Father of the dreams and abilities within them. It sounds good on the outside because of its selfless religious appeal, but it works against God's purposes on the inside. Most still don't see the difference between the entrance *to* the Kingdom, and life *in* the Kingdom. We enter on a straight and narrow road, saying, *"Not my will but Yours be done."* The only door is Christ Jesus. The only way to find life in Christ is to come in complete abandonment to Him.

But life in the Kingdom, which is past the narrow entrance of salvation, is completely different. It's bigger on the inside than it is on the outside. It is here we find the Lord saying to us that we're no longer servants, but friends. It's in that context He says that the Father will give us whatever we want. The emphasis is on *what you want*. Granted, we can't forget the context, or we'll just create more selfish people who confess Christ. Just as the Cross precedes the resurrection, so our abandonment to *His will* precedes God attending to *ours*. But the opposite emphasis also has dangers—if we never become people of desire, we will never accurately and effectively represent Christ on the earth.

THE TREE OF LIFE

"...*desire fulfilled is a tree of life*" (Proverbs 13:12 NASB). Solomon gave us this amazing statement. If there was anyone qualified to discuss *fulfilled personal desires* it was Solomon. In Second Chronicles 7:11, it says, "*Solomon successfully accomplished all that came into his heart....*" We can't allow his disobedience later in life to deter us from the profound lessons learned through his obedience early in life. He experienced the power of having his heartfelt desires accomplished.

Solomon's words revisit the subject of the tree of life found in Genesis. It connected Adam and Eve to eternity. (After eating the forbidden fruit, the angel of the Lord guarded the way to the tree of life so that Adam and Eve could not eat its fruit; it made eternal whatever it touched. It would make their sinful condition permanent—an eternal, unredeemable state.) Here we are told that a believer will experience the tree of life as their desires are fulfilled. This implies that those who taste the wonder of fulfilled desires in Christ will be given eternal perspective and identity through that fulfillment. The process of surrender, personal transformation, and fulfilled desires is the training ground for reigning with Christ forever.

In John 16:24, it says that God wants to answer our desires (prayers), "...*that your joy may be full.*" No wonder there's been so little joy in the church. Joy is the result of our redeemed heart reveling in its participation in God's unfolding plan for the earth through prayer. More specifically, joy comes through having our prayers answered.

Answered prayers, especially those that require supernatural intervention, make us happy! And happy people are fun to be with. Perhaps that's why Jesus was called the friend of sinners (see Luke 7:34). His joy exceeded all those around Him. Moment by moment, day after day, He saw His prayers answered by His heavenly Father. His joy was what many would consider extreme. In Luke 10:21, it says, "*Jesus rejoiced in the Spirit.*" The word *rejoiced* in that context suggests "shouting and leaping with joy."[3] Even proximity to Jesus brought joy. John the Baptist leapt for joy in his mother's womb because Mary, who was pregnant with Jesus, entered the room. Jesus' joy is contagious, and must become the mark of true believers once again.

David Sets a New "High Water Mark"

An extraordinary example of fulfilled dreams is illustrated in Solomon's building of a temple that his father, David, had planned. The building and consecration of Solomon's temple is one of the most significant events in the Bible. Yet at the temple's dedication, Solomon said,

> Blessed be the Lord God of Israel, who spoke with His mouth to my father David, and with His hand has fulfilled it, saying, 'Since the day that I brought My people Israel out of Egypt, I have chosen no city from any tribe of Israel in which to build a house, that My name might be there; but I chose David to be over My people Israel.' Now it was in the heart of my father David to build a temple for the name of the Lord God of Israel (1 Kings 8:15-17).

God said that He didn't choose a city, He chose a man, and the idea for a temple was in the heart of the man. God basically said: The temple wasn't my idea. *David* was my idea. Incredible! David's creativity and desires helped write history because God embraced them. David gave us many Kingdom principles, which set the direction in which we are to live. It is as if he said, "Dreamers! Come! Let's dream together and write the story of human history." You are God's idea, and He longs to see the treasure that is in your heart. As we learn to dream with God we become co-laborers with Him.

Adam—The First Co-laborer

God assigned Adam the task of naming all the animals (see Gen. 2:19). Names had much richer meaning in those days because they represented the nature of something. I believe that Adam was actually assigning to each animal its nature, its realm of authority, and the dimension of glory it would enjoy. In reality, Adam's assignment was to help define the nature of the world he was to live in. This co-laboring role was a creative role, complimentary to God the Creator. God brings us into these situations, not because He can't do it Himself. He delights in seeing all that He made come into its identity in Him by embracing its divine purpose. To embrace the privilege of creative expression is consistent with being made in the image and likeness of our Creator.

The Tool That Shapes History

The King James Bible highlights the role of our desires in the way it translates Mark 11:24, "*Therefore I say unto you, what things soever ye desire, when ye pray, believe that ye receive them, and ye shall have them.*" We are to pay attention to our desires *while we're enjoying the presence of God in prayer.* Something happens in our time of communion with Him that brings life to our capacity to dream and desire. Our minds become renewed through divine encounter, making it the perfect canvas for Him to paint on. We become co-laborers with Him in the master plan for planet earth. Our dreams are not independent from God, but instead exist *because of* God. He lays out the agenda—*On earth as it is in Heaven*—and then releases us to run with it and make it happen! As we grow in intimacy with Him, more of what happens in life is a result of our desires, not simply receiving and obeying specific commands from Heaven. God loves to build on our wishes and desires, as He embraced David's desire for the temple.

This truth is risky from our perspective because we see those who live independent of God and only want Him to validate their dreams. True grace always creates a place for those with evil in their heart to come to the surface through increased opportunity. But the richness of this truth is worth pursuing in spite of the perceived danger, because only this truth enables the Church to come fully into her destiny through co-laboring with the Lord.

This divine destiny was announced by the Psalmist long before the blood of Jesus made it a possible lifestyle. *"Delight yourself also in the Lord, and He shall give you the desires of your heart"* (Psalms 37:4).

DREAMERS WELCOME HERE

We were born to create, to build, and to advance. This requires an ongoing display of supernatural wisdom to succeed. Wisdom, and its unique expression, is the focus of the next chapter.

ENDNOTES

1. While this is not the etymological breakdown of the word, it does convey the principle represented by the word.
2. Quotes from Lance Wallnau.
3. Footnote in the Spirit-Filled Life Bible.

CHAPTER 2

The Creative Edge

*When unbelievers lead the way in inventions
and artistic expression, it is because the
church has embraced a false kind of spirituality.*

One of the most natural parts of being created in the image of God is the ability to dream. It's a God-given gift. Yet many believers, in their attempts to please God, kill the very capacity He gave them. They reason, "To really please God I must get rid of everything to do with self!" It sounds spiritual to many, but it's more Buddhist than Christian. If we pursue that line of thinking for long we end up with neutered believers. Self-mutilation need not be physical to be a perversion. Anytime we try to cut away at what God placed in us, we are entering a form of spirituality that the Scriptures do not support, and are contributing to a spirit that works against us having a truly effective witness. It is not wise to crucify the resurrected man and call it discipleship. The Cross is not for the new man; it's for the old man (Romans 6:5-9).

Many have even prayed, "None of me, all of You." God had none of us before we were born and didn't like it. He created us for His pleasure. A better prayer would be, "All of me covered by all of

You!" Even John the Baptist's statement, "He must increase but I must decrease" is often misapplied in order to endorse the self-depreciating form of Christianity. Look at the context; he was passing the baton to Jesus. His job was to prepare the way for the Messiah. It was important for him to be out of the way, as he closed out the Old Testament prophetic ministry. Jesus would bring about the fulfillment of all the prophets had announced and initiate God's manifest dominion on the planet. John the Baptist passed the baton to Jesus, who has passed it on to us *that we might increase.*

This confusion over our value and identity is sometimes most acute in revival, as the outpouring of the Spirit always brings an increased awareness of our sinfulness. Some of the greatest hymns of confession and contrition have been written during such seasons. But the revelation of our sin and unworthiness is only half of the equation. Most revivals don't get past this one point, and therefore cannot sustain a move of God until it becomes a lifestyle. It's difficult to build something substantial on a negative. The other half of the equation is how *holy* He is on our behalf and who we are as a result. When this is realized, our identity changes as we embrace the purpose of our salvation by faith. At some point we must go beyond being simply "sinners saved by grace." As we learn to live from our position in Christ, we will bring forth the greatest exploits of all time.

Throughout much of church history people have been stripped of their God-given gifts, talents, and desires, under the guise of *devotion to Christ.* This stripped-down version of Christianity removes the believer from ministry, and relegates that privilege to a certain class of Christian called "ministers." The regular believer's role is reduced to financial and emotional support of those in public ministry. To work without fulfilled dreams and desires is to partner with the religious spirit that exalts routine without purpose, and calls it suffering. The honor of giving to promote ministry must not be devalued, but its emphasis should never be at the expense of each individual carrying their own creative expression of the Gospel through realizing their God-given dreams and desires.

LIKE FATHER, LIKE SON AND DAUGHTER

Our heavenly Father is the Creator of all, and the Giver of all good gifts. His children should bear His likeness, which means they should be creative. When unbelievers lead the way in inventions and artistic expressions, it is because the church has embraced a false kind of spirituality. It is not living in a true Kingdom mentality, which is the renewed mind.[1] The renewed mind understands that the King's dominion must be realized in all levels of society for an effective witness to take place. Someone with a Kingdom mind-set looks to the overwhelming needs of the world and says, "God has a solution for this problem. And I have legal access to His realm of mystery. Therefore I will seek Him for the answer!" With a Kingdom perspective, we become the answer in much the same way Joseph and Daniel were to the kings of their day.

To be free to dream with God, one must learn to be a co-laborer. The desire of the true believer is never independence from God. The goal is not to find ways to shape God's thinking, as though He were in need of our input. Instead it is to represent Him well. Learning to display His heart instinctively and accurately is the passion of true lovers of God. His heart is to redeem all people, and the tools He uses to display His goodness are gloriously vast, reaching into the heartfelt needs of every individual. Only divine wisdom can meet that challenge.

Learning the dreams of God for this world is our beginning place. Dreaming can be expensive. We know that the Father's dream of redeeming humanity cost Him the life of His Son. However, partnering with Him in His dreams will release in us a new capacity to dream like Him.

WISDOM CREATES

Wisdom and creativity are related subjects in the Bible. In fact, creativity is a manifestation of wisdom in the context of excellence and integrity. Wisdom is personified in Proverbs 8, and is the companion of God at the creation of all things. Therefore wisdom and creativity must not be separated in the mind of the believer. They are the essential tools needed to complete our assignment of being an effective witness to the lost. It is wisdom that makes our role in this world desirable to them. While most Christians have a value for wisdom, most do not have an equal value for the role of creativity in their God-given responsibilities. Yet it is creativity that illustrates the presence of wisdom: *"Wisdom is vindicated by all her children"* (Luke 7:35 NASB).

The six days of creation saw the most wonderful display of wisdom and art imaginable. As God spoke, the worlds were made. Light and beauty, sound and color, all flowed together seamlessly as wisdom set the boundaries for creation itself. Solomon, the man known for supernatural wisdom, discusses the co-laboring effect that wisdom had on that day:

> *When He marked out the foundations of the earth; Then I was beside Him, as a master workman; and I was daily His delight, rejoicing always before Him, rejoicing in the world, His earth, and having my delight in the sons of men* (Proverbs 8:29-31 NASB).

Wisdom is given an artisan title of "master workman." Note the even more powerful phrases; *"rejoicing always before Him," "rejoicing in the world,"* and *"my delight in the sons of men."* Wisdom is not stoic as it is so often pictured. It's even more than happy; it is celebratory in nature and finds pleasure in the act of creation. But its greatest delight is in us! It has found perfect companionship with humanity. We were born to partner with wisdom—to live in it and display it through creative expression.

WISDOM, THE MASTER CRAFTSMAN

The first mention of a person filled with the Holy Spirit in Scripture was Bezalel. He was called upon to head up a building project for Moses. His assignment was to build God a house that He might dwell among His people. God revealed what He wanted that house to look like, but it would take a special gift of wisdom to know "how" to get it done. That is where Bezalel came into the picture. He was given supernatural wisdom to complete the task with artistic excellence. It was wisdom that qualified him to take on this assignment, and it was wisdom that enabled him as an artisan or master craftsman to design and build what was in God's heart.

Notice the bold print in the following verses. It is the cause and effect of being filled with His Holy Spirit:

*I have **filled him with the Spirit of God** in **wisdom,** in understanding, in knowledge, and in all kinds of **craftsmanship,** to make **artistic designs** for work in gold, in silver, and in bronze, and in the cutting of stones for settings, and in the carving of wood, that he may work in all kinds of **craftsmanship** (Exodus 31:3-5 NASB).*

*Then Moses said to the sons of Israel, "See, the Lord has called by name Bezalel the son of Uri, the son of Hur, of the tribe of Judah. And He has **filled him with the Spirit of God,** in **wisdom,** in understanding and in knowledge and in all **craftsmanship;** to make **designs** for working in gold and in silver and in bronze, and in the cutting of stones for settings and in the carving of wood, so as to perform in every **inventive work.** He also has put in his heart to teach, both he and Oholiab, the son of Ahisamach, of the tribe of Dan. He has filled them with **skill to perform every work** of an engraver and of a designer and of an embroiderer, in blue and in purple and in scarlet material, and in fine linen, and of a weaver, as **performers of*** *every work and makers of designs* (Exodus 35:30-35 NASB).

Artistic design, excellence, and *inventive work* are a few of the characteristics of wisdom in this passage. That is part of what being filled with the Spirit looked like in Moses' day. The New Testament adds the power element, because every believer now has access to the miracle realm through the outpouring of the Holy Spirit. This new emphasis does not abolish the original revelation of the subject, but uses it as a foundation to build upon. If we combine the two we end up with believers who walk in wisdom, making practical contributions to the needs of society, who also confront the impossibilities of life through the provisions of the Cross, bringing solutions through supernatural display of miracles, signs, and wonders. Perhaps it is these two things working in tandem that should be considered *the balanced Christian life.*

THE WAR OF ART

Then I lifted up my eyes and looked, and behold, there were four horns. So I said to the angel who was speaking with me, "What are these?" And he answered me, "These are the horns which have scattered Judah, Israel and Jerusalem." Then the Lord showed me four craftsmen. I said, "What are these coming to do?" And he said, "These are the horns which have scattered Judah so that no man lifts up his head; but these craftsmen have come to terrify them, to throw down the horns of the nations who have lifted up their horns against the land of Judah in order to scatter it (Zechariah 1:18-21 NASB).

This is one of the more alarming passages in the Bible. Not because it deals with spiritual warfare, but because God's tools for victory are not common knowledge for most of us today.

In these verses the people of God are being terrorized and scattered by abusive authorities and powers (horns). Hopelessness is the theme of the day, and the confidence that God is with them is at an all time low. The God of all wisdom illumines a truth that is to awaken the people of God to His end-time plans. He sends forth His army to tear down the military strongholds. Who are His soldiers? Craftsmen! Not since God first sent a choir into war[2] has there been such an outlandish strategy for battle. This is a plan that only Wisdom could design.

When creativity is the normal expression of God's people there is something that happens to all who oppose Him. They become disheartened. The devil himself has no creative abilities whatsoever. All he can do is distort and deform what God has made. God is made known through His works. When His works flow through His children their identity is revealed, and there is an inescapable revelation of the nature of God in the land. He is irresistible to those who have eyes to see.

The four craftsmen were God's answer to the four horns that had attempted to scatter His people. Those committed to skillful wisdom (artistic expression) will dismantle the strongholds of abusive power. Not only will they overcome them in a military sense, they will terrify supernatural and counterfeit powers to their core! This is the mission and outcome for entering God's Last Days strategy of infiltrating the world system with skillful wisdom—wisdom from above.

Craftsmen are not simply woodworkers and painters. Nor does that title belong only to actors and musicians. Everyone, doing their God-given task with *excellence, creativity*, and *integrity* is a craftsman in the biblical sense. Schoolteachers, businessmen and women, doctors and lawyers, and all those who have surrendered their gifts to the purposes of God need to display divine wisdom. The opposition that surrounds us seems great, but it cannot stand against the demonstration of God's people wielding this great weapon of war. From the housewife to the brain surgeon, from the preacher to the professor, all must be filled with the Spirit of God until we are known for wisdom, turning the heads of the *queens of Sheba* once again (see 1 Kings 10:1-10). She traveled a great distance just to see extraordinary wisdom. The Bible tells us that in the last days the nations will come to His holy nation asking us to teach them the Word of the Lord (see Micah 4:1-2). Is it possible that this is their response to seeing us filled with the Spirit until His wisdom is on display? I think so.

THE NATURE OF WISDOM

The world's definition of wisdom is focused on the attainment and use of knowledge. It's not wrong; it's just misleading. The church has adopted their incomplete definition, pursuing a wisdom that has no soul. Biblical wisdom sees with divine perspective, and is the creative expression of God, bringing practical solutions to the issues of everyday life.

Besides Jesus, Solomon was the wisest man to ever live. He caught the attention of his entire generation. People were in awe of his gift. The royalty in other nations envied his servants who had the privilege of being exposed to his gift on a daily basis. *A servant in the presence of wisdom is better off than being a king without wisdom.* The queen of Sheba was stunned by how wisdom affected simple things like clothing, buildings, and the like. Examine her perspective:

> *And when the queen of Sheba had seen the wisdom of Solomon, the house which he had built, the food at his table, the seating of his servants, the attendance of his ministers and their attire, his cupbearers and their attire, and his stairway by which he went up to the house of the Lord, she was breathless* (2 Chronicles 9:3-4 NASB).

The effects of his gifts brought Israel into the greatest time of peace and prosperity they had ever known. Wisdom, through one man, changed a nation. What could happen with millions embracing this God-given opportunity?

The wisdom of God will again be reflected in His people. The Church, which is presently despised, will again be reverenced and admired. The Church will again be a *praise in the earth* (see Jer. 33:9).

The manifestations of wisdom are varied. But as mentioned earlier, its nature can be seen in three words—integrity, creativity, and excellence. Divine wisdom springs from *integrity*, and becomes manifest through *creative* expression with *excellence* as its standard. Wherever we find ourselves operating in any of these three expressions we are being touched by divine wisdom.

Let's examine the three characteristics of divine wisdom:[3]

Integrity – a) Adherence to moral and ethical principles; soundness of moral character; honesty. b) The state of being whole, entire, or undiminished. c) A sound, unimpaired, or perfect condition. *Synonyms* – honesty, truth, truthfulness, honor, veracity, reliability, and uprightness.

Integrity is the expression of God's character revealed in us; and that character is the beauty of His perfection—His holiness. Holiness is the essence of His nature. It is not something He does or doesn't do. It is who He is. It is the same for us. We are holy because the nature of God is in us. It begins with a heart separated unto God and becomes evident in the Christ-nature expressed through us.

Creativity – a) The state or quality of being creative. b) The ability to transcend traditional ideas, rules, patterns, relationships, or the like, and to create meaningful new ideas, forms, methods, interpretations, etc.; originality, progressiveness, or imagination. c) The process by which one utilizes creative ability. *Synonyms* – originality, imagination, inspiration, ingenuity, inventiveness, resourcefulness, creativeness, and vision.

Creativity will not only be seen in a full restoration of the arts; it is the nature of His people, expressed in finding new and better ways to do things in any area of influence. It is a shame for the Church to fall into the rut of predictability and call it "tradition."

We must reveal who our Father is through creative expression. We do not become culturally relevant when we become like the culture, but rather when we model what the culture hungers to become.

The Church is often guilty of avoiding creativity because it requires change. Resistance to change in reality is a resistance to the nature of God. The statement, *"For I the Lord do not change"* (Mal. 3:6 NASB) refers to His nature, which is perfect and unchanging. Yet He is always doing a new thing. As the winds of change blow, it will be easy to distinguish between those who are satisfied and those who are hungry. Change brings the secrets of the heart to light.

Excellence – a) The fact or state of excelling; superiority; eminence; b) An excellent quality or feature. *Synonyms*: fineness, brilliance, superiority, distinction, quality, and merit.

Excellence is the high standard set for personal achievement because of who we are in God, and who God is in us. It is not the same as perfectionism. Perfectionism is the cruel counterfeit of excellence, which flows from a religious spirit.

Excellence is impossible without passion. An excellent heart for God appears to be wasteful to those on the outside. In Matthew 26:8 we find Mary pouring ointment upon Jesus that cost a full year's income. The disciples thought it would be put to better use if it had been sold and the money given to the poor. Yet that move was so valuable to God that He said her story would be told wherever the Gospel is preached (see Matt. 26:13).

In like manner King David was extravagant when he took off his kingly garments and danced wildly before God, humbling himself before the people (see 2 Sam. 6:14-23). His wife, Michal, despised him for it. As a result she bore no children to the day of her death, either from barrenness or the lack of marital intimacy with David. Either way it's a tragic loss, as pride destroys fruitfulness, and attacks the heart of true excellence. Her biblical epitaph describes her as *Saul's daughter*, not David's wife. Her rejection of the generous heart toward God caused her to be listed with those God rejected.

David, on the other hand, was fruitful in all he put his hands to do. He was extravagant toward God. In pursuing this virtue, we are to live generously by *doing all to the glory of God, with all our might.* Such is the heart of excellence.

DISQUALIFYING OUR DISQUALIFICATION

Many feel disqualified from creativity because they have narrowly confined it to the world of art and music. They fail to realize that everyone has some measure of creativity, which should be consistently expressed throughout life.

Every 5 year old is an artist. It's an expression of their bent to create. But something happens when they enter grade school. Many educational systems narrow the definition of creativity to include only those who can draw or paint. By the time children are around 10 years of age very few of them are still considered to be artists because of that narrow definition. Today's Kingdom-oriented teachers must embrace the value of true wisdom, and develop children's creative skills outside the traditional box called "art." It is divine wisdom displayed in creativity that brings individuals to the forefront in his or her field of influence.

There are others who feel disqualified because they think that creativity always means we are to make something new or do something novel. In reality, most great ideas are actually the offspring of other concepts. Years ago I bought a jazz album on a whim. I eagerly looked forward to something fresh and new as I placed the album on the turntable. But I was horribly disappointed. It sounded like a child randomly pounding on a piano, with no melody or harmonies, no consistent rhythm, nothing to give it purpose or direction. Coincidently, I found a magazine article by the same musician a year or so later. In that magazine he described a particular season of his life in which he tried to be completely original, without being influenced by any other musician. He referred to it as a dark season of his life. It was obvious to me that I had purchased the *bad fruit* of his *bad season*. He went on to give what has become for me a profound lesson on creativity. He said that to really be creative he had to go back to what he had learned from others, and use that as a platform from which to create.

It is wisdom that can take something that is an everyday item or concept and build upon it creating something new and better. This is exactly what Solomon did. All kings of the day had cupbearers, servants, banqueting tables, and nice clothing for their servants. But there was something about his use of wisdom for everyday life that made him stand out above the rest. The queen of Sheba became speechless in response to Solomon's wisdom. It's time for the Church to display a wisdom that causes the world to become silent again.

There is a misconception that often exists in the artistic community; creativity must come from pain. There's no question but that some of the greatest works of art came from people who were troubled with life, or experienced some of the worst tragedies. The reality is this—it often takes trauma to launch a person into a place of seeing the true priorities for life. The believer doesn't need that experience. Having our old nature crucified with Christ is the only tragedy needed to launch us into our proper roles of creative influence.

THE CHURCH REVEALS

> ...that now the manifold wisdom of God might be made known by the church to the principalities and powers in the heavenly places, according to the eternal purpose which He accomplished in Christ Jesus our Lord... (Ephesians 3:10-11).

The Church has a clear assignment: we are to exhibit the multifaceted wisdom of God, *now*! It must permeate all we are and do.

This neglected element is at the heart of our call to disciple nations. It is a part of the "witness" that turns people's heads in the same way as the nations were impacted by Solomon's wisdom. The spirit realm is watching, and more importantly, is affected by such a display. They must be reminded of their defeat, our victory, and the Father's eternal plan for the redeemed. It's our connection to wisdom that clearly manifests our eternal purpose of reigning with Christ. When we walk in wisdom, we mirror the reality of Heaven here on earth, and actually give Heaven a target for invasion. In the same way agreement with the devil empowers him to kill, steal, and destroy, so agreement with God releases God to accomplish His purposes in and through us to the world around us.[4] This is the reason He made humanity His delegated authority on this planet.[5]

A reformation has begun. And at the heart of this great move of the Spirit is the total transformation of the people of God as they discover their true identity and purpose. Great purpose elicits great sacrifice. Up until this time, many of our agendas have failed. Our attempts to make the Gospel palatable have had a serious effect on the world around us. The world has longed for a message they could *experience*. Yet many believers have simply tried to make the good news more intellectually appealing. This must stop! The natural mind *cannot* receive the things of the Spirit of God (see 1 Cor. 2:14). The wisdom of God is foolishness to men. It's time to be willing to appear foolish again, that we might provide the world with a message of power that delivers, transforms, and heals. This is true wisdom. It alone satisfies the cry of the human heart.

There are melodies that have never been heard by the human ear that would bring people to their knees in surrender to Jesus. Musicians must hear the musical sounds of Heaven and reproduce them here. I have a friend who is a wonderful worship leader. He was once taken to Heaven, where he heard them singing a song that he had written. He joyfully said, "Hey, you're singing one of my songs." But the angel replied, "No, we let you hear one of ours."

There are medical secrets that are only one prayer away from revolutionizing the way people live. Businesses strive day after day for success when the gift of wisdom can launch them into profound places of influence in a community. Politicians look to consultants on how best to run a campaign. Yet there is a wisdom in God that is so fresh and new that it will give them great favor with their constituents. There are methods of education that have been hidden in the realms of God's mysteries. He simply waits for one of His own to ask for the revelation. The list of heavenly answers is limitless. He looks for those who will ask.

THERE IS *NO* FAILURE IN FAITH

Many are discouraged because their dreams have failed. In their pain and frustration they oppose the message that a believer has the right to dream. "*Hope deferred makes the heart sick…*" but the verse doesn't stop there and neither should we: "*…but desire fulfilled is a tree of life*" (Prov. 13:12 NASB).

Here is a higher reality: when people pursue dreams but fail to see them fulfilled, they prepare the way for others who carry the same dream to eventually get the breakthrough that they were seeking. It is hard for many to take comfort in this thought, but that's because we usually think *it's all about us*. There is no failure in faith.

Often a tragic loss here on earth is viewed quite differently in Heaven. What is honored in Heaven is frequently pitied or mocked here on earth. When a person dies while trying to live out an expression of faith, people often criticize the foolishness of their decision. Few realize that their loss became the soil in which someone else could eventually realize their dream, because their loss actually paved the way to a breakthrough.

Those with failed dreams can take comfort in the fact that they prepared the way for others. It's a *John the Baptist* role. He prepared the way for the One to come. Countless times throughout history there have been those who never realized a fulfillment of their dreams. Many come to the end of their lives with the overwhelming conclusion that they failed. To our detriment, we have lived without the consciousness that a failed attempt at a dream often becomes the foundation of another person's success. Some water, others plant, and still others harvest. We all have an important role to set the stage for the King of kings to receive more glory. It's all about Him, not us.

THE NATURAL ILLUSTRATES THE SPIRITUAL

In the 1920s, a man named Mallory led an expedition to be the first to climb Mount Everest. He attempted this feat on two separate occasions, but failed. He went back to work assembling the best team of climbers available, with the finest equipment in existence. They gave extra attention to the details of their assignment, especially focusing on the issues of safety. In spite of their efforts, tragedy struck. Many in the expedition were killed in an avalanche, including Mallory. Only a few survived.

When the team returned to England, a banquet was held in their honor. The leader of the survivors stood to acknowledge the applause of those in attendance. He looked at the pictures of his comrades that were displayed around the room. Choking back the tears he spoke to the mountain on behalf of Mallory and his friends. "I speak to you, Mount Everest, in the name of all brave men living, and those yet unborn. Mount Everest, you defeated us once, you defeated us twice, you defeated us three times. But Mount Everest, we shall someday defeat you, because you can't get any bigger, but we can!" Death and disappointment could have been the end of such a quest. But instead it became the foundation for future success.

A SMALL DEVIL

There is a mountain of opposition against the purposes of God for this world. They are *principalities, powers, rulers of the darkness of this age, and spiritual hosts of wickedness in the heavenly places* (see

Eph. 6:12). But the devil's dark realm is not getting any bigger. When he rebelled against God, he was removed from his life source. He walks about as a roaring lion, hoping to intimidate through noise. His noise, the constant report of bad news, is designed to give the illusion of greatness. But it is not so.

Hell is not the realm that satan rules from. It is not a place where he takes people and torments them for eternity. It is a place of eternal torment designed for him and his demons. Those who are slaves of the devil will suffer the same demise.

On another note, demons aren't being made anymore. There's the same number wandering around the planet today as there were in Jesus' day, yet the population of people has increased into the billions, with believers numbering in the hundreds of millions. On top of that, we all know from Scripture that there are two angels for every demon. And since Jesus has *all* authority, that leaves none for the devil. The "all" that Jesus possesses has been handed over to us. His great plan is not designed so He will have to come and rescue us from the devil. It's the gates of hell that *will not* prevail against the advancing church (see Matt. 16:18). Jesus' authority has been given to us to do great exploits. With the Moravians, let's declare, "Let us win for the Lamb, the reward of His suffering!"

Our commission to pursue divine wisdom comes with mystery. That is the subject of the next chapter.

ENDNOTES

1. For more about this subject read my book *The Supernatural Power of a Transformed Mind*.

2. Even a choir is an artistic expression! See Second Chronicles 20:21.

3. Definitions for creativity, integrity, and excellence taken from Random House Dictionary. Synonyms taken from Microsoft Word Encarta World Dictionary.

4. If God is restricted in any way, it is a self-imposed restriction.

5. For more on this subject read Chapter Two of my book *When Heaven Invades Earth*.

The Value of Mystery

God hides things for us, not from us.

An intellectual gospel is always in danger of creating a God that looks a lot like us; one that is our size. The quest for answers sometimes leads to a rejection of mystery. As a result mystery is often treated as something intolerable, instead of a real treasure. Living with mystery is the privilege of our walk with Christ. Its importance cannot be overrated. If I understand all that is going on in my Christian life, I have an inferior Christian life. The walk of faith is to live according to the revelation we have received, in the midst of the mysteries we can't explain. That's why Christianity is called *the faith*.

All too often believers abandon or dilute their call in order to feel better about the things they cannot explain. To allow what we cannot answer to downgrade what He has shown us is to be carnal minded. Too many only obey what they understand, thus subjecting God to their judgments. God is not on trial; we are. A true *Crosswalk* is obeying where we have revelation in spite of the apparent contradiction in what we cannot explain. To obey only when we see that there will be a favorable outcome is not obedience. Obedience is supposed to be expensive. To embrace what He has shown us and to obey what He has commanded us, often in the midst of unanswerable questions, is an honor beyond measure. It is a great privilege to be a believing believer in the midst of a culture of unbelief. We must embrace this privilege. No Christian should be unmoved by the Lord's question, "When I return, will I find faith on the earth?" I have set my heart to be His pleasure by living in faith.

The Power of the Offended Mind

When Jesus felt it was time to minister in His hometown of Nazareth, He went to the synagogue. As He began to teach the people, they were quite amazed at His wisdom. They were also very impressed with the healings they were seeing. But when they realized they knew Him, having watched Him grow up, they were offended in their "reasonings." "It is Jesus. We know His brothers and sisters. He grew up here! How can He do this stuff? And where did He get this wisdom?"[1] They were not offended in the typical sense; their feelings were not hurt, nor were they caught up in bitterness. They simply could not put two and two together and arrive at the conclusion—*their Jesus was a miracle worker and a man of great wisdom*. It didn't fill them with wonder and awe. Instead it caused them to become hardhearted and reject Him. This unresolved question became the mental stumbling block that was strong enough to shut down Jesus' anointing to perform miracles and teach with power. To have questions is healthy; to hold God hostage to those questions is not. It sometimes creates an atmosphere that fulfills its own prophecy about the power of God not being for today. It shuts down the very anointing that would teach them otherwise.

Not understanding is OK. Restricting our spiritual life to what we understand is not. It is immaturity at best. Such a controlling spirit is destructive to the development of a Christ-like nature. God responds to faith but will not surrender to our demands for control.

Maturity requires a heart-felt embrace of what we do not understand as an essential expression of faith.

A person's heart is more clearly seen by what they're willing to embrace without offense, than by their expression of faith only in what they already understand.

THE DEAF PRAYING FOR THE DEAF

My oldest son, Eric, is 85-90 percent deaf in both ears. He has an amazing gift for life. He functions beautifully in the "hearing world" and has never had to learn sign language. His adjustments to life are miraculous, while his self-esteem is unaffected by this handicap. He is strong and Christ-centered. He is our Missions Pastor.

I was fasting and praying for his healing some years ago, and God spoke to me very clearly that He was going to heal him. It *has* happened in the atonement, and will be seen in my lifetime. We don't treat it as a *someday off in the future God will heal Him* kind of thing. We view it as a *right now* word. Yet he still can't hear without the assistance of a hearing aid.

It's interesting that the healing of deafness is one of the most common miracles I see in my meetings and in our church. Even more interesting to note is that in the last couple of months Eric has laid hands on two people who were deaf and God opened their ears. How could that happen without him being healed first? I don't know. But I do know that mental offense, stumbling over this apparent contradiction in our minds, will shut down this anointing. That is something we are not willing to do. Eric and I will continue to live in the understanding we have, and embrace the mystery we are required to live with, knowing that God is perfectly faithful and good beyond measure, all the time. He is worthy of our trust.

HOW WE LEARN

I'll never forget when God first began to open up the Scriptures to me. As I read, my heart leapt within me over the richness of what

I was reading. Yet I couldn't have taught on that particular passage if my life depended on it. My spirit was doing the learning and my mind would have to wait. The mind is trained through the experience of divine encounters and supernatural experiences initiated through the revelations from Scriptures. Revelation that doesn't lead to a divine encounter will only make us more religious, teaching us to embrace external standards without the internal realities.

God is not opposed to the mind; He created the mind to be a complement to all that He had made. He is opposed to the unrenewed mind. It is at war with God, being incapable of obeying Him (see Rom. 8:7). The believer who governs his Christian life through the mind is the carnal Christian that the apostle Paul warned about (see 1 Cor. 2–3). The soul can only lead us into religion[2]– form without power. It is what makes way for Ishmaels instead of Isaacs.[3]

It's important to understand the learning process. Our spirit is where the Holy Spirit dwells. Our spirit is alive and well and is ready to receive great things from God. When I filter everything through my mind and remove what isn't immediately logical, I extract much of what I really need. Only what goes beyond my understanding is positioned to renew my mind (see Phil. 4:7). If we can learn more about the actual voice and presence of the Lord, we will stop being so paranoid about being deceived by the things we can't explain. Usually those who use the natural mind to protect themselves from deception are the most deceived. They've relied on their own finite logic and reason to keep them safe, which is in itself a deception. They usually have an explanation for all that's going on in their walk with the Lord, but criticize those who long for more.

Our hearts can embrace things that our heads can't. Our hearts will lead us where our logic would never dare to go. No one ever attributes the traits of courage and valor to the intellect or the strength of human reasoning. Courage rises up from within and gives influence over the mind. In the same way, true faith affects the mind. Faith does not come from our understanding. It comes from the heart. We do not believe because we understand; we understand because we believe (see Heb. 11:6). We'll know when our mind is truly renewed, because the impossible will look logical.

MYSTERY—A CROSS FOR THE MIND

What we don't understand is sometimes as important as what we do. It's one thing to obey when He has given us understanding about a matter, and quite another to obey while facing questions and circumstances that seem to contradict what we understand. So many fail at this point, and then bring the Bible down to their level of experience. Many do this to feel better about the fact that they are living in compromise—a compromise of their revelation from Scripture. Our challenge is instead to bring our lifestyle up to the standard of God's Word.

To embrace revelation[4] with one hand, and embrace mystery with the other, forms a perfect cross. This is a cross that everyone who is hungry to do the works of Jesus will have to carry. God must violate our logic to invite us away from the deception of relying on our own reasoning.

GOD HIDES THINGS TO BE FOUND

When my children were small we hid Easter eggs for them to find. The measure of difficulty in the search was always determined by the age and capabilities of the child. We never went outside, dug a 3-foot deep hole and buried a chocolate egg hoping a 2 year old would find it. When my children were that young, we'd put the egg on a table, or on a chair. And as they got older we would make it more difficult, but never impossible. Parents delight in their child's curiosity, and love to see them enjoy the process of discovery. Children enjoy the pleasure of the search, and revel in the affirmation of their parent's delight in their searching and discovery. "...*Seek and you shall find...*" (Matt. 7:7). This curiosity and delight in discovery are meant to be a part of what it is to "*seek first the kingdom*" (Matt. 6:33) as well as to "*receive the kingdom of God as a little child*" (Luke 18:17).

> *It is the glory of God to conceal a matter, but the glory of kings is to search out a matter* (Proverbs 25:2).

People wonder why God doesn't always speak in more open terms—audibly, with visible signs, and other such ways. I don't know how or why it works this way, but the Bible indicates that *God receives more glory when He conceals*, rather than making things obvious. It is more glorious for Him to hide, and have us seek. In the introduction to the parable of the seed and the sower we find that Jesus did not merely use parables as illustrations, but at times to conceal truth so that only the hungry would understand (see Matt. 13:11,18-23). It is the mercy of God to withhold revelation from those who have no hunger for truth, because if they don't hunger for it, the chances are they won't obey it when they hear it. Revelation always brings responsibility, and hunger is the thing that prepares our hearts to carry the weight of that responsibility. By keeping revelation from those without hunger, God actually protects them from certain failure to carry the responsibility it would lay on them. And so He conceals. Yet, He doesn't conceal from us; He conceals *for* us!

But there's another part to this equation—"*it's the glory of kings to search out a matter*"! We are kings and priests to our God (see Rev. 1:6). Our royal identity never shines brighter than when we pursue hidden things with the confidence that we have legal access to such things. Mysteries are our inheritance. Our kingship, our role in ruling and reigning with Christ,[5] comes to the forefront when we seek Him for answers to the dilemmas of the world around us.

Jesus answered them, "*To you it has been granted to know the mysteries of the kingdom of heaven, but to them it has not been granted*" (Matt. 13:11 NASB). We, as believers, have legal access to the realm of God's mysteries. It's that simple. The hidden things are placed in waiting for the believer to discover. They are ours by inheritance.

The Value of Mystery

Truth Held in Tension

It is very hard to imagine the Church bringing answers to the issues of life when much of our eschatology anticipates world conditions getting worse and worse. When we also believe that the darkness of world circumstances is the signal for Christ's return, we have a conflict that ultimately costs us a practical vision—to invade and transform the world system. It's not my intention to declare when or how Jesus is returning for His Church. My only point is that wrong assumptions about the unobvious can harden us to the obvious.[6] If we assume we know what certain types and shadows used in the prophets mean it can incorrectly influence our understanding of the clear commandments of the Lord. Wrongly interpreting when and how He is returning can undermine our approach to the Great Commission.

Jesus is returning for a spotless Bride, whose Body is in equal proportion to her Head. The Father alone knows when that moment will be. We don't. Our job is to do everything possible to bring about, "*Thy kingdom come, Thy will be done, on earth as it is in Heaven.*" If my faith for His return has its anchor in the darkness of the world around me, then I will do little to change it. We will try to get converts, of course, but to bring answers to the issues of this planet will not be a priority. Yet this is the practical tool that turns the hearts of the kings of our day (see Prov. 22:29).

Our commission is clear: we are to disciple nations! And to insure that this seemingly impossible task would be possible, He caused the One called *the desire of the nations* to live within us. This revelation of Him is ultimately a revelation about us, for we are His Body. Being made in His image gives us the privilege and responsibility to reflect His greatness to the world around us. The nations are looking for a people who can bring the answers to the issues facing our world.

HANNAH'S MYSTERY

Hannah's womb was closed. She was barren and without hope of bearing children apart from a miracle. As cruel as it may sound to the natural man, God used this to bring her into her greatest success. In her barrenness she developed a desperate heart. The purpose of a promise is not to inspire us to strategize and make plans, but instead it works to make us desperate for God to show up. This means that barrenness in any area is our invitation to excel. Hannah became a co-laborer in fulfilling her own destiny. Solomon states, *"An inheritance gained hurriedly at the beginning will not be blessed in the end"* (Prov. 20:21 NASB). Not everything comes to us easily, nor should it. The God who hides things for us also gives us His Kingdom as our inheritance. Israel was given the Promised Land, but was told it would come to them little by little so that the beasts wouldn't become too numerous for them. His promises cover everything— His promises are yes and *amen!* (See 2 Cor. 1:20.) All is covered by the redemptive work on the Cross, but it is gained little by little, sometimes through our co-laboring effort.

This became a great personal lesson in my quest for miracles. Mario Murillo has had more to do in stirring up the passions of a revivalist in my life than any other person. Almost 20 years ago I asked him about the life of miracles, telling him of my frustration in having theory without fruit. I had never witnessed anyone getting healed, even though I tried many times. He encouraged me with one of the most powerful prophetic words of my life. In it the Lord spoke of His intent to make miracles a regular part of my life. I have prayed over that promise for many years. In recent years I have seen thousands of people healed.

Mario, and his wife, Mechelle, recently came to our home for lunch. I showed him the prophetic word he spoke over me in 1988. I did so to express my thanks to him for being such an encouragement to me. He brought up the story of Hannah and her closed womb. He said that God has closed up the realm of the miraculous to me, not as punishment, but to draw me into the desperation needed to maintain it as a lifestyle once I received my breakthrough. It was a long and painful lesson. But I got it. And I think I really understand.

MARY'S MYSTERY

Mary, the mother of Jesus, lived with mystery in a most notable fashion. She carried revival better than anyone, since Jesus is revival personified. Mary was given the ultimate mystery—both in word and experience.

Mary gave birth to the Christ-child as declared by the angel Gabriel. The things spoken of by those who recognized Jesus' purpose and divinity were pondered in her heart. The word *things* in this story is the word "rhema" in the original language, which is the *freshly spoken word of God.* She pondered the things *spoken to her by God,* even though she didn't understand them. Her pondering gave place for the roots to be established and the word to grow until the promise became manifest. God's Word grows in the heart of the yielded believer.

Her encounter with mystery could be summarized as follows:

1. As a young girl Mary had an angelic encounter with Gabriel.
2. Gabriel gave Mary a word that was incomprehensible; she was to give birth to the Messiah while she remained a virgin—a biblically unprecedented experience.
3. She yielded to what was beyond understanding by saying, *"Be it unto me, according to Thy word."*
4. Mary nearly lost Joseph, her fiancé, to the news that "God made me pregnant." An angel appeared to Joseph to convince him it was true, thus saving their marriage.
5. She began to "manifest" under the influence of the ultimate revival—Jesus. (You can only hide the reality of pregnancy/revival so long.)

6. Those who knew that her son was the Messiah would often speak to her of His greatness. She pondered the things they said in her heart, thus becoming pregnant again—this time with promise.

In essence, the glorious story of Mary is repeated every time we are impregnated with God's Word of promise. Christ is still being formed in His people. This spiritual reality is not to be thought inferior to the natural reality that Mary experienced. In no way do I mean to dishonor Mary. She will be considered "highly favored of the Lord" forever! Rather, I want to increase respect for the work of the Spirit of God in every heart.

THE KINGDOM NOW, BUT NOT YET

When I first heard this phrase, *the Kingdom now but not yet*, over 20 years ago, it was used as a statement of promise. It was helpful for me to realize that we have access to things right now that I had always thought were inaccessible. The phrase helped to bring into focus the reality that some things will be enjoyed in time, and some things only in eternity. But that same phrase has also been used to define limitations and restrictions, and not instill hope. It is used to ease people's dissatisfaction with unrealized promises now. But I have a problem with this approach. It makes people satisfied with less than is available now. I rarely hear it used to describe our potential or promise; it carries with it boundaries and barriers that Jesus did not teach or make.

It is true that a full manifestation of the Kingdom of God is more than our physical bodies can endure. But it is also true that when we are in Heaven we will still be able to say, *now, but not yet*, about the Kingdom, because there is no end to the increase of His government. Throughout eternity the Kingdom will be expanding, and we will always be advancing. I teach our people that if *now, but not yet* is used to define promise and potential, accept it. If it is spoken to build awareness of our limitations and restrictions, reject it.

We don't need more people without authentic Kingdom experiences telling us what we can and cannot have in our lifetime. Those who walk out their faith with an experiential paradigm understand that we will always live in the tension of what we have seen and what we have yet to see, and that we are always moving on to *more* in God. This is an *understanding by experience* issue.

Someone has to go beyond the boundaries of historical accomplishments and attempt something that has been considered impossible by their contemporaries. The Church is often known as the group that *changes not*. Very little of what exists today would exist at all if those who preceded us did not seek to surpass the boundaries experienced by their predecessors. And so it is with the Church. It is this adventure that God has called us to. And it is this adventure that we call *the normal Christian life*.

THE LANGUAGE OF MYSTERY

As God draws us into a place of embracing the realm of His mysteries, He establishes the life of faith in us. Yet He longs to unlock the mysteries for those desiring to make a difference in the world around them. Hidden things are revealed to those who hunger for Him, and can recognize His voice. That is the subject of the next chapter.

ENDNOTES

1. My paraphrase.

2. The most common definition of the soul is the *mind, will,* and *emotions.*

3. Ishmael was the son of Abraham's efforts, while Isaac was the son of God's promise.

4. More on this in the chapter called, "The Spirit of Revelation."

5. It is important to note, *ruling* from God's perspective means to be the servant of all. Too many have embraced this theology, and have used it as an excuse to pursue ruling over others in the way Jesus warned against. Our strong suit has been, and always will be, serving.

6. One of the greatest errors in end-time theology comes from working to interpret types and symbols (the unobvious) until they redefine the clear commands of the Lord (the obvious). For example, many know much more about Gog and Magog, the ten nation confederacy, the seven years of tribulation, the anti-Christ, etc. than they do about the simple command to pray "*on earth as it is in Heaven.*"

CHAPTER 4

The Language of the Spirit

"God hides things for you, not from you."

A yielded imagination becomes a sanctified imagination; and it's the sanctified imagination that is positioned for visions and dreams. There is great paranoia over the use of the imagination in the Church of the Western world.[1] As a result; unbelievers often lead the way in creative expression—through the arts and inventions. They have no bias against imagination. The imagination is like a canvas to a painter. If it's clean, the artist has much to work with. God would love to use our imagination to paint His impressions upon; He just looks for those who are yielded. However, those who are preoccupied with "not being worthy" are too self-centered to be trusted with much revelation. At some point it has to stop being about us long enough to utilize the benefits of being in Christ for the sake of those around us. Such a position gives us unlimited access to the mysteries of God that enable us to touch the needs of a dying world.

Jesus is the Word of God. It's hard for Him to not have something to say. Occasionally, we go through times when we feel God is not speaking to us. While that may be so, most of the time He has simply changed His language, and He expects us to adjust with Him.

MISSING THE AUDIBLE VOICE OF GOD

"Father, glorify Your name." Then a voice came from heaven, saying, "I have both glorified it, and will glorify it again." Therefore the people who stood by and heard it said that it had thundered. Others said, "An angel has spoken to Him" (John 12:28-29).

The audible voice of the Father came from Heaven while Jesus was speaking to a crowd. The people acknowledged hearing something, but none of them knew what it was. Not only did they fail to realize it was the voice of God, it never occurred to them that this unusual event had any meaning for their lives. Jesus responded to their unbelief by saying, *"This voice did not come because of Me, but for your sake"* (see John 12:27-30). In His mercy God spoke to provide a way out of the lifestyle of unbelief for every bystander. But their hardness of heart blocked their perception of what was said, who was speaking, and made what they heard unintelligible. We know that God spoke clearly (see 1 Cor. 14:9). Yet the people did not *understand* because of their predisposition toward unbelief (see John 12:37). Some thought it was thunder—an impersonal act of nature. Others thought it might have been an angel—spiritual, but just not for them.[2] It is a true statement that it's the hungry heart that hears best.

UNBELIEF MASQUERADES AS WISDOM

The story of John 12 addresses one of my greatest concerns for the church in the Western world—the prevalence of unbelief. It has masqueraded long enough as wisdom and must be exposed for being the great sin that it is. Unbelief has the outward appearance of a conservative approach to life, but works to subject God Himself to the mind and control of people. It feeds off the opinion of others, all the while stroking itself for not falling into the extremes that others have stumbled into. What is seldom realized by those who live in such a religious trap is that an unbelieving mind-set is completely unable to represent Jesus in His power and glory.

It is troubling to me that so many Christians need me to prove that God actually does what I say I've seen Him do—as though the Scriptures were not enough proof. What is even more astonishing is that when the miracles happen before their eyes, they still want doctors' reports, x-rays, etc. before they will give God any praise. It is grievous to see an empty wheelchair with someone walking, a formerly depressed person rejoicing, or one who could not hear now hearing and giving praise, but the bystander still wants proof those were really miracles. I realize that charlatans exist. But the massive effort to protect ourselves from being fooled is more a sign of unbelief than it is of our wisdom keeping us from deception. Such a fear only exists where unbelief has reigned for a long time.

However, "*Love believes all things*" (1 Cor. 13:7 NASB). A deeper encounter with the love of God frees a person from the tendency to protect themselves out of fear through unreasonable caution. And considering that "*faith works through love*" (Gal. 5:6), it is reasonable to say that even the faith to believe God for miracles can come by experiencing His love. Overwhelming encounters with the extravagant love of our heavenly Father will do much to dismantle unbelief.

It is not wisdom that continually asks God to demonstrate Himself for us so that we might believe. While there is no question that exposure to the miraculous can help us grow in faith, such a demand is not a hunger for Him but is instead an effort to put God on trial. He is not on trial. We are. The un-renewed mind is at war with God and puts demands on Him to perform for us. That unhealthy attitude puts us in the role of a judge. Such arrogance is the father of unbelief. Jesus confronted these attitudes in his many encounters with the religious crowd.

The Ultimate Meal

The heart of abiding faith "leans into God," anticipating His voice, looking for His next move. Like Jesus, we are to be able to say, "*My food is to do the will of Him who sent me*" (John 4:34 NASB). I am strengthened in hearing God speak. I am nourished through my own obedience to His voice. The situations of life take on meaning and purpose because of the abiding faith to follow Jesus. Hearing from God is the essential element of the Christian life, for "*man shall not live by bread alone, but by every word that proceeds from the mouth of God*" (Matt. 4:4). His voice is our life.

There are many tables to eat at in life. There is the table of *public opinion*. The food is sweet, but it sours in the stomach. There is the table of *personal achievement*. That's a power meal for sure, yet the crash is as rapid as the ascent. There's only one table with rich food that settles well and brings supernatural strength; it's the table of God's will.

My Personal Story in Revival

When I became the pastor of Bethel Church, in Redding, California, I came because of a cry for revival by the leadership of the church. I was the pastor of Mountain Chapel, in Weaverville, California, where we were experiencing a wonderful outpouring of the Holy Spirit. Bethel was the mother church of our church in Weaverville, where my family and I had been for 17 years. The invitation came for me to return and be Bethel's Senior Pastor. When I spoke to the new congregation about my coming, I told them that I was born for revival; if they didn't want the move of the Spirit of God, along with the messes that come from such an outpouring (see Prov. 14:4), they didn't want me, because this was not negotiable! They responded positively with close to unanimous support.

The outpouring began almost immediately. Lives were changed, bodies were healed, divine encounters increased in amazing proportions—and approximately 1,000 people left the church. What was happening was outside their point of reference and off the map of their own experience.

Few things are more devastating to pastors than when people leave the church. It feels like personal rejection (and often times it really is). Those in ministry are certainly not immune to these feelings. Pastors are a unique breed—there are times when people who hate us leave the church and we still feel bad. Yet during this strange season of *exodus*, my wife and I were immune to the devastation, which is only possible if God has actually given a supernatural grace to joyfully live *opposite* of your circumstances. (The counterfeit that many fall for is to be callous of heart to the point that no one can affect you, good or bad. And still others choose to live in denial about the impact that such a loss is causing in their hearts. Neither is healthy or acceptable.) Because of the grace given to us, not one day was spent in discouragement or questioning God. Our food really was doing His will, which provides all the nourishment and strength we need.

It was the generosity of God that made this possible. Along with the increased manifestation of His presence, He made His will too obvious to ever miss. God often spoke to us in a dream, a vision, or a clear impression in our minds. Sometimes He brought forth a prophetic word that confirmed or added understanding to a direction we were to take. There was never a question. The fruit of the increased measure of His presence, along with the bounty of transformed lives, was all we needed to smile in the face of such apparent loss. To this day, we've considered it a privilege to gain that kind of increase through such a loss.

Today we are growing fast. The miracles are increasing in astonishing ways. Yet I secretly savor the moments of the initial outpouring when it was illogical to the natural mind to be so happy when so many things appeared to be so wrong. The opposition was fierce at times. The slander and rumors increased daily with a vengeance. For close to a year our denominational office received complaints and accusations about us every single day. Yet only God can make such a season so wonderful, because only His will is so completely nourishing. It has been, and continues to be, my favorite meal.

The beauty of His will is lost for the person who does not know the language of the Spirit. It is vital to learn how God speaks. His first language is not English. In fact, it would be safe to say it's not Hebrew either. While He uses the languages of men to communicate with us, He is more inclined to speak through a myriad of other methods. In the remainder of this chapter I will attempt to address some of the "languages of the Spirit." There are many great materials written on this subject, so I will only emphasize the areas that are a bit more obscure, such as the section called "Dark Sayings." This is far from a complete list. It represents the limited discoveries of my own adventure with God.

THE LANGUAGE OF THE SCRIPTURES

The Scriptures are the basis for all "hearing" from God. While God will not violate His Word, He often violates our understanding of His Word. Remember, God is bigger than His book. The Bible does not contain God; it *reveals* Him.

This truth can be represented by two Greek words for *word*, "logos" and "rhema."

Logos is often used to speak of the written Word, our Holy Bible. Bible reading is the most common way of receiving instruction and learning to recognize His voice. Page after page is filled with practical instructions for life. Learning the principles of God's Word helps us to learn to recognize His voice by establishing truth in our hearts. The Psalmist affirmed that purpose, saying, "*Your word I have treasured in my heart, that I may not sin against You*" (Ps. 119:11 NASB). This is where we find the Kingdom principles for life. They work for anyone who applies them.

Rhema is the freshly spoken word. It is always an expression of that which is *being uttered*. Therefore it carries an aspect of immediacy

The Language of the Spirit

with it. Often times God breathes upon His Word and gives life to something written for "now." The spoken word is never to replace the written Word. The more of the written Word we have in our hearts, the greater capacity we have to hear the spoken word, because He speaks to that which has been deposited in our hearts and calls it forth.

THE LANGUAGE OF THE AUDIBLE VOICE

The voice of the Lord is not an impression that we have to find language for. It is a direct word-for-word communication from God to us. The audible voice may come to the natural ear while we're awake or while we're asleep. It can also come to our spiritual ears. (The reason I make this distinction is that after it has happened, you can't always remember if it was out loud or internal. It is far more than an impression. It is as clear as hearing someone speak.)

On at least two occasions I have been awakened with the audible voice of the Lord. But in reflection I never thought that my wife would have heard it. She didn't. That's why I say it can come to the natural ear, as it did in John 12, or in our spirit. He once woke me with His voice, saying, "He watches over the watch of those who watch the Lord." That phrase then ran through my mind the rest of the night. It became apparent that He wanted my full attention so I could learn to watch Him only. In doing so He would watch over all that concerned me.

THE LANGUAGE OF THE STILL SMALL VOICE

This is the quiet voice or impression of the heart. This is probably the most common way that people hear from God. It is sometimes thought to be our own "inner voice" in that it is our own thoughts and ideas. While we do have such a voice, it is wisdom to learn to recognize *His* still small voice. It is quiet. So we must become quiet to recognize it consistently. Someone gave me a helpful clue to discerning His voice; they said, "You know you've heard from God whenever you have an idea that's better than one you could think up yourself."

The Language of Visions

Visions come both to the natural eye and to the eyes of the heart. The second are the pictures in the mind, which are the visual equivalent of the still small voice—they are as easy to miss as they are to get. *Leaning into God* is what makes this one come into focus.

External—Many people refer to this as an "open vision." Though I have never had one, I have many friends who have, including my senior associate, Kris Vallotton. One such method that God has used with him is when something like a movie screen appears over a person's head, and God plays back portions of that person's life. Describing it to them tends to get their attention, preparing the way for them to receive significant personal ministry.

Internal—On a ministry trip to Germany, preceding the evening healing meeting, I was praying with the leadership of a remarkable ministry. I had a "snapshot" picture flash in my mind. In it I saw someone seated to my right, and then saw only their spine, as in an x-ray. I somehow knew it was arthritic. In this vision I pointed to them and said, "The Lord Jesus heals you!" This vision sounds much more dramatic than it really was. It was a brief snapshot that I gave attention to. It was one that I could have easily missed. When it was my time to speak, I started by asking if there was anyone there with arthritis in the spine. A woman to my right raised her hand. After asking her to stand I declared, "The Lord Jesus heals you!" She began to tremble. When I asked her "where is your pain?" she responded with intense weeping, saying, "It's impossible! It's impossible! It's gone!" She was healed through a declaration that was brought about by an internal vision.

At another time, during a tent meeting with Todd Bentley in Roseville, California, I had a unique experience involving another internal vision. During the worship I saw the vertebrae of a neck and realized it was injured. But I also saw the number 94 float by. It was not dramatic, but very subtle—easy to miss. When I got up to speak, I asked for those to come forward who had injured their neck in 1994 in some sort of accident. To my surprise 12 people came to the front for prayer. I was able to speak to eight or nine of them following the time of prayer and each one had been healed.

THE LANGUAGE OF DREAMS

Obviously, dreams mostly happen at night. But there is a form of dreaming that is similar to a *daydream*. They happen when you're awake and are more likely to be ignored because you think it's *your imagination*. In their more intense form they are more like a trance. Once again, leaning into God brings this tool into a clearer perspective, giving us the needed discernment to recognize what is from God and what is actually our imagination.

Daydream. While sitting in a conference, I began to daydream about a prayer house. I could see four walls of windows to the north, south, east, and west. Over each window was the phrase from Isaiah, "*Say to the North, 'Give them back!'*" The same appeared over each of the windows facing their respective directions. In the carpet was the compass star, again pointing to the north, south, east, and west. In the center of the room was a fountain that flowed continuously. I knew it was to be called the Alabaster House. (An alabaster vial is what was used to contain the priceless—actually worth about a year's salary—ointment that the woman poured over Jesus before His death as the ultimate expression of worship (see Mark 14:3). The disciples became angry because this woman *wasted* her perfume with such a senseless act, when it could have been sold and the money given to the poor. Jesus had a different perspective; He called it worship.) I felt we were to build a place where people could *waste themselves on Jesus!* When I shared this experience with our church board, one of the members[4] asked to meet with me the next day. He was a contractor who brought in plans he had drawn two years earlier of the very prayer house I had described. Needless to say, we built the Alabaster House, even though its construction was during the time when about 1,000 people were leaving the church. We built it with cash—another testimony of God's wonderful mercy and grace.

Night Dream. As I was preparing to come to Bethel Church to be their new pastor, I had a dream warning me of the potential danger in the coming transition. In the dream I was taking an exit off of a freeway. I was then to cross over the roadway on an overpass, and get back on the freeway going in the opposite direction. When doing so I noticed that the road was icy and that I would need to be cautious as to how fast I made the turn or I would roll my vehicle off the embankment back onto the freeway. I woke up realizing that God just warned me not to make the needed changes too quickly. While some might have felt our transition happened rather fast, it was much slower than it would have been without that dream. Each step was preceded by a clear Word from God.

He let me know when that season of "cautious turning" was over through another dream. In it I saw the same freeway, but this time I was going the opposite direction. There was bright green grass on both sides of the road, and the pavement was wet from the melted ice. As strange as it may sound, the water didn't pose any danger to traveling at high speeds but instead was a sign of His fresh outpouring. The ice, that made a quick transition dangerous and unwise, had melted. There were no other cars to slow down or impede our progress. In giving me this dream He spoke, saying, "It's time to pull out the stops." This second dream occurred around 18 months after the first one. The majority of the people had left that were going to leave and I was now given liberty to go at a pace more suitable to the increasing winds of change.

THE LANGUAGE OF DARK SAYINGS (PROV. 1:6 KJV)

God sometimes speaks to us by hiding truths in phrases, stories, riddles, and circumstances. The meaning is there for us to find. When we *lean into God*, anticipating His voice, it becomes easier to discern when those circumstances are from God, or are merely unusual events in life. This unique language from God is an invitation to enter His great adventure.

Parables. At my request, a member of our maintenance team took a dear prophet friend and me around our church's near 70 acres to find the corners of the property line. We drove stakes into the ground at the corners. Each stake had a different colored flag attached, representing a particular gift and calling upon our church. This was not something I had done before and found it to be a unique experience to walk the grounds and pray according to what the prophet sees. While it was different for me, I trusted him.

Upon driving the last stake into the ground, four geese flew by. The prophet told me the goose is the *watchdog* of the old world, and they represented the angels who stood at the four corners of the property guarding what God is doing there.

Jesus was teaching through the use of parables when He gave the disciples the promise that the Father has given us access to His mysteries (see Matt. 13:11). There are patterns of interpretation that can help us to find His intended message. For example, the number four represents the earth—the four corners of the earth; north, south, east, and west; etc. Understanding these things can help us to more clearly hear everything from simple words of affirmation to great words of revelation.

Riddles. I include this story in the *riddle* category because it needs an interpretation. Sometimes the Lord speaks in ways that can be researched through biblical principles of interpretation. For example, the number 50 means Jubilee. It comes from the Jubilee principle (forgiving all debt and releasing all slaves) that Israel was instructed to follow every 50 years. The following story could not be interpreted in that way. God alone could explain.

In October 2003 I woke up at 5:55 A.M. after running into those numbers several times in just a few days. While lying in bed I said out loud, "What are you trying to tell me?" Immediately I was asleep as though someone knocked me out. He then spoke audibly saying, "The anointing for the day of the cancellation of debt is upon you." I instantly woke up realizing that I had been asleep for maybe three minutes. Since that day, all debt is gone from our lives, with the exception of our mortgage, which we believe is next. The numbers were like a puzzle that needed explanation from the manufacturer.

There are great books that give us principles of interpretation for numbers and symbols in the Bible and in life. However, I doubt that any of them would say that 555 means the cancellation of debt. I recommend people use those books as guides, but seek the Lord to see if there is something else He wants to say. Parables tend to be more symbolic, while riddles need divine explanation.

Unusual Coincidences. I have paid little attention to these for most of my life. It's only been in the last couple of years that His language has become more obvious to me in this way. While it would be wrong to say that every coincidence has the voice of God in it, God is speaking through them more often than you might think.

He got my attention recently with the following chain of events. I checked into my hotel preparing for some meetings in the great state of Texas. The man behind the counter gave me room key #308. I gave it no thought. When I went to the next city I noticed I was again given a key for room #308. It seemed like a strange coincidence, but I can't say I felt it was anything but an unusual coincidence. Then I woke up at 3:08 in the morning. God finally had my attention. I asked, "What are you trying to tell me?" The answer didn't come for several days; while sitting at my desk in my office it hit me, about 18 years earlier I had been seeking the Lord whether or not I should attempt to write.

It had been in my heart for quite some time, but I was never a great student, and had missed much of what I would need to know in order to be a writer. But I had this desire that wouldn't go away. In response to my question about writing, He woke me in the middle of the night and said these words, "Isaiah 30, verse 8." When I opened the Bible to see what it said I read, *"Now go, and write."* Very soon afterward, I began to write small articles for our church bulletin. I made time for it in my regular schedule so that I could learn more of what I needed to know through experience.

Now 18 years later I had written a fair amount, but I had filled my most recent schedule with conferences and other traveling engagements. At the time of the "308" word, it had been months since I had set any time aside for writing. In fact, my schedule was making that goal more and more impossible. The number 308 was a reminder of my question to God, His answer, and the subsequent call on my life. The conviction of the Lord came upon me and I repented. I met with my staff to go over my calendar for the next several months and set aside blocks of time for writing. Even the writing of this book is in response to that word.

During that same trip to Texas I had another experience that was new to me. I had a word of knowledge in a meeting about someone with a broken tailbone. A woman yelled out that it was her and that she broke it giving birth to her child. She was instantly healed without prayer. Moments later I had a word of knowledge about someone with broken ribs. The same woman spoke loudly from the back of the room, "I broke my ribs carrying my child (in pregnancy)." She was again healed instantly. In the next town someone came to me to testify that they had just been healed of an injury they suffered while giving birth to their child. (I don't remember ever having someone healed of something of this nature—now, two cities in

SECRETS TO IMITATING GOD

a row women were healed of birth-related issues. That is the language of the Spirit—unusual coincidences.) I stopped the meeting and asked for all those who had ongoing physical problems caused either by pregnancy or giving birth to stand up. Around ten women stood. Over the next few minutes at least eight of them testified that they were healed.

Unusual Circumstances. The burning bush of Moses' experience would fall into this category. These are highly unusual situations that usually seem to have no meaning in and of themselves. God brings those events into our lives to get our attention, hoping we will "turn aside" from our agendas and plans. *"When the Lord saw that he turned aside to look, God called to him from the midst of the bush and said, 'Moses, Moses!'"* (Exod. 3:4 NASB). When Moses turned aside, God spoke.

We have a pre-service prayer meeting on Friday nights. Many meet in the church dining room to pray for the meeting. One night I got there a bit early to pray alone. Soon after my arrival, a roadrunner with a lizard in its mouth came up to the wall of windows facing the west. He started to dance and jump at the window as though he were trying to get inside. I live in Redding, California, and have spent quite a bit of time outdoors. I had never seen a roadrunner in my life and never even heard of one in northern California. I got within 3 feet of him and thought, "This is too strange to not be prophetic." Minutes later he left. The time came for others to come to pray, and the room began to fill up. Then the roadrunner returned. One of my staff members said, "Oh, the roadrunner's back." I asked him what he meant. He said, "Yeah. He was here last week." I responded, "You're kidding!" He obviously wasn't.

For the next several months the roadrunner came to most every prayer meeting, usually with a lizard in its mouth. Some of our youth leaders began to meet in the dining room to pray before their main meeting on Wednesday nights. The roadrunner started to come to that prayer meeting as well, usually with a lizard in its mouth. I used to have a Signs and Wonders class on Sunday morning. One morning I talked about the *signs that make you wonder*, and used the roadrunner as an illustration. Almost on cue he came up to the window as before. The people pointed and said, "You mean him!" I was shocked. He came almost "on cue."

News began to spread about this strange recurring event. Many tried to help by doing research to find the meaning. I was told that in the natural the roadrunner is related to the eagle. They're one of the few animals that will kill and eat a rattlesnake, which we do have in our area. (I was happy about that.) I already knew that eagles represent the prophetic and snakes usually speak of the devil. Knowing that the enemy would be trampled down through the increase of the prophetic brought great joy.

During this time we starting building our 24-hour prayer chapel called The Alabaster House. The roadrunner started to shift his focus from our prayer meetings to that building. He would actually perch himself on a rock which many of our folks had taken to calling the Eagle Rock, because of its unusual resemblance to the head of an eagle. It was as though the roadrunner, who loved prayer meetings, was overseeing the prayer house building project.

One day he got inside the church facility, right above the original prayer room. One of our custodians, Jason (an extremely prophetic student in our school of ministry), found the bird in a large second story meeting room. Jason turned on some worship music and sat in the middle of the room on the floor and worshiped the Lord. The roadrunner came over right in front of him and seemed to join him. He would occasionally leave Jason and go to the window as though he wanted outside, but then he came back and stood right in front of Jason as he worshiped.

Jason started to feel bad for taking so much time for worship while he was supposed to be cleaning that he turned the music off and went downstairs to clean other rooms. The roadrunner went with him. Suddenly someone opened the door in the long hallway and startled the bird. He flew to the end of the hall, hit our plate glass window, and died instantly.

This bird had become like a beloved mascot to us, reminding us of the importance of prayer. He loved prayer meetings and had become a prophetic symbol of God's promised increase for us as a church family. He came during a time when many members had already left or were leaving, and the finances were extremely tight. The lizard in his mouth spoke to us of God bringing all that was needed for this move of God. As eagles represent the prophets, it was obvious that the prophetic was actually getting stronger and stronger within our church body.

Jason found me to tell me this horrible news. I asked him to show me where he had put the bird so we could go and raise it from the dead. With a sense of purpose and confidence we walked around back where the roadrunner was laying. It made perfect sense to me that God would want the roadrunner alive. Why should He want our living prophetic message dead? Strangely, I actually felt the anointing lift when I got around 5 to 6 feet away from the bird. It was puzzling to me. God's presence was upon me in a strong way until I got close. It was like He was saying my resolve was good, but my application and timing was not. The roadrunner was not raised from the dead. We were quite sad. Then the Lord spoke, "What I am bringing into the house has to have a way of being released from the house, or it will die in the house."

That word applied to the money we desperately needed, the manifest gifts of the Spirit we were crying out for, the specific anointings we were growing in, and the people who were being saved. The word was costly and clear; *we only get to keep what we give away.*

Prophecy. This is one of the most important areas of my life. God has been very faithful to put prophetic people in my life at just the right times—people of great integrity. As a result, we have a strong prophetic culture. To encourage risk on the part of prophetic people we emphasize the responsibility of the hearer to discern whether or not a word is from God. In the Old Testament the Spirit of God was upon the prophet alone, so he bore all the responsibility. Today the Spirit of the Lord is within every believer, so the responsibility is now given to the people of God to discern whether or not a specific word is from God. When it is from God, we respond according to the direction given in the Word. When it's not from God, we try to learn from it and sharpen our prophetic skills.[5]

Prophecy comes to us from another person. While this can be a very dangerous form of hearing from God, it can also be one of the most dramatic and faith-building. Once it has been confirmed as having its origins from God, we must act accordingly.

Kris Vallotton prophesied over me early one Sunday morning saying that God was going to support me publicly by bringing in the total amount of money needed to build our prayer house in one offering. This was the very day we felt we were to present the project and follow the presentation by receiving an offering. In the natural this was the worst time to expect a large offering as this was toward the end of the mass exodus—our lowest point in numbers. The amount needed to build the prayer house was an unheard of amount for our church to give in one offering, even before so many people had left. By the end of the service our CPA totaled the offering and we announced to the whole church that we surpassed our goal by $8 and some change.

Testimonies. In the Old Testament the word testimony comes from the word, "do again." The implication is that God wants to repeat His wonderful works when we speak of what He has done. In the New Testament we have a confirmation of that principle in Revelation 19:10 (NASB): "*The testimony of Jesus is the spirit of prophecy.*" This says that if God has done it once, He is ready to do it again. The spoken or written record of whatever Jesus has done carries the prophetic anointing to cause a change in events in the spirit realm so that the miracle spoken of can happen again. Indeed, a testimony often carries the actual voice of the Lord. Learning to recognize it will enable us to accommodate and cooperate with the move of His Spirit that was released in the testimony.

One Sunday morning I was teaching about the power of a testimony and telling the story of a little boy that was healed of clubfeet. A family was visiting from out of state. They had a little girl, almost 2 years old, whose feet turned inward so severely that she would trip over her feet when she ran. The mother heard the testimony and said in her heart, "I'll take that for my daughter." When she picked up her little girl from our nursery, she noticed her feet were already perfectly straight! No one prayed for her. God spoke in the testimony, the mother heard, and the daughter was healed.

Senses. Our five senses are not only instruments that help us to enjoy life, they are tools that enable us to hear from God better. In the Psalms we are told that the songwriter's body actually hungered for God (see Ps. 84:2). In Hebrews, the writer states that the senses were to be *trained to discern good and evil* (see Heb. 5:14 NASB). In that passage, this ability is actually used as a mark of maturity—being able to use the senses to recognize God.

During one of our Sunday morning worship services, a young lady came and stood in front of me. I sit on the end of the aisle, in the first row in the sanctuary. (The front of the auditorium fills up with people who want to give a more exuberant expression than you can do while stuck in the middle of a row.) As people raised their hands or danced with joy, she made all kinds of different motions with her hands and arms. We have quite a number of people involved in the occult who come to our meetings—some come out of hunger, some come to disturb. We don't make a big deal out of it, but we do stay on the alert.

I was puzzled by her and tried to discern what was going on. It was as though my discernment was shut off. But I did notice that it got cold where I was standing. I remembered a demonic encounter that my brother had several years earlier where his office turned very cold and remained so for several hours. So I walked about 15 feet away and noticed the temperature was normal. I went to Summer, who heads our prophetic dance ministry, and asked her to please go up on the stage and dance. I told her, "We need to break something." When she did, the young lady collapsed right in front of me. The demonic power that inspired her was broken through the prophetic act of the dance—*physical obedience brings spiritual release*. My wife knelt down next to her and brought deliverance to her and then led her to Christ.

CONNECTED TO ANOTHER WORLD

Having the heart and the ability to hear from God leaves us with an unlimited potential in resourcing earth with Heaven's resources. That connection to His world will prove necessary as we boldly invade the kingdoms of this world that are becoming the Kingdom of our Lord and Christ! That is the subject of the next chapter.

Endnotes

1. Many prominent authors and conference speakers add fuel to this fire of fear assuming that because the new age movement promotes it, its origins must be from the devil. I find that form of reasoning weak at best. If we follow that line of thought we will continue to give the devil the tools that God has given us for success in life and ministry. In doing so we will be building a confidence in the power of darkness above the Spirit of God.

2. We had many people in the revival of this hour speak to us in this way—"We know this is a move of God, it's just not for us." It's a shocking thing to see believers acknowledge God is among them, but watch them not respond to Him by crying out for more.

3. This is a phrase I use to describe *anticipating God to act or speak at any time.*

4. Cal Pierce, now of the Spokane Healing Rooms.

5. Kris Vallotton's Prophetic Manual, *A Call To War*, provides much practical instruction about this subject.

CHAPTER 5

Invading Babylon

Any gospel that doesn't work
in the marketplace doesn't work.

We have been given authority over this planet. It was first given to us in the commission God gave to mankind in Genesis (see Gen. 1:28-29). and was then restored to us by Jesus after His resurrection (see Matt. 28:18). But Kingdom authority is different than is typically understood by many believers. It is the authority to set people free from torment and disease, destroying the works of darkness. It is the authority to move the resources of Heaven through creative expression to meet human need. It is the authority to bring Heaven to earth. It is the authority to serve.

As with most Kingdom principles, the truths of humanity's dominion and authority are dangerous in the hands of those who desire to rule over others. These concepts seem to validate some people's selfishness. But when these truths are expressed through the humble servant, the world is rocked to its core. Becoming servants to this world is the key to open the doors of possibility that are generally thought of as closed or forbidden.

Neither our understanding of servants or of kings can help us much with this challenge for both are soiled in our world, probably beyond repair. That is where Jesus comes in. He is the King of all kings, yet the Servant of all. This unique combination found in the Son of God is the call of the hour upon us. As truth is usually found in the tension of two conflicting realities, we have an issue to solve. Like our Master we are both royalty and servants (see Rev. 1:5; Mark 10:45). Solomon warns of a potential problem, saying, *"the earth cannot bear up under a slave when he becomes king"* (Prov. 30:21-22 NASB). Yet Jesus contradicted Solomon's warning without nullifying the statement, by being effective at both. *Jesus served with the heart of a king, but ruled with the heart of a servant.* This is the essential combination that must be embraced by those longing to shape the course of history.

Royalty is my identity. Servanthood is my assignment. Intimacy with God is my life source. So, before God, I'm an intimate. Before people, I'm a servant. Before the powers of hell, I'm a ruler, with no tolerance for their influence. Wisdom knows which role to fulfill at the proper time.

INVADING THE MOUNTAINS OF INFLUENCE

There are seven realms of society that must come under the influence of the King and His Kingdom. For that to happen, we, as citizens of the Kingdom, must invade. The dominion of the Lord Jesus is manifest whenever the people of God go forth to serve by bringing the order and blessing of His world into this one.

The effort by many believers to simply obtain positions of leadership is putting the cart before the horse. Servanthood remains our strong suit, and it's through service that we can bring the benefits of His world into the reach of the common man.

The Kingdom is likened unto leaven (see Matt. 13:33). As yeast has an effect on the dough it is "worked into," so we will transform all the kingdoms of this world as we are worked into its systems.

From there we must display His dominion and rule. As the people of God move into these realms of society to show forth the benefits and values of the Kingdom, His government expands.

For this invasion to work effectively, we must correct a few misconceptions. In doing so, it is equally important to establish the necessary Kingdom principles in their proper order.

There is no such thing as secular employment for the believer. Once we are born again, everything about us is redeemed for Kingdom purposes. It is all spiritual. It is either a legitimate Kingdom expression, or we shouldn't be involved at all.

Every believer is in full-time ministry—only a few have pulpits in sanctuaries. The rest have their pulpit in their areas of expertise and favor in the world system. Be sure to preach only good news. And when necessary, use words!

The call of God is important, not because of the title it carries (or doesn't carry). It's valuable because of the One who called us. An assignment to be in business is as valuable in the Kingdom as is the call to be an evangelist. The privilege to be a stay-at-home wife and mother is equal in importance to being a missionary. Embrace your call with the faithfulness and thankfulness worthy of the One who has called you.

Our eternal rewards do not come because of how much money we made, how many souls were saved, or how many homeless people we fed. All rewards are given based on our faithfulness to what God has given and called us to be and to do. The honor we give to one another must not be only to those who have obvious spiritual occupations. Honor must be given to those who are faithful in the call, no matter what it is.

Prophetic ministry is not to be focused on the sins of the world. It takes very little discernment to find the dirt in people's lives. The prophetic in its purest form is designed to find the gold in people's lives and call it to the surface. This approach changes the attitude of the world toward the Church, and makes it possible for us to be contributors to society, not just confronters of all that is evil.

COVERT VS. OVERT MINISTRY

Our church and ministry school is most often known for its overt ministry—outward and aggressive. We have seen hundreds of people healed and delivered in public places. We've even had words of knowledge[1] given over the intercom of a local grocery store. The results were amazing. People responded by gathering around cash register number 10 and received the healing ministry of Jesus through one of our young men named Chad. Following God's merciful display of power, they were invited to give their lives to Christ. Many did.

Overt ministry is very common for us. Whether it's in the mall, neighborhoods, schools, or places of business, the Gospel is brought to those in need. But this is only half of the needed ministry equation. The other half is covert ministry. The word *covert* means "hiding place." This refers to ministry that is more subtle in nature. It is hidden not because of cowardice but rather out of wisdom. It works within the systems of this world to bring about change by reestablishing the proper norms of thought, beliefs, disciplines, and relational boundaries. In other words, we work to change the culture. This requires more time, as the goal is not a specific healing or conversion. The goal is the transformation of society itself by invading the systems of the city in order to serve. Serving for their benefit, not ours, is the key. As someone once said, "*We shouldn't try to be the best in the world. We should try to be the best for the world!*" When we set aside our religious agendas to make others a success, we have learned the Kingdom mind-set, and have become a part of the transformation movement.

DUMPING RELIGIOUS AGENDAS

The Church is sometimes known for its willingness to serve, but usually with well-meaning spiritual agendas as the ultimate goal. It almost sounds blasphemous, but serving simply to get people saved is a religious agenda. As pure and noble as it may seem to us as believers, it is manipulative to the world, and is viewed as impure service. The world can smell it a mile away. We put them on the defensive when we carry such reasons for serving into their sphere of responsibility. But, for example, when we volunteer in our local school to help the principal succeed, then we've crossed the line into territory seldom visited by the Church. It is serving for the benefit of another. It's that kind of a servant that the world welcomes. The amazing bonus is you also end up influencing the school in ways you never thought possible, including bringing people to Christ.

What would happen if parents volunteered in their local schools to help the teacher succeed? Generally teachers have an authentic interest in children succeeding in life. They invest themselves for the sake of another generation. They deserve honor for their commitment; and we can help them succeed.

School districts are accustomed to Christians seeking positions on local school boards. Sometimes parents will work with another parent to get a principal to fire a teacher because they're an atheist, or to change a particular curriculum. But what would happen if we actually invaded the systems of this world to give honor where it is due instead of dishonor those whom we think deserve expulsion? The former brings transformation through favor. The latter is a self-fulfilling prophecy of rejection as the world has few options but to protect what they are stewards over from the *outside group* (us) that wants to be in control. Christians are notorious for trying to take over schools through political maneuvering.[2] It may work from time to time, but it is not Kingdom. Nor is it long-lasting. There is a better way.

Interestingly enough, the fullness of the Spirit can also be seen in these two distinct approaches to ministry. As stated in Chapter 2, the fullness of the Spirit makes way for "believers that walk in wisdom, making practical contributions to the needs of society, who also confront the impossibilities of life through the provisions of the Cross—solutions through supernatural display. Perhaps it is these two things working in tandem that should be considered *the balanced Christian life.*"

THE SEVEN MIND-MOLDERS OF SOCIETY

Both Dr. Bill Bright, founder of Campus Crusade for Christ, and Loren Cunningham, founder of Youth With A Mission, received the same revelation from God around the same period of time: there are seven major realms of influence in society that shape the way we live and think. These mountains of influence must be invaded by Kingdom-oriented people for the transformation of society to take place. These mountains are:

- Home.
- Church.
- Education.
- Media (Electronic and Print).
- Government & Politics.
- Performing Arts (including Entertainment and Sports).
- Commerce (including Science and Technology).

It is interesting to note that God gave this insight to two men who lead significant youth movements. It is obvious that God wants an entire generation to value their call regardless of what title it brings, teaching them how to invade a culture for its total and complete transformation. God fully intends for there to be a fulfillment of His Word about *"the kingdoms of this world have become the kingdoms of our Lord"* (Rev. 11:15).

The following list is a little different from the original. It is not an improved list, but it does have a slightly different emphasis to more accurately represent our application of these principles. They are: *Business, Education, the Church, Family, Arts/ Entertainment, Science & Medicine, and Government* (not listed in any order of importance).

Wisdom is the vital ingredient to be effective in this invasion. As a reminder, we've defined wisdom with these three words: Integrity, Creativity, and Excellence. It is the display of the mind of God, always in the context of integrity that brings forth the creative solutions for life while holding to the standards of excellence. These play a vital role in manifesting the Kingdom in ways that honor God and solve the issues of life for humankind.

BUSINESS

Many Christians have tried to gain favor and position in the business world, but have failed miserably. It is hard to gain favor in that world without prosperity. Prosperity is a primary measure for success in that arena. With that in mind, the world is also full of stories of great financial success that were disasters in every other way. People instinctively want both—outward and inward success. The Kingdom businessperson has the chance to display a more complete picture of success by focusing not only on money. Their celebration of life, with all its many facets, will grab the attention of those hopelessly trapped in the "money is success" daily grind.

While there is room for overt ministry in every part of life, it is generally not the outward preaching of the Gospel that secures the place of favor in the eyes of the unbelieving businessperson. It is divine order (Kingdom) in the overall approach to life—to self, family, business, and community.

Even the world knows that money is not the only measure of true success. Most of those in business want much more than money for their labors. Simple things like joy, a happy home life, recognition, and meaningful friendships are an important part of the life of true prosperity. John, the Beloved, referred to this as "prosperity of soul" (see 3 John 2). Mixed into this quest is the cry for significance. The Kingdom businessperson is poised to illustrate that element by their approach to life. The extra efforts in world relief, along with the personal participation in helping the poor of our own cities as well as other projects requiring giving and sacrifice, help to give definition for the favor of God that is upon the Kingdom businessperson.

One of our men sold cars at a local used car lot owned by believers. When a woman came in to buy a car, he noticed that she was very troubled. Through the direction of the Holy Spirit, he was able to minister to her quite profoundly. She opened up to God and received major healing in her heart. When they were through he told her, "Because you have opened up your heart to me, I cannot sell you a car. It would be unfair for me to do so. Instead I will introduce you to another salesman who will help you find the kind of car you are looking for." He was unwilling to come close to the possibility of taking advantage of this woman by selling her something when she had become emotionally vulnerable to him.

Kris Vallotton used to own an automobile repair shop and several car part stores. A man once stole some tires and rims from his shop. However, he didn't realize that Kris knew he was the thief, and brought his car in to Kris's repair shop. When that customer came in to pick up his car and pay his bill, Kris took him into his office and told him, "I know you stole my tires and rims. And to show you that I forgive you I am giving you the work we did on your truck for free." The man went to his vehicle and sat in silence for about five minutes without doing anything, just staring off into space. (Occasionally, a person receives a Gospel tract that they will never forget. This man received one stamped "Paid in Full.")

Then there is the humorous story of an employee wanting to get one of his workmates in trouble. He told his boss, "Every time I pass his office he's just staring out the window. He needs to be fired!" His boss responded, "Leave him alone! Just the other day he came up with an idea that saved us over $300,000—by just staring out that window."

Creativity is a necessary component for the Kingdom businessperson. It brings fresh ideas that keep adventure as a central part of their assignment. Witty inventions are going to increase in the Christian community, as God is using that expression of wisdom to bring about a transfer of wealth for Kingdom purposes.

"Do you see a man who excels in his work? He will stand before kings; He will not stand before unknown men" (Prov. 22:29). This verse tells us two things: One, the result of lives pursuing excellence; they will influence the influencers. Two, kings demand excellence. Many compromise in this area to make a quick buck, but it is excellence that provides wealth for the long term. It's a wealth that has no sorrow (see Prov. 10:22). Excellence is a Kingdom value, and is not to be confused with perfectionism, which is a counterfeit and comes from the religious spirit. One of the clearest paths of promotion is through excellence.

EDUCATION

Often times the Church reacts to the abuses of the world system and creates an error equal in danger to one we've rejected. This was never truer than in the realm of education. The Western mind-set, that values reason as the only proper measure of truth, has undermined the Gospel. This worldview, which Paul battled in First Corinthians, has been embraced by our educational culture. It is anti-Christ in nature. The supernatural then becomes subject to the evaluation of ignorant people. But the solution to this problem is not to reject education; the answer is to invade. Our rejection removes us from our place of preservation as *the salt of the earth* (Matt. 5:13).

God is willing to debate anyone (see Isa. 1:18). He is very secure in His understanding and arguments. He also backs up His insights with evidence that will bear up under scrutiny. Invading the educational system is essential as it's this mountain that greatly shapes the minds and expectations of the younger generation. While it could be argued that today entertainers have a greater role in shaping the minds of the young, it is the educators who generally shape the minds of the entertainers in their way of thinking.

Our young people need to believe they will be able to live their entire lives on this earth, and plan accordingly. Get educated, married, have children, all with a Kingdom mind-set. Too many generations who experience the outpouring of the Spirit forfeit their desires for training and education in order to do "the Lord's work." As noble as that sounds, it comes from a misunderstanding of real ministry aided by the idea that we will be taken out of here at any moment. This is a tender subject, as we must be ready to be with the Lord at any given moment. But, as the Church regains the value for *no job is secular for the believer*, the esteem will return for the positions in society that had little value in prior generations. The desire for Heaven is right and healthy, but it must not replace our commission; *"Your kingdom come. Your will be done, on earth as it is in heaven"* (Matt. 6:10 NASB). We were not commissioned to look into the clouds for His coming (see Acts 1:11). We were commanded to "occupy" until He comes (Luke 19:13 KJV). *Occupy* is a military term. And according to Kingdom values, occupation is always for the purpose of advancement.

Our children must become educated, and become educators. But that goal is not complete without the Kingdom mind-set. We are sending them into dangerous territory to get their training. Choose their schools carefully. Each teacher that trains your child is a delegated authority—delegated by you. The Bible does not give the authority for training children to the government, no matter how noble their intent. It rests upon your shoulders, so pray, pray, pray, and educate, educate, educate.

We would never send our child to a restaurant where only one in ten die of food poisoning. Yet we do that daily in our educational system, with odds that are much worse than one in ten. We often send them out, unguarded, into a system that works to undermine faith and ultimately their relationship with God. The answer is not to withdraw from society and move into the mountains to preserve the family unit. The answer is to train and invade. Our training is superior to theirs if it's authentic, because it is driven by a personal relationship with God, and includes transforming divine encounters.

As for the believers who are already in the educational system, bravo! Invade with a Kingdom mind-set. Such a way of thinking provides the mooring needed to stay stable in storms and conflict. It also puts you in place to provide the answers to the dilemmas created by the inferior "Greek" mind-set. Most bad ideas (including bad theology) are only one divine encounter away from oblivion. We owe people an encounter with God. And that is what you carry into that mountain of influence.

Most people in our culture unknowingly live under the influence of a dark kingdom. Yet they suffer with problems that have their answer in the Kingdom of God and the believer. Both wisdom and power are available to us that we might provide solutions from another world that meet their needs.

At Bethel Church, we have a waiting list of schools wanting us to be part of their after-school program. Why? We have come alongside to serve, not take over. The liberty that is given to our teams (presently seven schools a week) is really quite amazing. There are many who believe that what we are doing is impossible. And as long as the Church maintains an adversarial relationship with the educational system, it will remain impossible.

Throughout Scripture we see that when God's people step forward to serve, God backs it up with power. The schools are asking for our help. They face problems on a daily basis that were unheard of 30 years ago. It is our hour to invade, serve, and shine for His glory!

Moral values are the basis for integrity. And moral values are rooted in the character of God. The supernatural educator has access to a realm of stability that others don't have. That is not to say one has to be a believer to have integrity. Many unbelievers do. But the supernatural element available in the realm of character is reserved for those who have the Spirit of the resurrected Christ living in them. Young people need educators with integrity, but they also need those who believe in them. Calling out the treasure in a young person can mark them for good forever. Often times such an educator plants a seed that another person will harvest, but that is the joy of this Kingdom—no words return void. (See 1 Cor. 3:5-9 and Isa. 55:11.)

We have a team of educators in our church who, through Kingdom principles, have tapped into ways of defeating learning disorders in many children. This creative expression came to them through divine inspiration. It is the result of people realizing they have legal access into the mysteries of the Kingdom, and have a responsibility to bring those secrets into play in the lives of those with great needs. This affects all the lives within their sphere of influence. There are answers to every problem we face. There are methods of training people that are far superior to what we know now. Kingdom-oriented people, who know who they are in Christ, will access these secrets for the benefit of all who are around them.

Excellence is more than exhorting students to get good grades. It is a gift from God that uses the full measure of resources from both the natural and spiritual realities. Some just seem to be good at everything, while others appear to have been absent the day gifts and talents were given out. In reality, each person has an area where God has gifted them to excel and it's the wise educator who discovers that area in a child. An excellent teacher will bring excellence out of the one who can't find it in themselves.

ENTERTAINMENT

Entertainment includes the arts, professional sports, and the media.

It wasn't too long ago that the world of entertainment was deemed so unholy that believers were forbidden to enter. The Church has often fallen to the notion that darkness is stronger than light. Entertainment is a mountain of influence that must be invaded. The indictment of that realm being 'unholy' was accurate, but unfortunately, it is also a self-fulfilling prophecy—anywhere we do not invade becomes darker in our absence. We are the "*light of the world*" (Matt. 5:14). The realms of society that we fail to invade are hopelessly lost to darkness. Invasion is the responsibility of light.

This is a realm which ought to have edification as a primary objective. When it is perverted, it steals and plunders. But in its primary function, it creates. Recreation comes from this—re-creation! It must not only be creative, it must create.

Heaven has what we want. Every creative dream is fulfilled in Heaven. The great news is that we have access to that realm through prayers of faith. For example: there are sounds in Heaven that earth has never heard. When a musician taps into that reality and communicates that sound here, Heaven will have found agreement and will invade. All art finds its origins in the person of God; more specifically, it's found in His holiness. The Scripture says, "*in the beauty of holiness*" (Ps. 29:2). It's tragic that holiness gets such poor treatment from the people of God. It is God's nature, His person. Beauty pours forth from that one attribute (see 2 Chron. 20:21).

When I was growing up there were few Christians in this mountain of influence. Baseball was my love, and I only knew of two Christians in all of baseball. I'm sure there were more, but the point is it wasn't common. Today there are many teams that have a large percentage of genuine believers. The same is true of the arts. No field is left untouched. God is planting His last days' army in these strategic places of influence.

Mel Gibson's movie *The Passion of the Christ* is testimony to the turning that is taking place in this mountain. The doors of this realm are open wide, as creativity is at an all-time low. Immorality, jealousy, hatred, and revenge are poor substitutes for real creativity.

There's such a vacuum in the area of integrity in this mountain that all true Kingdom people will quickly stand out. However, we can't be nonchalant about the pressure to conform to worldly standards that the believer will face. Being a stumbling block to others has been become an art form for many. People receive justification for their own immoral lifestyles by getting others to fall morally. But for those who have true foundations, the sky is the limit. In crisis, people will always turn to those who are stable. Integrity will be a beacon of light to those wandering through this land of disappointment and shame.

It might seem that creativity is where we have the biggest challenge in this mountain of influence. The opposite is true. Writers, designers, and the like have substituted sensuality for creativity. This has left a huge gap in the area of real originality. Anyone who has escaped the pressure to duplicate trash will automatically be positioned to create. Learning how to pray in the Spirit and *soak* in His presence will give great advantages to those wanting to invade this mountain. Heaven has what we're looking for. And you'll have to go there to get it. The best novels and plays have yet to be written. The most beautiful melodies to ever grace the human ear are yet to be discovered. Those with an ear for God, discovering the experience of "being seated in heavenly places" will have access to things no other generation has ever seen before.

Many have mistakenly thought that the devil has all the good music. He is not creative. Tragically, he receives credit for too many things, even by the Church. How is it that an ungodly person can write a beautiful piece of music, or a brilliant script for a movie? How is it they can paint a masterpiece or design buildings that take our breath away? They were made in the image of God, and He doesn't remove that distinguishing feature when a person rebels against Him (see Rom. 11:29). In recent days, believers who have adopted the Kingdom mind-set have caught up to, and in some cases surpassed, the world in the area of excellence and will continue to do so.

THE CHURCH

Jesus gave His disciples a warning about the potential influence of religion on the mind, saying, "*Beware of the leaven of the Pharisees and the leaven of Herod*" (Mark 8:15). The mentality of the Pharisee places God at the center of everything, but He's impersonal and powerless. Their God dwells mostly in the realm of theory and sup-position. They excel at traditions that are convenient, and reverence that is self-serving. But there's not much in the religious community that is actually Kingdom. It has a wide-open door for people with a renewed mind.

Many in the religious community have a lot of sincerity. And when they see someone who actually practices the purity and power from the pages of Scripture, something comes alive in them. They hope it's true. They just lack examples. Kingdom-oriented people have great opportunities in the midst of great opposition. But the rewards are worth every risk.

Success is often measured by numbers of people attending serv-ices, copies of books or CDs sold, or how many watch their TV show. One of the most common fears in this world of influence is that "someone will steal my sheep." Being committed to another leader's success, with no personal agenda for gain, is essential for invasion into this mountain. Ignoring the external measurements of success will enable the leader in this realm to value what the King values—passion, purity, power, and people.

Compassion is one of the greatest tools we possess to invade this mountain of influence. One of the churches in our network wanted to touch a local Catholic orphanage. They live in a country where

Protestants and Catholics do not work together. In fact, they are known for preaching against one another from their pulpits. When the pastor went to the priest to talk, the priest was naturally guarded. Yet the pastor worked hard to share with him that they wanted the opportunity to honor them for their heart for the orphans. He noted that they were doing something important that none of the Protestants had been willing to do. The pastor asked if there was anything the children needed. The priest told them of their need for shoes. In spite of their very limited resources, the Protestant church bought shoes for each child. The sacrifice needed for this particular church family to do such a thing is beyond what I can write about on these pages. Yet they did. From this simple act of love, the entire Church in this region has been rocked by this display of an authentic Gospel. And a city is being healed from the religious animosity that has ruled over that area for decades.

The area of morality and integrity should be the area in which we have little problem. But that is not the case. While I don't believe the statistics that claim the Church (authentic believers) is equal to the world in divorce and immorality, the numbers are admittedly far too high. Divine encounters, accurate teaching from Scripture, and accountability to other members of the Body can help change this problem. Righteous people can provide a righteous peer pressure. When fellowship becomes valuable enough that it is sacrificial, then those in fellowship begin to walk in the light—openly, with integrity and accountability. (See Heb. 13:15-16.)

The Church is known for its ruts, not its new ideas. Thankfully a great transformation is taking place in that area. While change for change's sake is not always healthy, those resistant to change are usually resistant to the Holy Spirit. If anyone should be known for creativity, it should be those in whom the accurate image of the Creator has been formed—born-again believers. There are better ways of doing things. Always. And the Church is in the place of leading the way. Cultural relevance is rightfully the cry of the hour, but it must be relevance *with* power!

The Church has often taken the low road in the realm of excellence because of a misunderstanding of humility. But the choice of that road usually flows from low faith, and humility gets the blame. Excellence can and must be the expression of true humility as humility declares, "Our best, for His glory!" Most of the areas that can bring the greatest results have the greatest risk. This is no exception. Excellence is Kingdom. Perfectionism is religion. Poverty is demonic.

FAMILY

The pressure being exerted on the family today makes this one of the easiest and most important areas to invade. Even those who seem to work overtime to destroy the family unit instinctively hunger for healthy relationships, significance, and a legacy. All a family needs to do to have influence in this mountain is to be healthy, and not hidden. When relationships are good and the boundaries of godly disciplines are intact, there is no limit to the influence of the Christian home. The problem has often been a false standard of holiness wherein the Christian doesn't associate with the unbeliever, yet maintains similar values and habits to them. The opposite should be our goal—mingle and associate with the lost, but don't take on their values or habits. That way we, as both salt and light, have our proper effect of preserving and exposing in order to bring them into their destiny. Healthy families that are intentional breed healthy families.

One of our local high schools was having a problem with some of their students. Some parents had lost control of their kids and were clueless as to what to do. The school was considering removing these students permanently from their program. The principal recognized an unusual gift for family life in a couple of our pastors. Their heart was not to dominate or take over; they simply wanted to serve. The principal took a huge risk and asked them to come and mentor these parents about functional home life. The transformation within the families' relationships was amazing. Teenagers who had previously cursed their parents to their face were suggesting the whole family play a board game before they all went to bed. Some of them requested a regular time to talk each evening. The turnaround was so astonishing that there is a waiting list of public schools that want this team to come and work with their parents.

When parents have godly character and wisdom for raising children, they produce a family that reflects the love and integrity of Christ. If children grow up seeing one standard in church and another at home, they tend to rebel against standards all together. Conversely, when integrity is genuine both in and out of the public eye, children grow up willing to pay the price needed to follow in their parents' footsteps, as long as they have been given room for individuality.

This is one area where an ounce of effort translates into a pound of impact. Few families actually purposely live the adventure of life together. Embracing such an adventure together is what gives place for creative expression to surface. My wife has been so good for our household in this area. She is adventurous by nature and tends to add joy to the things I might unintentionally crush by my intensity. I learned from her, because I wanted to learn. My family is better...and I am better, because of her quest for creativity in the home.

This simply means that we always do things to the best of our ability. Sometimes money is tight. Excellence can't be measured in buying the finest car or the most expensive clothes. Rather it is displayed in our approach to life—all of us, for all of Him. It's a great deal!

GOVERNMENT

Knowing that Jesus is the "desire of the nations" encourages us as we approach this mountain of influence. It means our simple task is to make the desired One visible.

Government usually lives in a crippled state because of the fear of voters. Noble people enter that world and end up losing their dreams on the altar of intimidation. The *leaven of Herod* poisons many (see Mark 8:15). But there is a new breed being groomed for this hour who fears only God and lives with a wisdom that enables one to dance through the minefield of public opinion. Such is the price of working effectively in government.

Those who climb this mountain of influence must realize that it is necessary to increase "*in favor with God and men*" (Luke 2:52), just as Jesus did. Proverbs is probably the most practical book of instruction on this subject. Reading a chapter a day, according to the date, will give leaders in this realm a compass bearing so that no issue arises that doesn't have a Kingdom solution.

One of the women in our congregation was recently working in an Arab country for the U.S. State Department. She was invited to give input into the educational system in that country. They had a problem with the discipline of high school boys, and though they rarely empower women in their country at that level, the favor upon her life was larger than the cultural barrier. She addressed the instructors and then wrote a paper on the subject, based on the principles we live by in our church—all Kingdom principles of discipline. Their educational leaders were so impressed with the report that they adopted it as the standard of discipline for their school system for the entire nation. The U.S. embassy responded in like manner, sending the report to their embassies around the world.

It is unfortunate that the words *integrity* and *politician* are considered an oxymoron. The Word of God remains true—"*when it goes well with the righteous, the city rejoices*" (Prov. 11:10). People instinctively want to be governed by people who are honest and righteous.

They want leaders who are not self-serving, but will actually govern sacrificially for the benefit of the whole. Here again is where we need to embrace the standard of Jesus, which is to serve like a king and rule like a servant. It is His way.

It is sad to see believers who fall to the political tactics of unbelieving opponents because their popularity has declined in the public opinion polls. There are better ways of doing things, from running a campaign to surrounding oneself with people of wisdom for good decisions. All of these things are marks of a person committed to the wisdom of creativity.

Two of the most basic roles of government are to create a realm of safety and a realm of prosperity. When governmental leaders use their position for personal gain, it amounts to prostituting their charisma for themselves. Excellence is found in doing our best for the sake of others.

SCIENCE & MEDICINE

This is becoming a bigger influence in the world all the time. Diseases are on the increase, with little sign of cures. I believe in divine healing and have seen thousands healed through Jesus Christ, but I'm not opposed to medical intervention. The entire medical community is gaining power, credibility, and influence throughout our society.

One of our ministry targets is to pray for all those who are with the dying. That includes doctors and nurses, ambulance workers, convalescent hospital employees, police, firefighters, etc. We are praying that the righteous are assigned to those places of influence, because we want to make it nearly impossible to get to hell from our city.

We have a person in a place of authority in one of the convalescent hospitals in our area. It is written on the medical charts that the nurses must call her when anyone is dying so she can be with them. If necessary she will even remove the family members from that patient for a few minutes while she prays with them to receive Christ. We don't want people politely going to hell from our city. You've heard the saying; *there are no atheists in foxholes*—the same could be said of those on the edge of eternity. People are very receptive to the Truth when they are facing death. Authentic love and compassion for people, expressed by those planted within that system, brings forth a wonderful harvest. It's amazing what we are allowed to do when we go in low just to serve. People know the difference between authentic love and a person fulfilling their religious obligations. Real love has very few opponents.

Christ-like character always puts others first. This highly respected industry has fallen on hard times due to the great number of doctors who make questionable decisions based on profit margins. Hospitals are often in the crosshairs of critics as they often operate without compassion. Yet that is not the norm. Most of those in this profession at least started out with sincere compassion and a desire to help others. Kingdom-oriented people will once again be easy to spot as the need is so great. And if those individuals believe in the power of God to heal, all the better. Miracles occur through the hands of medical professionals at an increasing rate. The number of doctors who attend our healing conferences is growing dramatically. It's a beautiful combination when we see a whole segment of society raised up that can work in both the natural and the supernatural realms to bring about good health.

More and more Christian doctors are being trained by God to find answers to health issues. As wonderful as healing is, divine health is greater. Believers have been given access to the mysteries of the Kingdom regarding this subject. It would be tragic to come to the end of time and have the only generation to experience divine health be the Israelites. They lived under an inferior covenant and were in rebellion against God. Inferior covenants cannot make superior promises. Those in this mountain of influence have access to things that the entire world is aggressively asking for. Asking God for specific solutions will enable those involved in medicine to give true creative expression to a dying world.

This group of professionals has a head start in the area of excellence, as they are accustomed to paying a significant price for their role in society. If they can maintain passion and discipline, while embracing a humble heart, nothing will be impossible for them.

Passion for God Creates Passion for Other Things

Keeping passionate and encouraged is vital while facing the privilege of ascending these mountains of influence. Passion wears out when it relies solely on self-motivation. God has fire in His eyes! Frequent encounters with Him will keep any flame in us burning. But encouragement is another matter. "*One who speaks in a tongue edifies himself*" (1 Cor. 14:4 NASB). Dr. Lance Wallnau adds an interesting twist to this word *edifies*. He points out that *edifice* is a related word, and that one who prays in tongues *builds the edifice from which the purposes of God for their life becomes manifest!* Perhaps this is why the apostle Paul claimed that he spoke in tongues more than anyone else. He was building something big for God!

We often still think in terms of spiritual and secular, thus eliminating our influence in areas that are not overtly spiritual. This next chapter will deal with the practical application of these truths and expand on this concept of *how our love for God affects our love for other things.*

ENDNOTES

1. A word of knowledge is when a person knows something about someone else that they couldn't know without God revealing it to them. In this case, it was knowing about specific illnesses of those shopping in that store whom God wanted to heal.

2. Being involved in the political process is not only acceptable for the believer, it is essential. We just cannot lower our standards by thinking that our strength is in the political process. Natural efforts in obedience to God bring spiritual release. His invasion is our strength.

CHAPTER 6

The Practical Side of Things

If it matters to you, it matters to Him.

Perhaps you've heard it said, *God is number one, the family is number two, and the Church is number three....* That unofficial list is important as it outlines a few of the priorities in a Christian's life that have become confused through the years. I know of many tragedies in pastor's families because they ignored these priorities of Kingdom living. Yet, as good as this list is, I don't believe it is technically accurate. When God is number one, there is no number two.

Out of my love for God I give myself to my wife and kids. It's not separate from the Lord, but is unto Him. It's not that I can't love my wife without loving God—many unbelievers do that well. But in knowing and loving God, I am released to a measure of supernatural love that is unattainable apart from God. It should be said that anyone who is completely abandoned to God should love others more than they thought possible. It is because of my passion for Jesus that I love the Church the way I do. My love for God *is* my love for life. They cannot be separated. Loving my family, church, ministry...is an expression of my love for God. God being number one, the only One.

Religion is what destroys this process because it implies that only overtly spiritual activities are acceptable as service to God and that anything that doesn't have to do with Bible reading, witnessing, church attendance, etc. is not true Christian service. Religion takes us back to the concept of spiritual and secular parts of the Christian life. The person living this dual life needs a list of priorities to survive; otherwise they will not take care of other matters of importance. Their concept of God doesn't allow them to actually have a passion for something that is not viewed as a Christian discipline.

What may appear to be semantics for some has purpose for this reason: we must have a shift in thinking whereby we recognize that passion for God *gives birth* to a passion for other things. And it's those other things that are often to be pursued *as unto the Lord*. We shouldn't experience them as something in competition with, or separate from, our devotion to God. Perhaps the best example of this in Scripture is found in First John 4:20. It says that if we love God it will be measurable by our love for people. This is such an absolute principle that God says if we don't love others, we don't actually love Him. The point is this: in the wake of our passion for God, passion for other things is created. It is often in giving ourselves to those things that we prove and manifest our love for God.

In my case my love of the outdoors is part of my devotion to Christ. While some worship nature, I worship the One it points to—the Creator. My love for my family, for hunting and fishing, the mountains and the ocean, fountain pens, and French roast coffee, are all part of the enjoyment of life for me; and that joy is born completely through a relationship with Him.

> *The heavens are telling of the glory of God; and their expanse is declaring the work of His hands. Day to day pours forth speech, and night to night reveals knowledge* (Psalms 19:1-2 NASB).

For since the creation of the world His invisible attributes, His eternal power and divine nature, have been clearly seen, being understood through what has been made, so that they are without excuse (Romans 1:20 NASB).

DAVID'S CHIEF JOY

Throughout Scripture David is known as "the man after God's heart." His passion for God seems unparalleled in Scripture; yet he also illustrates a love for life that is without equal. In Psalms 137:6 (NASB), he says, *"May my tongue cling to the roof of my mouth if I do not remember you, if I do not exalt Jerusalem above my chief joy."* In today's religious community this statement would probably not be accepted. How can Jerusalem, the community of the redeemed, be called his chief joy? Isn't God supposed to be his chief joy? The apparent paradox fits perfectly into the Jewish culture that looks for practical expression of spiritual truths. David's love for God needed expression, and Jerusalem was a perfect target.

When we live with genuine passion for God, it creates a passion for other things. *While it is possible to value other things above God, it is not possible to value God without valuing other things.* This is the key point confronting the religious mindset, which dismisses everything not considered sacred. The effort to accomplish the goal of loving God with no other passions has had to create a monastic lifestyle to survive. And while I admire many of the monastic believers in the past, it is not the model that Jesus gave us. The way we steward the rest of life becomes the litmus test that demonstrates an authentic love for God.

MY PRIORITIES VS. GOD'S

Like most people, I have a list of things I pray for. They represent the basic desires and needs of my life and those I love. If they're not written down on paper, they're at least written in my heart. On the list are things which have obvious eternal significance—prayer for our cities, for the salvation of certain people we've ministered to, for healing breakthrough in tough cases, provision—both personal and the church. Following the urgent is the "it would be nice" section of the list. It is long and has varying degrees of importance. But I've noticed that God sometimes bypasses the list and goes directly to the "I haven't even bothered to ask" part that dwells somewhere deep in my heart. It is a pleasant and sometimes offensive move.

On one such occasion a friend came up to me and said, "Hey, would you like a hunting dog?" I've always wanted to have a well-trained hunting dog, but never had the time or money for such a luxury. Nor was it on my list. He went on to say, "A dog trainer owes me a big favor and said he'd get me any kind of dog I want. I don't need another dog. So tell me what kind of dog you'd like and I'll get it for you." Just like that, I was to be the owner of a dog that wasn't on my prayer list. It wasn't even on the "it would be nice" part of my list. It wasn't important enough. It was, however, a secret desire in my heart. God bypassed all the stuff that had such eternal significance and went to something temporal and seemingly insignificant.

It offended me at first. Not that I wasn't thankful; I was. But it made no sense. I would have preferred He let me use that *trump card* for something that is more important to me.

It took awhile, but eventually I got it. My requests were important, but my view of Him was more important. It was then and there I started to see that *if it matters to me, it matters to Him.* His bypassing my "urgent" prayer list, my "it would be nice" list, and entering the "secret desires of the heart" list told me more about my heavenly Father than answering all the other things I had been praying about.

A RESTORED VIEW OF PRAYER

People frequently come asking me to pray with them for someone else's healing. Sometimes they have an obvious physical need themselves, but will ask for their friend's healing instead. When I press them about their own condition, they usually say something like, "Oh, I'd rather have God heal them than me. They have cancer. I only have a ruptured disc in my back." Their compassion is wonderful because they are putting another person's need before their own. But their concept of God is wrong. Really wrong!

He doesn't have limited power. In other words, He won't run out of power after He heals their back. He'll still have enough power left to heal their friend's cancer. Also, you don't just get one wish and run out after the first one is used up. The desire for a friend is noble, but it's not an "either/or" situation. Besides that, His attention span is excellent; so good in fact that He can give His undivided attention to every human being on the planet, all at the same time. Neither does He view our prayers on the same priority scale that we do. Some would see it this way: "Of course God heals cancer. That's important. My ruptured disc is not as important. I have learned to live with it." We think of cancer being urgent (which it is) and everything else should be put on hold. In reality, it's often the blown disc that gets healed first. And the increase of faith in that one experience helps to bring about the faith needed for healing of the cancer. Our logic is not consistent with His, and He isn't going to change.

DREAMS THAT MATTER

In this chapter I bring to you three stories, and an unusual experience in a hotel. They are true, simple, and yet profound. Out of the hundreds of stories that could be written, I chose these because they have no obvious eternal significance in themselves. Yet they are rife with meaning for those wanting to impact their world. The reports of God invading governments and various systems of the world to bring change are increasing daily. Many are included in other wonderful books. While they have great importance for us, for me, the nature of God is seen more clearly in His answer for the simple, temporal things.

Toxic Furniture Polish

Barry and Julie Schaffer had a wood finishing company, which they opened in 1987. They pre-finish woodwork for homes and commercial properties. The materials they used were toxic and quite hazardous. They were concerned for all the obvious reasons and began to search for a high-quality, water-based product. They decided that if they couldn't find a good water-based product to use they would quit the industry. The search was on, yet nothing they tried had the same quality as the toxic materials they were using.

After several years of working with products that did not work well, they decided to try to develop one themselves. Barry contacted people in the business as well as get formulas from chemical companies. He tried over and over to work with what they told him but nothing looked right or worked well.

After the tragic death of their third child, Amy, Julie and Barry came to know Jesus. Once again we see the wonderful grace of God to use the very thing sent to destroy us to actually bring us to Him. Following their conversion, Julie still had several miscarriages. She became pregnant with their fourth child but began to bleed. She told Barry that she would not be back to work until she knew that they were going to have this baby. Julie went home to pray and seek the Lord for as long as it would take. Each day Barry would come home to make lunch for her. She didn't leave the couch for almost two months. They prayed each day, and then he would return to work. On one of those days they began to pray and the Holy Spirit gave Julie a sequence of letters and numbers with instructions to tell Barry. She was hesitant, feeling very awkward since this had never happened before. When she did, he said, "I think I know what that means." He went back to their shop and used it as the formula for making the topcoat that he had been trying to make for years. It worked! He used this formula to manufacture their non-toxic, water-based product for the next several years. The same formula became the foundation for many other products.

They always gave God all the glory for their radical conversion, and this creative idea. They also believed that God would receive even more glory if things would continue to develop, and tried many times to expand their business. Neither of them had the time, money, or ambition to pursue the big marketing arena. Then, in 2001, a man built a log home in upper Michigan, and used their products. He was a 44-year-old retired businessman who had made a lot of money in the computer industry. He used their stains and finishes on the interior of his home and was so impressed that he talked to the contractor about them. When he heard that they were a small town company, owned and operated by two people, his entrepreneurial mind was activated. He contacted them about selling the company. They prayed and prayed about this because they knew God had given it to them. After two years of seeking the Lord they agreed to discuss a possible sale. When they finally agreed on an amount, it was more than they could have imagined making in their entire lifetime. They agreed to sell the company to begin a new life of serving the Lord in missions and in evangelism.

It was God's creative ability that brought these things to pass. Barry doesn't hold a chemistry degree. He prayed whenever he got stuck in the creative process, and God always had the right person call or the right sample show up. The major breakthrough came when the "Holy Spirit impressions" that Julie had actually contained a formula for the ultimate product—a mystery contained in the Kingdom realm, but out of reach until it was sought after.

For them, the greatest miracle of all followed. After being told they would never have another child, the Lord gave them their fourth, a son.

A BETTER BOW

Matt McPherson is known as a man with great passion for God. His love is to minister the Gospel through music and leading in worship. However, after being handed a $15 check for a weekend of ministry, he realized that it would be a very challenging way to support his family. Soon after that experience, the Lord gave him this wonderful promise: I am going to prosper you in business, so you can be self-sufficient in ministry. The following is a brief report of God's faithfulness to that promise.

Matt's approach to life is refreshing, as he is bothered by mediocrity. The thought of being average is frightening. He has no desire for fame or power, but refuses to be passive with his life. He wants to make a difference. His love for God has created a passion for excellence and creativity that is admirable.

One day God spoke something to him that would forever change his life. He said, I know every answer to every problem in the world. If men would only ask me, I would give them the answers. Matt was overwhelmed with the promise and the sense of awe he had for God in that moment. He dropped to his knees and cried out to God about the things that concerned him. As a young man Matt developed a hobby of making and shooting compound bows. He obtained the love of archery, while hunting with his father and brothers, in his early years. Following the revelation about God having the answers to every issue in life, he asked God about how to build a better bow. He knew hundreds of ways not to build one, but wanted to take God's invitation to ask for answers for any problem. Several weeks later, at around three o'clock in the morning, he woke up seeing a piece of paper suspended before his eyes. It looked as though it was torn from a notebook. On it was a sketch of a compound bow, revealing a new concept. When his wife, Sherry, asked him what he was doing, he said, "I think I'm having a vision." He was. In response to his prayer, God gave him the initial concept for what would eventually launch the Mathews Archery Company, changing the archery industry forever.

Compound bows have an intrinsic problem to them: they have two cams/pulleys that must be properly synchronized to get the bow to work correctly. The idea that God put on the suspended sheet of paper was a whole new concept in bow design. It was a single-cam bow that eliminated the synchronizing issues. This idea alone turned the archery industry upside down.

Today, Mathews Inc. is the largest archery manufacturing company in the world. They not only sell volumes of bows; they sell a product of superior design and excellence in craftsmanship. The combination of quantity and quality is a rare blend seen in the business community today. But the commitment of the McPherson family to honor God in all they do has increased the favor of God on all they do.

Not all creative ideas have to come from a suspended piece of paper. As exciting as Matt's story is, the bigger picture is of a man and wife who have given themselves completely to God, for His glory. It is because God found them trustworthy that He entrusted ideas of great worth to them. Matt is the owner of at least 20 patents, with more pending. They have embraced the call to ministry through business. He was inducted into the Bowhunters Hall of Fame in 1998.

Before his breakthrough in the archery industry, Matt ran a body repair shop that shared space with another repair shop. One day he observed one of the other tenants deliberately damaging a vehicle, so he could collect more insurance. Matt addressed the situation; the other tenant's response to Matt was that no one was getting hurt, and that you had to be willing to compromise in that business to make a living. Matt told him he was wrong, and set out to prove that success can come without the loss of personal integrity. Today, as far as Matt knows, that man is still eking out a living while Matt is demonstrating the blessing that comes from honorable living—a wealth that has no sorrow.

The same excellence and creativity used for designing and manufacturing archery equipment is also used for making acoustic guitars. As a result of their innovation and quality, their master craftsmen make some of the finest guitars in the country. Many of the industry's top recording artists play the McPherson guitar. This is yet another testimony of the McPherson story of God's promised blessing. When Matt once asked God why he was chosen for a particular assignment, he discovered that while he wasn't God's first choice, he was the first willing. The assignment was challenging, but successful.

Today Matt and Sherry McPherson are living what God had promised many years ago. They are free to do their music ministry, travel, and support the Gospel around the world. They have also discovered the joy of bringing God-ideas to their sphere of influence. As a result, their business is ministry. Countless numbers of people are touched by their love and example in the business world through their integrity, creativity, and excellence.

ANSWERS FROM A HOMELESS SHELTER

One of the more unique expressions of innovation comes from a most unlikely place—a homeless shelter in Southern California. It is called Hope for Homeless Youth, and is pastored by Clayton Golliher, a member of the Harvest International Ministries network. Clayton and his group have tapped into God's creative nature, and have made that privilege a part of their discipleship training. As a result they already have 12 patents that have captured the attention of major toy makers and manufacturers around the country. The shelter sees these open doors for business as open doors for the ministry of the Gospel. Executives of major corporations have been amazed by their inventions, which have produced an openness to their message. To say they are shocked by *who God gives the ideas to is a great understatement.*

One of the toys already in production is their *anti-gravity hovercraft* flying machine. It is being made in China and will most likely be sold nationwide through a TV marketing network. This *one-of-a-kind* toy has opened doors for ministry that has already resulted in conversions to Christ in that communist nation. It's remarkable; creativity turns the heads of those in big business, resulting in conversions to Jesus Christ!

One expert told them their idea for the hovercraft would be "aerodynamically impossible to fly." So they went to prayer, where God gave them a vision showing them how to make it, what materials to use, and how it would fly. It was up and flying within two days.

Besides the unique toys, they have over 50 "household type" inventions. They have amazing ideas that range from a *cure for diaper rash* to a device that dramatically *cuts a household's water consumption.*

They attribute their success to three things:

1. They believe that they live under an "open Heaven." Because of what Jesus did on the Cross they can be one with God. His creativity has been interwoven into them through Christ.
2. They believe they have dominion over this world: over the economy and the technologies of this earth.
3. They pray in the Spirit up to three hours a day. They believe that when they pray in tongues they tap into the Holy Spirit's creative nature.

Their amazing story is more than simply a bunch of Christians learning how to be creative. That story in itself would be worth telling. But this is a story of this nation's "throwaways" bringing solutions to everyday problems and challenges. It is a marvelous reflection of God's grace and one man's vision functioning outside the box of normal ministry expectations. Perhaps this is part of what the Lord had in mind when the prophet declared, "*I will make the lame a remnant, and the outcast a strong nation…*" (Micah 4:7).

A Traveler's Prayer

Not every creative expression has to do with inventions, or solving problems. Sometimes this characteristic is seen in the caring way we express the love of God to others. The previous three stories were all about the influence of the Kingdom on invention and design; this next story is about communication.

On a recent visit to Dallas, Texas, I returned to my room at the Embassy Suites Hotel following the evening meeting. Leaning against my pillow was a laminated card that one of the hotel staff left after cleaning my room. Thinking it was just another notice about a particular feature of the hotel, I started to lay it aside. Then I saw it was a prayer. Out of curiosity I began to read. I've never seen anything so simple, yet so profound, which actually has the potential to bring great impact to a person or even a city. It represents the responsibility of Kingdom-oriented people to be a contributor to society for their good. Once again we see that creative Kingdom influence can and must be demonstrated in all we do, big and small. It's called an *Ancient Prayer* – "The Stranger Within Our Gates."

> *Because this hotel is a human institution to serve people,*
> *and not solely a money-making organization,*
> *we hope that God will grant you peace and rest*
> *while you are under our roof.*
>
> *May this room and hotel be your "second" home.*
> *May those you love be near you in thoughts and dreams.*
> *Even though we may not get to know you,*
> *we hope that you will be comfortable and happy*
> *as if you were in your own house.*
>
> *May the business that brought you our way prosper.*
> *May every call you make*
> *and every message you receive*
> *add to your joy.*
> *When you leave, may your journey be safe.*
>
> *We are all travelers. From "birth till death"*
> *we travel between eternities.*
> *May these days be pleasant for you,*

*profitable for society, helpful for those you meet,
and a joy to those who know and love you best.*

It is amazing to me that something with that level of Kingdom principle would be left on a pillow in a hotel room...particularly a major hotel chain. This is especially noteworthy when you consider the *politically correct* conflict that exists in the minds of most CEO's. I honor the person who decided to take this risk by impacting lives with such a compassionate prayer of blessing. It not only functions as a powerful prayer, it gives an opportunity for people to adjust their thinking to Kingdom principles, while potentially gaining a sense of purpose for why they are on planet earth.

How and what we communicate has the potential to change the atmosphere, creating the context for people to be released to their destiny. Therefore our communication skills must come under the influence of the Holy Spirit. Done correctly, our words are able to release the presence of God into people's lives through the expressions of compassion and concern.

THERE'S MORE

To consistently bring these kinds of solutions to the forefront of society, we will have to learn how to access the realm of Heaven; for it is in Heaven where our answers lie. The spirit of revelation has been given to make this possible. That is the focus of the next chapter.

The Spirit of Revelation

We thrive with the spirit of revelation,
but we perish without it.

People who see what is unseen have the advantage over every-one else who desire a place of significance.[1] They are the ones who are able to *live from Heaven toward earth.* When we live conscious of Heaven and eternity, it changes the way we live and rad-ically increases our measure of impact on society. It's really quite amazing that the ones who see Heaven most clearly have little desire for this world, yet they are the ones who have the greatest impact on the world around them.

Awareness of unseen things is a vital aspect of the Christian life. In fact, we are instructed to, *"Set your mind on the things above, not on the things that are on earth. For you have died and your life is hid-den with Christ in God"* (Col. 3:2-3). The abundant life that Jesus promised to His disciples is found in this unseen realm. The display of His dominion through miracles and various supernatural expres-sions are all rooted in this heavenly world. We must access His world to change this one.

The Impossible Assignment

Changing the course of world history is our assignment. Yet we have gone as far as we can with what we presently know.[2] We need signs to get where we want to go. Signs are realities that point to a greater reality—an exit sign is real, but it points to something greater—the exit.[3] We don't need signs when we travel on familiar roads. But, if we're going to go where we've never gone before, we'll need signs to get there. These *signs* will restore the *wonder*.

To go any further we need to hear from God anew. We must see the things that are before our faces day after day, yet are presently hidden from our eyes. The ever present need to see and hear has never been greater. The key to staying current with the shifting seasons of God is the spirit of revelation.

The apostle Paul understood this need as he prayed for the church at Ephesus. He asked the Father to give them the Spirit of wisdom and revelation (see Eph. 1:17). Many would consider the church in Ephesus to be the most significant church in the Bible. They were experiencing one of the greatest revivals in history; second perhaps only to Nineveh (see Jonah 3). There was a public confrontation with the occult, which resulted in satanic materials being destroyed by repentant citizens (see Acts 19:19). Some of the New Testament's most notable miracles also happened there.

It is also the only church to receive a letter from the apostle Paul in which he gave no word of correction. In their letter he unveiled what is arguably the Bible's greatest revelation of spiritual warfare, husband and wife relationships/the Bride of Christ and Jesus, the fivefold ministry, and the nature and function of the church, are a few examples.

For this victorious body of believers he prayed, "*That the God of our Lord Jesus Christ, the Father of glory, may give to you the spirit of wisdom and revelation in the knowledge of Him*" (Eph. 1:17). What do you give to the one who has everything? Prayer for their eyes to open to see what is still unseen (revelation), and the insight to know what to do with it once they see it (wisdom).

A fundamental lesson for us in this historic fact is that even a church in revival, known for great teaching and citywide impact, needs more revelation. It is not automatic. To say, "The Spirit of God is welcome here, and free to do as He pleases" is not enough. Many of the things we need and long for must be prayed for specifically, and pursued relentlessly. Such is the case with the spirit of wisdom and revelation. Only when wisdom and revelation are passionately pursued do they take the place they deserve in the Christian life. These two elements become the safeguards that keep us from the peril of religion. The foremost apostle prayed this for the foremost church.

WHY DO WE NEED REVELATION?

What I know will help me. What I think I know will hurt me. It's the spirit of revelation that helps me know the difference.

The prophets warned us about what would happen to a people who did not increase in knowledge through revelation. All knowledge is useful, but can be general. But when God releases revelation, it releases knowledge that enables us to address specific issues at crucial moments. It often is the difference between life and death. It can be said that we thrive with revelation knowledge but perish without it.

> My people are **destroyed for lack of knowledge**. Because you have rejected knowledge, I also will reject you from being My priest. Since you have forgotten the law of your God, I also will forget your children (Hosea 4:6 NASB).

And,

> Therefore My people **go into exile for their lack of knowledge**; and their honorable men are famished, and their multitude is parched with thirst (Isaiah 5:13 NASB).

The Old Testament prophets Hosea and Isaiah understood the challenge and spoke to the issues we would be facing. In the two passages there were two calamities mentioned. *Destroyed* means to "cease; to be completely cut off." Without revelation we are completely cut off from the purposes of God on the earth. It is possible to be busy about the Lord's work, yet still separated from His purposes. *Go into exile* is very similar in its meaning as it can also be translated as "remove." The picture here is of one who suffers an "official expulsion from a home, country or area as a punishment." Here we are exiled from His purposes, as we are unfit to carry the weightiness of such a responsibility apart from the spirit of revelation working in our lives. It is costly to have access to *sight*, and not use it (see Luke 12:56).

Knowledge in this context is experiential knowledge. It is more than mere concepts or theories. The word knowledge here comes from the word used in Genesis describing the experience of intimacy – "*And Adam knew Eve; and she conceived and bare Cain*" (Gen. 4:1 KJV).

It is foolish to think, "Because we have the Bible, the full revelation of God has already been given. We don't need anymore." First of all, while the Bible is complete (no more books are to be added) it is a closed book without the help of the Holy Spirit. We must have revelation to see what is already written. Secondly, we know so little of what God wants us to understand from His Word. Jesus said as much. He couldn't teach His disciples all that was in His heart (see John 16:12). This is the knowledge that comes from the Spirit of God as He breathes upon the pages of Scripture. It leads to divine encounters; truth experienced is never forgotten.

Another passage to examine in this line of thought is:

"*Where there is no vision, the people perish*" (Proverbs 29:18 KJV).

The New King James Version says, "*Where there is no revelation, the people cast off restraint.*" That clarification is huge. Many have thought this passage was about goals and dreams. It's not! It's about the impact of the spirit of revelation upon a person's life, enabling them to joyfully restrain themselves from everything that works against the dream of God for us. As someone once said, *vision gives pain a purpose.*

THE ASSIGNMENT

Not all truth is equal. Truth is multidimensional—some things are true, and some things are truer. If you touched a leper in the Old Testament, you became unclean. A primary revelation of the Old Testament is the power of sin. In the New Testament you touch the leper and the leper becomes clean. A primary revelation of the New Testament is the power of God's love. Both statements are true (*sin is powerful* and *love is powerful*) but one is clearly superior.

The Holy Spirit has been given to lead us into all truth. But one of the things He is so clearly in charge of is taking us into the truths that the Father wants emphasized in a particular season. Peter understood this when he wrote:

> *For this reason I will not be negligent to remind you always of these things, though you know and are established in the present truth* (2 Peter 1:12).

Present truth implies *truth that is at the forefront of God's thinking.* It is a wise man who learns to recognize where the winds of Heaven are blowing. Life and ministry are so much easier when we involve ourselves in what God is already blessing.

GREEN LIGHT DISTRICT

Many believers live with the concept that God will lead them when it's time for them to do something. And so they wait, sometimes for an entire lifetime, without any significant impact on the world around them. Their philosophy—I have a red light until God gives me a green one. The green light never comes.

SECRETS TO IMITATING GOD

The apostle Paul lived in the *green light district* of the Gospel. He didn't need signs in the heavens to convince him to obey the Scriptures. When Jesus said, "Go!" that was enough. But He still needed the Holy Spirit to show him what was at the forefront of the Father's mind concerning missions.

He had a burden for Asia, and tried to go there and preach. The Holy Spirit stopped him, which also means He didn't lead him. He then tried to go to Bithynia, but again, the Holy Spirit said no. He then had a dream of a man pleading with him to come to Macedonia. He woke up concluding that this was the direction he was looking for, and went to Macedonia to preach the Gospel. It's a wonderful story of God's leading (see Acts 16:6-10). But it's easy to miss the point; Paul was trying to obey what was on the pages of Scripture because he lived carrying the commandment *to go into all the world!* (See Matt. 28:19.) The old adage comes into play here; it's easier to steer the car when it's moving than when it's standing still. Paul's commitment to the lifestyle of *going* put him in the place to hear the specific directions God had for him in that season. It was the Holy Spirit who was trying to keep him from going to certain places in wrong seasons.

THE PURPOSE OF REVELATION

Revelation is not poured out to make us smarter. Insight is a wonderful benefit of this encounter, but our intelligence is not God's primary concern. His focus in revelation is our *personal transformation*. Revelation leads to a God encounter, and that encounter forever changes us. The encounters can be stunning experiences, or the simple moments of being immersed in His peace; but they are markers along the journey of, "*Thy kingdom come....*" Without the encounter, revelation makes us proud. This was the nature of Paul's warning to the church at Corinth: "*Knowledge puffs up...*" (1 Cor. 8:1). The actual effect on our intelligence is according to the measure of transformation we've experienced. Revelation comes to *enlarge the playing field of our faith.* Insight without faith being released to have the truth realized through experience keeps truth unproven— only theory. It is the birthplace of religion. When God shows us that He wants people well, it is not to give us a theology on healing. It is so we will release our faith into the very area in which He's given us insight that we might experience the fruit of revelation—in this case, to heal people! *Revelation* means "to lift the veil" or "remove the cover." Revelation gives us access to the *realms of greater anointing available* to us to make that truth a personal experience and lifestyle. The greater the truth, the greater the anointing needed to demonstrate that truth to the world. Anointing must be pursued, not assumed (see 1 Cor. 14:1). The measure of anointing that we carry reveals the measure of revelation we actually live in.

THE HEART THAT RECEIVES

One of the more offensive concepts that Jesus taught and believed is that children are more ready to enter the Kingdom than grown-ups. Many of us have adjusted to the concept for the most part, but still struggle with certain applications. The following is a case in point:

> *At that time Jesus answered and said, "I thank You, Father, Lord of heaven and earth, that You have hidden these things from the wise and prudent and have revealed them to babes* (Matthew 11:25).

Can it be true that children are more open to revelation than adults? We tend to think that the weightier concepts are reserved for the mature. In part, that is true. But the really mature, from God's perspective, are those with a child's heart.

Many people ask me to pray for them to receive greater revelation from Scripture. While it's always an honor to bless someone with prayer, it is seldom understood how revelation comes, or to whom it comes. One of the greatest joys in life is hearing from God.

There is no downside. But there is a cost that comes with the impartation.

The following is a list of practical suggestions for those wanting to grow in revelation from God.

Become childlike. Simplicity and humility of heart helps qualify a person to hear from God, while the desire to be profound is a wasted desire. What many discover after years of teaching is that the word that is simple is often the most profound. *"At that time Jesus answered and said, "I thank You, Father, Lord of heaven and earth, that You have hidden these things from the wise and prudent and have revealed them to babes"* (Matt. 11:25).

Obey what you know. Jesus taught His followers, *"If anyone wills to do His will, he shall know concerning the doctrine, whether it is from God or whether I speak on My own authority"* (John 7:17). *"If anyone wills…he shall know"*—Clarity comes to the one willing to do the will of God. The willingness to obey attracts revelation, because God is the ultimate steward, investing His treasures into fertile ground—the surrendered heart.

Learn the biblical art of "meditation." *"I call to remembrance my song in the night; I will meditate within my heart, and my spirit makes diligent search"* (Ps. 77:6). Biblical meditation is a diligent search. Whereas religious cults teach people to empty their minds as the means of meditation, the Bible teaches us to fill our minds with God's Word. Meditation has a quiet heart and a "directed" mind. Mulling a word over in our heart, with a pursuit that springs from the inquisitive child's heart, is meditation.

Live in faith. Living by faith in my present assignment makes me ready for more. *"Whose minds the god of this age has blinded, who do not believe, lest the light of the gospel of the glory of Christ, who is the image of God, should shine on them"* (2 Cor. 4:4). Notice that the light of the Gospel comes to the person who believes. Revelation comes to the one expressing faith! Live with the understanding that God has already willed to give you His mysteries (see Matt. 13:11), and ask accordingly. Then thank Him in advance.

Acquire an understanding heart. This sort of heart has the foundations in place for something to be constructed upon it. These are the basic concepts of the King and His Kingdom. Proper foundations attract the builder (revelator) to come and add to those foundations. *"But knowledge is easy to one who has understanding"* (Prov. 14:6 NASB). God wisely stewards fresh insight to those who have the basic principles in place. When fresh insights come, the understanding heart has a "slot to put it in." It is not lost as seed spilled on the ground.

Give God your nights. I try to end each day with my heart's affection stirred up and directed to the Holy Spirit. What an amazing way to go to sleep. The Song of Solomon reveals this poetically, *"I sleep, but my heart is awake"* (Song of Sol. 5:2). God loves to visit us in the night and give us instruction that we would have a hard time receiving during the day (see Job 33:15-16). The desire to give God our night season flows naturally from the child's heart that knows revelation cannot be earned. Ask Him specifically to minister to you in the night through visions and dreams. Once you have a dream or vision, write it out, and ask Him for understanding.

Give away what you have already received. Never underestimate what hungry people can "pull" from you while you minister the Word. Being in a place of continual giving is a sure way of getting more. When we're in "over our heads" in a ministry situation, we find out what God has been putting into us during the night. He draws out of the deep places in our hearts things that are not yet a part of our conscious thought processes (see Prov. 20:5).

Become a friend of God. God shares His secrets with His friends. *"No longer do I call you servants, for a servant does not know what his master is doing; but I have called you friends, for all things that I heard from My Father I have made known to you"* (John 15:15). He makes all things known to His friends. Not only does He want to share all, He's invited us to ask anything of Him. But be accustomed to hearing more than you can share with others. Listen as He speaks, but speak only what He gives you freedom to speak about. Some things are revealed only because we're friends, and are not to be shared with others.

Inheriting the Family Stories

One of the fun parts of growing up was hearing stories of my family. It didn't matter if it was Grandpa talking about the Northern Pike he caught in Minnesota, or it was my dad talking about his days playing football in high school, they were the stories I loved to hear. And it didn't matter that we may have heard them last week. I wanted to hear them again and again, hoping each time I might get more detail. They were worth repeating, and are a part of my inheritance.

In this light, Jesus made some alarming statements. He said, *"Truly, truly, I say to you, we speak of what we know and testify of what we have seen, and you do not accept our testimony. If I told you earthly things and you do not believe, how will you believe if I tell you heavenly things?"* (John 3:11-12 NASB).

"We" refers to the Father, the Son, and the Holy Spirit. It is NOT a reference to Jesus and His disciples or even Jesus and the angels. Jesus said what He heard His Father say. The Spirit of God was upon Him, and made it possible for Him to succeed in hearing and seeing His Father clearly. God has a testimony, and is trying to pass on His story to anyone who would listen. He repeats His cry later in this chapter, *"What He has seen and heard, of that He testifies; and no one receives His testimony"* (John 3:32 NASB). Because it's our responsibility to *"loose here what is loosed in heaven"* (Matt. 16:19), we need to have a revelation of Heaven along with the heart to hear His testimony. That is the benefit of *"being seated in heavenly places in Christ."* He desires to give us His testimony, but can't find anyone ready to hear it. He has spoken of earthy things (natural birth and the nature of wind; see John 3:1-8) and the people struggled—His desire is to speak to them of heavenly things, which have no earthly parallel.

HEAVY WORDS

Jesus couldn't teach His disciples all that was in His heart. He ached to give them more, but didn't because the weightiness of His words would crush them.

I have many more things to say to you, but you cannot bear them now (John 16:12 NASB).

Their "weight-carrying capacity" was insufficient for what Jesus had to say. When God speaks, He creates. The realities created from what Jesus would have liked to declare were far too significant for them. And the realms of glory released over their lives would require a strength and stability that they did not yet possess.

While it's true that God does not give His glory to another, we're not *another*—we are members of His Body. The ability to carry more has to do with both character and faith. Character enables us to receive glorious promises of destiny without taking the glory to ourselves. And greater faith responds to the declarations with the great courage needed for fulfillment.

The Holy Spirit was given to prepare them for revelation at a whole new level. He would take them where Jesus couldn't. Perhaps this is part of the reason Jesus said, "*It is to your advantage that I go….*" The indwelling Holy Spirit enables us to bear more of the revelation of Jesus than was possible for the original twelve disciples.

But when He, the Spirit of truth, comes, He will guide you into all the truth; for He will not speak on His own initiative, but whatever He hears, He will speak; and He will disclose to you what is to come. He will glorify Me, for He will take of Mine and will disclose it to you. All things that the Father has are Mine; therefore I said that He takes of Mine and will dis-close it to you (John 16:13-15 NASB).

The Holy Spirit is assigned to take us into *all truth*. The word *all* here is staggering, and should be. What makes this even more stunning is the realization that truth is to be experienced; the Holy Spirit is therefore leading us into experiencing *all truth*. He receives all of His instructions from the Father. It was the Holy Spirit upon Jesus that enabled Him to know what the Father was doing and saying. That *same gift* of the Spirit has been given to us for that *same purpose*.

One of the assignments of the Holy Spirit is to let us know *what is to come*. If you read commentaries and various reference materials, you'll notice most think the promise of *knowing what's coming* is all about us being aware of coming calamities. Theologians tend to focus on problems because few truly believe in the glorious church. Everyone from world leaders to musicians, to actors and business leaders, are telling us of the coming calamities. We don't need the Holy Spirit for that purpose when people without God can do it. Rather, we need Him to see the coming *glory*! The warnings of difficulties are necessary as they help us keep our priorities straight. But it's the Father's good pleasure to give us the mysteries of the Kingdom. And there's no pleasure in speaking of the death and destruction of the unrighteous (see Ezek. 33:11). It's still called the *good* news for a reason.

He goes on to say, "*He will glorify Me, for He will take of Mine and will disclose it to you.*" A most touching thing takes place in this verse—Jesus inherits that which He previously gave up when He became a man and died in our place. It is also true that the Holy Spirit was given the task of not simply revealing all that Jesus possesses, but to actually "disclose" it to us. Disclose means to *declare*! There is an amazing transfer of resources taking place in this statement. Follow this; all belongs to the Father—the Father gives everything to the Son—the Son gives everything to us through the Holy

Spirit who transfers the resources of Heaven into our account through the declaration. This is astonishing! This is why hearing from God is so vital. He transfers Jesus' inheritance into our accounts every time He speaks. Every declared promise is a transfer of heavenly resources that enable us to fulfill the purpose of our commission.

DISCOVERING OUR INHERITANCE

One of the Holy Spirit's primary functions is to discover what lies in the depths of God's heart for us. He leads us into an understanding by experience to help us realize our inheritance.

> *For to us God revealed them through the Spirit; for the Spirit searches all things, even the depths of God. …Now we have received, not the spirit of the world, but the Spirit who is from God, so that we may know the things freely given to us by God, which things we also speak, not in words taught by human wisdom, but in those taught by the Spirit, combining spiritual thoughts with spiritual words* (1 Corinthians 2:10, 12-13 NASB).

This inheritance is freely given to us; it is the Holy Spirit who brings us into that *land of promise* that we might correctly navigate our way through life realizing the height, depth, length, and width of God's extravagant love for us. He unveils what is ours.

He is also the one who makes the Scriptures come alive; it is the *living* Word. Learning to recognize His presence, His ways, and His language will help us to succeed in our impossible assignment. That is the focus of the next chapter.

Endnotes

1. Significance is a God-given desire. Living to be famous is its counterfeit.
2. Quote from Martin Scott.
3. Quote from Dick Joyce.

CHAPTER 8

Celebrating the Living Word

It's difficult to get the same fruit
as the early church when we value a book they
didn't have more than the Holy Spirit they did have.

God spoke and the worlds were made. His Word creates. The ability to hear God, especially from His Word, is a mandatory skill if we are to enter divine purpose and true creative expression. It's as necessary as breathing. A yielded heart is impressionable as it studies Scripture and receives God's impressions (fingerprints) easily. Within that sort of tender soil, the Lord plants the seeds of Kingdom perspective that grow into global transformation.

The insights and empowering nature of Scripture provide solutions applicable to every society and culture. The Bible is limitless in scope, timeless, and complete, containing answers to every dilemma of humanity. The study of Scriptures must take us beyond the historical setting, beyond language studies in the Hebrew and Greek, and at times beyond the context and intent of the human authors of Scripture. It's time to hear from God afresh—that His Word would once again become the living Word in our experience.

I believe the Bible to be the Word of God, inerrant, fully inspired by the Holy Spirit. It is without equal, not to be added to, nor subtracted from. Not only did God inspire the writers, He inspired those who selected which respective writings should be included to make up the full 66 books of the Bible. I do not believe there will be any new revelation that has the same authoritative weight as Scripture. It alone stands as judge of all other wisdom, be it the wisdom of man or an insight or book purported to be revealed directly from God or given by an angel. God is still speaking but everything we hear must be consistent with what He has spoken to us in His Word. In light of these burning convictions, there are standards and traditions instituted by the church for our protection that practically suck the life and impact out of God's living Word. Though not the original intent, it has been an unintended result.

Being unaware of His presence has cost us dearly, especially as we approach Scripture. King David, who authored and sang songs of His love for God's Word, "set" the Lord before himself daily. He purposed to be regularly conscious of God's nearness and lived from that mind-set. The sanctified imagination is a tool in God's hand that enables us to tap into true reality. My approach is this; since I can't imagine a place where He isn't, I might as well imagine Him with me. This is not vain imagination. Rather, it's vain to imagine otherwise.

LIVING BY PRINCIPLE OR PRESENCE

There is a style of Scripture reading that is mainly concerned with finding and applying principles rather than enjoying His presence. This is good but limited. Kingdom principles are real and powerful. They can be taught to anyone. When they are applied to life, they bring forth fruit for the King. Even unbelievers will experience blessing when they live by His principles. My friend was having financial problems. He confided in a neighbor, who also happened to be a pastor, and the minister told him that his problems could be due to the fact that he wasn't honoring God with the tithe—10 percent of his income. He then challenged my friend to test God by tithing to see if his counsel was accurate. When my friend tithed in response to the challenge, blessing starting pouring into his life. He ended up giving his life to Christ because he saw and tasted God's love. But notice the Kingdom principle functioned even before his conversion. Finding and applying principles is something even an unbeliever can do.

I am not knocking the principles. The transformation of cities and nations depends on the receptivity of Kingdom principles. However, this is not the core of the Christian's experience with the Bible. Rather, more often than not, we should read to have a God-encounter.

LEARNING TO HEAR GOD

I began learning to recognize God's voice through the study of Scripture. During one season of my life I spent considerable time in the Book of Ephesians. When I read, *"and to know the love of Christ which surpasses knowledge, that you may be filled up to all the fullness of God"* (Eph. 3:19), the Holy Spirit spoke to me. He told me that it meant that I could know by experience what would be beyond the reach of comprehension. Later I was able to do a word study and found that this was exactly the meaning of the verse in the original language.

Often I would come to the Bible with a need and God would address it clearly from His Word, again and again. There were times when He spoke so clearly from a verse, yet I knew that what was ministering to me wasn't what the writer originally intended. But it was a *living word*, a sword, ministering to the very need of my heart. It wasn't until years later that I learned that God didn't speak that way anymore.

I'm thankful I learned to hear God through the Scriptures before I found out what the rules were. It's like being told there are no miracles today. That laughable statement might have gotten my attention many years ago, but it's way too late now. I've seen thousands.

THE ERROR THAT BREEDS ERRORS

To value the Scriptures above the Holy Spirit is idolatry. It is not Father, Son, and Holy Bible; it's the Holy Spirit. The Bible reveals God, but is itself not God. It does not contain Him. God is bigger than His book. We are reliant on the Holy Spirit to reveal what is contained on the pages of Scripture, because without Him it is a closed book. Such dependency on the Holy Spirit must be more than a token prayer asking for guidance before a Bible study. It is a relationship with the third person of the Trinity that is continuous, ongoing, and affects every single aspect of life. He is the wind that blows in uncertain directions, from unknown places (see John 3:8). He is the power of Heaven, and cannot be controlled, but must be yielded to. He eagerly reveals His mysteries to all who are hungry— truly hungry. He is so valued in Heaven that He comes with a warning. The Father and Son can be sinned against, but sinning against the Holy Spirit has unforgivable eternal consequences.

The Holy Spirit is de-emphasized and almost removed from many Christian's daily approach to life and the Word. The fear of becoming like some mindless fanatic has kept many a Christian from interacting with their greatest treasure in this life—the Holy Spirit. We are heirs of God, and the Holy Spirit is the down payment of our inheritance (see Eph. 1:13-14). Some teach that we shouldn't talk much about the Spirit as the Holy Spirit doesn't speak of Himself. However, both the Father and Son have a lot to say about Him. It is wise to listen to them. God is to be praised, adored, boasted in, and interacted with—and the Holy Spirit is God.

The approach of many believers to Scripture is inconsistent with the Spirit who inspired those sacred writings. Much of what we have a heart to accomplish cannot be done without reexamining our relationship with God through His Word. We have gone as far as we can go with what we presently know. Not only are we in need of the

Spirit of God to teach us, we are in need of a different view of the Bible.

The God who speaks through circumstances and unusual coincidences wants to talk to us again through the pages of His Word, even when it appears to be taken out of context or is not exactly in line with what appears to be the author's original intent.

THE LIVING WORD

The Word of God is living and active. It contains divine energy, always moving and accomplishing His purposes. It is the surgeon's knife that cuts in order to heal. It is balm that brings comfort and healing. But the point I wish to stress is that it is multidimensional and unfolding in nature. For example, when Isaiah spoke a word, it applied to the people he spoke to—his contemporaries. Yet because it is alive, much of what he said then has its ultimate fulfillment in another day and time. Living words do that.

God said we were to choose whom we would serve, yet Jesus said He chose us; we didn't choose Him. We are predestined from before the foundation of the world, yet are told that *whosoever will* may come. Jesus said we had to sell all to follow Him, yet He instructs the wealthy to be rich in good works.[1] The Holy Spirit knows what truth to breathe on according to the particular season of our life.

A classic conflict to the Western rational mind is found in Proverbs' instruction on how to treat a fool. It says, *"Do not answer a fool according to his folly, or you will also be like him."* The very next verse says, *"Answer a fool as his folly deserves, that he not be wise in his own eyes"* (Prov. 26:4-5). One verse says *not to answer a fool,* and it tells you why. Then it says to *answer a fool,* also giving us the reasons why. This is not a contradiction to the Hebrew mind-set, which understands that truth is often held in the tension of two conflicting ideas.

The mind-set that wants static, unmovable, tidy boundaries, and interpretations gets offended over the lines of reason and expectation that seem to be in flux. Herein lies our great challenge—can we hear what He is saying now, for now? And can we accept that He may speak differently to each of us?

ALL TRUTH IS NOT CREATED EQUAL

Truth is multidimensional. Some truths are superior to others. Lesser truths are often the foundation of greater truths. "I no longer call you servants, but friends." Friendship with God is built on the foundation of first being a servant. Truth is progressive in nature—line upon line, precept on precept.

For example, the primary message of the Old Testament is to reveal the power of sin. For that reason when a person touched a leper, they became unclean. Sin is overpowering. Flee from it! The primary message of the New Testament is the power of God's love. So when Jesus touched a leper, the leper became clean. "Love covers a multitude of sin." Both messages are true. One is greater. Love is overpowering!

Much division takes place in the church when people are devoted to different levels of truth. We tend to prefer static rules and boundaries, not things that flex and change. This desire for static rules is our basic preference for the law. Preset boundaries are what keep us *obedience focused* instead of *relationship focused*. One is set on memorized rules and regulations. The other is entirely set on His voice and presence and the rules and regulations sit at a different level. When the woman caught in adultery was brought before Jesus, He decided to enforce His own rules and law in a way contrary to what the law demanded. And Jesus only did what He saw the Father doing. Obedience will always be important for us. But obedience out of love looks a lot different than obedience because of rules. Israel discovered they couldn't do it, and neither can we.

To say the Scripture changes is an uncomfortable concept. It doesn't change in the sense that it passes away or contradicts itself, but it does change in the same way a wineskin expands to reflect the ever-increasing move of the Spirit of God. In Deuteronomy 23:1 the Lord commands that an emasculated man *shall not enter the assembly of the Lord.*" Yet in Isaiah 53:3-5, the eunuch who holds fast to the covenant will be given an everlasting name which will not be cut off. Finally, in Acts 8, Phillip converts a eunuch who becomes the very first evangelist to Ethiopia. Peter called this sort of movement "present truth."

OUT OF CONTEXT

In studying the Old Testament prophecies quoted in the New Testament, it doesn't take long to realize that Jesus and other writers of Scripture took many Old Testament passages out of context to prove their point. The common thought today is that the Holy Spirit worked that way for the Scriptures to be written, but it is unacceptable to do this today because the canon[2] is complete. How could it be wrong to use the same principles used to write the Scriptures to interpret the Scriptures? That *rule* is designed to keep us from creating doctrine by experience and contradicting orthodox Christianity. While the reason is noble, the rule is not biblical. It keeps us from some of the fruitfulness that has been assigned to the church of this hour.

The rule was written because we are unfamiliar with the presence and voice of Holy Spirit. The problem is not our tendency to incorrectly interpret Scripture; it's that after 2,000 years with the Holy Spirit being on the earth and in us, we still don't know Him! The rule is not the answer. Repentance for ignoring the third person of the Trinity is the beginning of the much-needed solution. That alone can take us into realms in God that have previously been thought impossible for an entire generation to experience.

How is it possible to set a rule of Bible interpretation that the Holy Spirit Himself did not follow in inspiring the Bible? And to say that it is no longer allowed because the canon is complete has little merit as the Holy Spirit is with us, and He knows what He meant when He wrote it. This is potentially dangerous because of the bent of some toward creating unholy and/or inaccurate doctrine, but it does not justify removing a necessary tool of the Spirit that He uses to speak to His people. There is danger, but there is also great treasure. This is the necessary tension.

A NEW NON-BURSTING WINESKIN

Doctrine must be a wineskin kept elastic by the oil of the Spirit. If it is rigid and unmoving, it will not yield to God's habit of opening up more of His Word to us. God loves to add to our knowledge things we think we already understand. Too much rigidity bursts our doctrinal wineskins under the weight of ongoing revelation. The end result is the church becomes irrelevant and powerless to the world around them.

It is easy to prefer a particular theological slant, build a monument around it, and become deaf or adversarial to its important counterpoint. For example, I am much more Armenian in background than I am Calvinist. Yet some of my dearest friends are Calvinists. I love to hear the Holy Spirit work through them, because there is freshness to what they teach. I become convinced of God's sovereignty and leave that meeting with a conviction that "God chose me, I didn't choose Him!" Conversely, when I sit in a meeting where the opposite point is stressed, I also leave with conviction—that of freewill, the power of our choice, my responsibility as a delegated one on this planet, and that the outcome of His purposes depends upon the faithfulness of God's people. Which is true? Both are.

The Holy Spirit has to be free to speak to us about the things that are on His heart; especially to those things we have a natural resistance. We must be open to truth when it has a biblical basis and is accompanied by the breath of God making it come alive for a specific purpose. The error is building a theological monument around a particular point of view that conveniently excludes certain portions of Scripture to help us feel secure in a doctrinal bent.

I am also concerned with our tendency to gather around doctrines instead of around spiritual fathers. The former builds denominations, while the latter creates movements. Even our most valued doctrines can be expanded under the inspiration of the Holy Spirit. Usually, it's not the expansion that we have the most difficulty with. It is when He begins to speak about what is, at first glace, a contradiction to what we have learned. The desire for rigid doctrine is in direct proportion to our inability to actually hear His voice. It's essential to be able to recognize His voice so we can embrace His revelation, even when it contradicts our traditional upbringing.

God is big enough to feed me from a particular verse everyday for the rest of my life. The Word of God is infinitely deep. I must come to that which I understand with a childlike heart because what I know can keep me from what I need to know if I don't remain a novice. Becoming an expert in any area of Scripture is the very thing that often closes us off from learning the new things that God is opening up in His Word.[3] Again, it's the childlike heart that attracts revelation from God (see Matt. 11:25).

Jesus Christ, the Ultimate Revelation

The one revelation that is about to change everything is the revelation of Jesus Christ. Paul declared as much when he said that there was something we would come to know by revelation (see Eph. 1:17) that would bring us into the fullness of Christ, saying *"until we all attain to the unity of the faith, and of **the knowledge of the Son of God**, to a mature man, to the measure of the stature which belongs to **the fullness of Christ**"* (Eph. 4:13). Notice that coming into maturity is the result of gaining the *knowledge of the Son of God*. This revelation will completely change the church as we know it today, *because as we see Him we become like Him.* This will enable us to accurately represent Jesus.

Jesus Christ is perfect theology. He is the "...*exact representation of His nature...*" (Heb. 1:3 NASB), the ultimate portrayal of the Father. Questions that exist about God's nature in the Old Testament were clarified in the New Testament. When I teach about God's absolute desire and provision to heal, I am asked, "what about Job?" I respond, "I'm not a disciple of Job, I'm a disciple of Jesus." Job's life helped create the awareness for the need of a savior. Job is the question. Jesus is the answer. If our study of Job (and other Old Testament issues) doesn't lead us to Jesus as the answer, it reveals we never really understood the question. The types and symbols of the Old Testament do not override the clear manifestation of God through Jesus in the New Testament. Any understanding we have about the nature of God that can't be seen in the person of Jesus, must be questioned.

How many people came to Jesus for a miracle and left disappointed? None! He was 100 percent successful as a man dependant on God. Jesus also messed up every funeral He attended, including His own. When the disciples asked Him about their failed attempt to bring deliverance to a child, He gave them instructions on how to get their breakthrough. He said it would come through *prayer and fasting* (Mark 9:29). It's time to respond to His counsel and discover for ourselves how to get the breakthrough that appears to be so elusive. He manifested the will of God. And we must not change it to fit our experience. It is time to manifest the will of God again.

THE REALITY AND VALUE OF DANGER

It is obvious and easy to assert that those who try to hear God from the pages of Scripture will not always hear clearly. Some of us will make huge mistakes and claim to have heard from God when it wasn't Him at all. Yet, to succeed, one must be willing to fail.

Early in our first pastorate, one of the elders of the church announced that he and his wife were expecting a child. It would be their third, and quite a surprise. We all rejoiced with them because of this wonderful news. As the time of delivery drew near, the doctor gave them the worst news possible—the baby in her womb was dead. When they came to us with the news, we all rallied together in prayer. It seemed that everywhere I looked in the Bible I found verses on resurrection. So, based on this, as a church we declared that this baby was not dead but alive. We prophesied the best we knew how. When the day of delivery came, the baby was in fact born dead. There was great mourning; first because of their heartbreak and loss, and second, because we didn't actually hear from God and missed it with all of our prophetic pronouncements. We met as a church family to review the tragedy and our mistakes. And as carefully as I knew how, I addressed where we missed God and tried to encourage everyone to press on in spite of our disappointment and loss.

We have since had at least two babies whom the doctors pronounced dead in the womb be resurrected and born alive and well. (One mother had been examined by five different medical professionals, all with the same conclusion—the baby is dead. Each of them gave her the warning that she would die if they were not allowed to remove the child. Jesus, in His mercy, raised the baby to life in her womb.) The area of our greatest risk, though we have previously failed, can become our greatest area of authority, if we won't give up.

Early in the 20th century there was a gathering of believers who had tasted the power of God and were hungering for more. Many went to foreign countries to become missionaries but didn't bother learning the language because they knew that God would give it to them because they spoke in tongues. Great disappointment soon followed when they arrived and were unable to speak the national language. "*Hope deferred makes the heart sick,*" is a verse that was never truer than in those years of well-intentioned missionary efforts. Yet today there are many who have had such a miracle—receiving the miraculous ability to speak in a foreign language without training. I know of a couple of people who speak over 10 completely different languages, many of which they received when they went into the new area to evangelize. While it's not an excuse to neglect training, it is a reward for the previous generations' efforts, even though they thought they had failed.

Many years ago a notable leader in the Body of Christ told me he had consciously gotten rid of the prophetic ministry in his church. He felt there was too much danger and too many potential problems. I respected him too much to voice my disagreement, but I quietly got excited in my heart because in the natural, counterfeiters don't make fake pennies; it's not worth the effort. I knew that if the enemy worked that hard to create a counterfeit, the original must have great value. Only things of eternal consequence are worth the devil's attention. For that reason I get encouraged when I see areas of danger, like the prophetic.

My solution is to find people of like mind to work with, realize the danger involved in our common pursuit, and stay humble and accountable in our pursuit of the authentic.

THE APPROPRIATE RESPONSE TO DANGER

Often times the charismatic or Pentecostal groups are blamed for having poor theological foundations. Granted, the hunger for more takes some people "over the line." While this has been the cause of some of the mistakes in church history, it's certainly not the reason for most of them nor the most serious of them.

The most dangerous heresies are not usually from a zealous desire to hear and obey the rhema word of the Lord. Most often these tragedies involve a demonic (angel of light) visitation, either real or imagined, and the subsequent elevation of that so-called revelation to the authority of the Bible. However, it's a fact that many times throughout history there have been those who are wrongly inspired over a verse or a phrase in Scripture. The result has been the creation of wrong or poor doctrine. The need to be different and original has sponsored a lot of bad theology.

For instance, last century a gentleman was reading the account of the Mount Transfiguration experience. After Moses and Elijah disappeared, it says the disciples then saw "Jesus only" (see Matt.17:8). It seemed to him to be the rhema revelation that the church had been missing for all these years. There was no Trinity—Father, Son, and Holy Spirit. There was *only Jesus*. The Father and Holy Spirit were essentially Jesus in different forms. And so, another heresy was born.

The rules mentioned earlier were created, I'm sure, to protect us from such mistakes. But sometimes the rules that keep us from error also keep us from our destiny. I believe this to be one of those times. The appropriate response to dangerous, and intrinsically important ideas is to stay low, stay hungry, take risks, and keep accountable.

But the answer for many has been to take a more analytical approach to the Christian life, one that is stable in doctrine and disciplines but lives without personal experience, denies the opportunity for risk, and resists emotional expression and passion. Christianity was never to be known by its disciplines. It's to be known by its passion; and those without passion are in far more danger than they know. Demons are attracted to religiously sanitized environments where there is no power.

Furthermore, the focus of many denominations within the church upon proper theological foundations as the center of faith has not led them into an encounter with God that demonstrates the life, power, and glory of Christ. Jesus warned the Pharisees saying, "*You are mistaken, not understanding the Scriptures nor the power of God*" (Matt. 22:29). Both the Scriptures and the power of God are essential! There is no justification for lack in either area. The stream of theological accuracy and the stream of experiential Christianity will merge as we learn to give honor to one another in our pursuit of a full demonstration of the Gospel.

MEDITATION: THE THINKER'S WAY TO A NEW WINESKIN

Biblical meditation is a completely different animal than what is encouraged in the New Age culture. Theirs is a counterfeit because it encourages us to empty our minds, making them vulnerable to any *angel of light* to enter, and eventually control. Unfortunately, there are many evil spirits looking for a vacancy. True meditation feasts on God's Word. That absolute foundation for thought sets a course of direction that is sure to take one on the journey of a lifetime. It is interaction with the Holy Spirit. It's a good start for obtaining the new wineskin of thought addressed in Scripture, by giving time for the seed to germinate in a person's heart. *"Tremble, and do not sin. Meditate in your heart upon your bed, and be still"* (Ps. 4:4 NASB).

THE FRUITFULNESS OF MEDITATION

There is a very strange story in Genesis about Jacob and his deceitful father-in-law, Laban. He had worked for Laban, for what seemed like forever, and had been cheated over and over again. He wanted to break away from this costly relationship and establish his own home for his growing family. Jacob made a deal with Laban for a portion of the flocks to be given to him for his years of service. It would enable him to leave with something to start *life on his own.* They agreed that he would take all the spotted and speckled sheep and goats as his wages. Laban agreed to the terms knowing that spotted and speckled animals were an aberration. Genesis 30:37-39 (NASB) speaks of Jacob's cunning plan in this way:

> *Then Jacob took fresh rods of poplar and almond and plane trees, and peeled white stripes in them, exposing the white which was in the rods. He set the rods which he had peeled in front of the flocks in the gutters, even in the watering troughs, where the flocks came to drink; and they mated when they came to drink. So the flocks mated by the rods, and the flocks brought forth striped, speckled, and spotted.*

As the animals came to drink, they would see spotted and speckled rods in the ground near their watering hole, which was also their breeding ground. As they came to the water and bred, they did so while looking upon the spotted rods. The result was that they reproduced spotted and speckled offspring. And it was all because of what they saw when they came to the water.

More than once the Word of God is referred to as water. It cleanses us from the impurities of life in much the same way as the laver was used to purify the priests of the Old Testament before going into the presence of the Lord. The blood deals with sin, but it's water that addresses impurity (see Eph. 5:26). It's not an accident that the laver of water was made from the mirrors of the women, as the Bible tells us that the Word of God is like a mirror (see 1 Cor. 13:12; 2 Cor. 3:18; James 1:23).

I don't believe it to be a stretch in the intention of God to derive the following lesson from Jacob's story: when we come to God's Word, we will reproduce what we see. Even more interesting is this, which has become my personal experience—whatever my heart is set upon when I come to the Bible, will determine much of what I see in the Bible. That can be good or bad, depending on whether or not I have "*watched over my heart with all diligence*" (Prov. 4:23). Those with evil in their hearts can find the confirmation they are looking for through the misreading of Scripture. The problem is not the method or approach to the Bible; it is whether or not we are willing to stay humble, honest, and hungry before the Lord. Our desperation for truth makes us available for things that others seem to continually miss. Keeping a pure heart makes the journey to God's Word a journey where nothing is impossible.

If I come to God's Word with evangelism on my mind, it seems that evangelism is on every page of my Bible. All the stories reaffirm my understanding of God's heart for people, but open up new Scriptures that I never previously considered to be evangelistic. The same is true of finances. If I come to God's Word with money on my mind, it appears that the whole Bible teaches about stewardship. This principle is true of most any subject you could mention. What you carry to this watering hole will determine much of what you see and reproduce.

God desires for us to bring forth His solutions for the difficulties and traumas of life on this planet. When we carry our concerns before the Lord, which come from our place of influence and authority on this earth, He begins to open up His mysteries that are concealed in His Word. For example, if there's a conflict on the job between two friends, God will give you specific insight through His Word about how to bring peace. If there is a need to expand your business, but you're not sure about how or when, He will speak from the pages of His Word. It is living, immediately applicable, and unlimited in its scope and power.

His Word comes to life. He breathes on the pages of His book, and something happens in our hearts. It comes to life! In the end it comes down to this: we will reproduce what we see as we come to the water of His Word.

LEARNING TO SPEAK

As we study God's Word, the heart of God is revealed. All that He has declared will come to pass. His Word will not return without bearing the fruit that He intended (see Isa. 55:11). We have the privilege of saying what the Father is saying, and thereby learning how to shape our world through biblical declarations. That is the subject of the next chapter.

ENDNOTES

1. Jesus did that with the disciples. First they left all to follow: Matthew 19:29. Then He instructed them what to do with their money, and to make sure they owned a sword: Luke 22:36. God did the same with Israel; during their time in the wilderness they had to learn to trust Him for everything. Having no land of their own was their training ground to learn how to possess the Promised Land once they entered it.

2. The complete set of sacred writings forming the Bible, made up of 66 books.

3. When God reveals truth to us, it is always built on the foundation of previously revealed truth. The former is not discarded. It is what the fresh word is built upon.

CHAPTER 9

Redesigning Our World

*The Holy Spirit is imprisoned
in the bodies of unbelieving believers.*

In Chapter 1 we glanced at Adam's role in naming the animals. He was given the unique responsibility of co-laboring with God in designing the nature of the world he was going to live in. Is it possible we have been restored to that level of authority once again? Would the blood of Jesus do anything less? We have been given this amazing tool to fulfill our stewardship role; *"Death and life are in the power of the tongue..."* (Prov. 18:21 NASB). With our speech we design and alter our environment. Realities are created that didn't exist a moment earlier through simple proclamations. With this tool we can build up or tear down, edify or discourage, give life or destroy it. The declared word has the capacity to resource earth with Heaven's resources. As reformers we must first pay attention to what we say, realizing that we are actually building the world we have to live in. We have the ability to speak *from* God, revealing His world and His ways. As Bishop Joseph Garlington says, *"nothing happens in the Kingdom until something is said."*

Jesus describes one of the primary roles of the Holy Spirit in this way; "*He will take of what is mine and declare it to you*" (John 16:14). He says this after revealing that all things belong to Him. Jesus is telling us how His inheritance (all things) would be transferred to our account. It would be done through the declaration. Every time God speaks to us, there is a transfer of heavenly resource from His account into ours. Hearing God is essential to the release and the discovery of the vastness of our inheritance in Christ. It is beyond comprehension. It is *all things* (1 Cor. 3:21).

The transfer of "all things," our inheritance, begs this question, "Why would God give us all things?" Because *all things* will be necessary for us to fulfill the commission that God has given us. Our assignment from God will require the use of "all things" to be under our supervision to accomplish His purposes on earth.

TOOL TIME

One of the essential tools necessary to redefine the nature of the world around us is the gift of *encouragement.* This profound instrument has all of Heaven's attention. When angels perceive its use, they know their assignment has been released. It is more than a natural use of words to make someone feel good about themselves or their circumstances; it is supernatural in nature and partners with Heaven to bring forth Heaven's response.

In the same way the Holy Spirit transfers our inheritance to us through the declaration, so we release heavenly realms through our speech. In God's economy, without declaration there is no creation (see Ps. 33:6). Deliberate declarations in line with the covenantal promises of God are essential for the transformation of the kingdoms of this world.

THE SET TIME OF FAVOR HAS COME

"*And Jesus kept increasing in wisdom and stature, and in favor with God and men*" (Luke 2:52 NASB). I understand why Jesus needed to increase in favor with man, as it would give Him access and influence within society in ways He wouldn't have without favor. But how is it that the Son of God, who is perfect in every way, needs to increase in favor with God? I don't have an answer. But I do know this—if Jesus needed more favor from God to complete His assignment, how much more of an increase do I need!

As with most everything related to the Kingdom of God, we receive increase through generously giving away what we have. It is no different with favor—grace. *"Let no unwholesome word proceed from your mouth, but only such a word as is good for edification according to the need of the moment, so that it will give grace to those who hear"* (Eph. 4:29 NASB). In this passage we find that speaking words of edification brings grace into the life of the person we are speaking to. Grace is the favor of God; a highly valued heavenly commodity. This is a significant tool because it brings transformation through words of encouragement by attracting the favor of God to the one we choose to serve.

I have a prophet friend who has told me that if I want him to go to particular church, just tell him and he will go. The favor I have in the eyes of this wonderful man is transferable. He has given me the liberty to choose a place, and because of the favor I have in his eyes, he will give that favor to a church he doesn't even know. In a similar fashion we get to choose who to encourage, realizing that God will extend to them the favor we have received from Him. It is an issue of stewardship. If we question whether believers have actually been given such a role of eternal consequences, I remind you that Jesus said, *"If you forgive the sins of any, their sins have been forgiven them"* (John 20:23 NASB).

A CULTURE OF HONOR

Encouragement is the initial tool used to create what we call a *culture of honor*. We use honor to train believers to step into their destiny, to strengthen our community in righteousness, and even for evangelism. We have honored those in the various facets of our community with amazing results. The average unbeliever is not accustomed to Christians having something nice to say about them. Christianity is known more for what we don't like than for what we do like. In spite of our shortcomings, we have been given this wonderful gift to distinguish us from the rest—the grace to encourage. When we encourage, it is more than a *feel-good moment*; it actually releases the favor of God.

The truth that encouragement releases the supernatural activities of God into the environment is a big issue in the Kingdom. In Isaiah 35:4, the people of God are told to minister to others with these words, "*Be strong, do not fear! Behold, your God will come with vengeance, with the recompense of God; He will come and save you.*" That is encouragement founded upon the covenantal provision and promise of God. It is taking what is available by promise and declaring it into reality in a person's life. The angelic hosts recognize their assignment through the words spoken to insure they come to pass (see Ps. 103:20). The amazing response from Heaven is noteworthy: "*Then the eyes of the blind shall be opened, and the ears of the deaf shall be unstopped. Then the lame shall leap like a deer, and the tongue of the dumb sing...*" (Isa. 35:5-6). Impossibilities yield in the supernatural atmosphere of encouragement.

This atmosphere of honor creates a health from which we serve those around us with life. Instead of becoming the victim of our circumstances, our circumstances become our victims, bringing them under a covenantal purpose (see Rom. 8:28). We become the answer to the heartfelt cry of society.

Living Inside Out

Contained in the realm of the Kingdom of God are all the answers to life's problems. It doesn't matter if it's the crisis with the ozone layer, frustration in dealing with contentious neighbors, or a problem with a failing marriage or business; the realm of the King's dominion has the answer. That realm of dominion is the realm of the Holy Spirit manifesting the lordship is Jesus Christ, which is first realized in our hearts.

Jesus taught us that, "...*the kingdom of God is within you*" (Luke 17:21). All the Kingdom issues are heart issues. Properly dealing with attitudes, ambitions, and agendas is key to enjoying the reign of God displayed in our lives. Our relationship with the Holy Spirit is foundational to the breakthroughs that we all want to see.

"*To you it has been granted to know the mysteries of the kingdom...*" (Luke 8:10 NASB). The secrets of God are our inheritance. We have access to this reality for the sake of those around us. The wonderful things that are to become manifest to the world are to flow from us. God intended that His expression to the world spring from *within* His people.

Israel was called upon to manifest the reign of God in their departure from Egypt and their entrance into the Promised Land. Normally this journey should have only lasted a couple of weeks at most, yet it took Israel 40 years. They *wandered* through the wilderness for 40 years. In reality, they were only doing on the outside what they were experiencing on the inside. "*Therefore I was angry with this generation, and said, 'They always go astray in their hearts, and they did not know my ways'; as I swore in my wrath, 'they shall not enter my rest'*" (Heb. 3:10-11 NASB). The phrase *go astray* means "to wander." They wandered in their hearts first. What was going on inside of them defined and shaped the world around them. In other words, their internal realities became their external realities. The lesson is simple: What is going on inside of us affects what goes on around us. This principle affects health, relationships, success in our occupation, and our gifts and ministries. All things flow from the heart. Solomon realized this and taught:

> *Watch over the heart with all diligence, for from it flows the issues of life* (Proverbs 4:23).

Stewardship of our heart is one of life's primary responsibilities. Successfully doing this guarantees success in other areas of life. When attitudes are properly guarded, godly conduct is insured. Careless attitudes give place to wrong thinking; and it's wrong thinking that gives way to sinful actions.[1]

PEACE ON EARTH

In Mark chapter 4 Jesus was in a life-threatening storm with the disciples. To their surprise, He was asleep. I've heard people say He slept because He was exhausted. I'd like to suggest that He slept because the world He was living in had no storms. Jesus was demonstrating what it was like to be *seated in heavenly places*. It is the exact application of what He meant when He said that, "*...He who came down from Heaven, that is the Son of Man who is in heaven*" (John 3:13), even though He was clearly standing right in front of them on planet Earth.

They woke Him and said, "don't you care we are perishing?" which is an astounding question to ask the Savior of the world. He responded by speaking "peace" over the storm and the storm ended. The peace that enabled Him to rest in the middle of a conflict became the very substance He released that stilled the storm. In other words, His internal reality became His external reality. If it's in you, and it's genuine, it can be released through you. We have authority over any storm we can sleep in, as we can only give away what we've received.

DIVINE HEALTH AND PROSPERITY

This principle of the Kingdom affects all we are and do. It seems to be the heart behind "*Beloved, I pray that you may prosper in all things and be in health, just as your soul prospers*" (3 John 2). Once again we note that what is ruling on the inside of us affects the outside. Health in my emotions, mind, and will affects my physical well-being. It is also important to note that a prosperous soul attracts the blessing of the Lord materially and financially.[2] This is the nature of life. The reality of the heart helps to define the nature of the world around us.

ON EARTH, AS IT IS AT HOME

A stumbling block for many children raised in Christian homes is the fact that Mom and Dad act differently in church than they do at home. Sometimes it's an issue of out-and-out hypocrisy. But most of the time it is well-meaning believers who never learn to watch over their hearts. When anxiety and unrest rule over a person's heart, they automatically create that atmosphere in their home. The joy that is sung about in the corporate gathering is foreign where it's needed most—in the home.

This is actually the source of much burnout for Christians. There is a pressure to produce on the outside what doesn't exist on the inside. It manifests in a works-oriented Gospel that tries to obtain favor through labor rather than working from the place of favor.

Sometimes we focus on merely changing our words knowing that they carry creative force. Still it's out of the heart that the mouth speaks. Changing the external without dealing with the heart is the way of religion. The push for miracles is the same. Trying to obtain a measure of Kingdom expression on the outside that is not manifest on the inside is the sign that the cruel taskmaster of religion is present. In the command to do the miraculous we find the key, "*Freely you have received, freely give*" (Matt. 10:8). We can give away *kingdom* in the measure we experience the *King's dominion* within us. What reigns on the inside rains on the outside. As it was with Peter's shadow, whatever overshadows me will be released through my shadow (see Acts 5:15). The heart is capable of all sorts of evil as well as all sorts of significant spiritual breakthrough. Stewardship of the heart is what determines what is produced there.

PARTNERS WITH THE CREATOR

The soul that is bound by worry, jealousy, anger, resentment, and the like is incapable of creativity on a consistent basis. It's impossible to thrive in that divine privilege because we are functioning separately from our design. Full potential is only found by carrying what God gave us to carry—"*my burden is light*" (Matt. 11:30). It is common knowledge that when a person's mind is not encumbered with these things, they are free for creative expression. Picture it like this—if I have an automobile with an eight-cylinder engine, I need all eight of them to reach full power. It is possible to run on only six cylinders, but it's not healthy. Nor is it the way the car was designed. People constantly learn to live with worry, fear, and other emotional pressures all the time and end up thinking their "motor" is running fine. The problem is that they've learned to define what is normal by their sub-normal lifestyle. Holding on to resentment and the like actually drains power from our engine and disqualifies us from significant spiritual breakthrough. Repentance is the beginning of the answer. It brings us into forgiveness and into our purpose.

HUNDRED-YEAR VISION

We believe God has required us to have a 100-year vision for our church. In other words, we constantly make decisions with the knowledge they will affect a generation that we will never see. "*A good man leaves an inheritance to his children's children*" (Prov. 13:22). God's righteousness makes us good. And it's His righteousness that causes us to see the effect of our decisions today on the generations that follow.

This vision is possible only through the discovery of divine purpose. As we see the eternal purpose of God for His people, we are able to develop lifestyles that are consistent with such a purpose. The end result is that we make His purposes perceivable to the unbeliever.

We are first and foremost a people of God's presence. The Church is the eternal dwelling place of God. As such we are known for our ministry *to God*, which positions and equips us for more effective ministry *to people*. For example, evangelism in its purist form is simply an overflow of worship. If the glory of God could be seen on and within the house(s) of God in the Old Testament—though the hands of man built them—how much more is that glory witnessed in this house called the church; for God is building His Church (see Matt. 16:18).

We are to display the wisdom of God to be seen by all those in positions of power—including the principalities and powers in heavenly places. The creative expression that comes through wisdom is a reminder to all that exists that this company of believers is commissioned to bring heavenly answers to earthly problems. This will turn heads from the inferior wisdom of this world to the divine wisdom that answers the cry of the human heart.

As His delegated authority on earth we have the responsibility to carry on the assignment that Jesus received from the Father—"...*destroy the works of the devil*" (1 John 3:8). The devil is defeated, but many of his works remain unchallenged. Before Jesus was taken to Heaven, He passed on the same commission to us that His Father gave to Him (see John 20:21). This is the overt ministry style of addressing those parts of people's lives that have been affected by the one who came to "*kill, steal, and destroy*" (John 10:10).

Mountains to Move

There are two basic mountains of opposition to the way of thinking that has us build for another generation to enjoy. The first is our own selfishness. It's easy to think in terms of what is best for us and lose sight of the ones that have to sleep in the bed we make. Hezekiah made such a mistake. He sinned by showing his complete treasury to foreigners. When the prophet rebuked him, he did so by saying, "'*Behold, the days are coming when all that is in your house, and all that your fathers have laid up in store to this day will be carried to Babylon; nothing shall be left,' says the Lord. 'Some of your sons who shall issue from you, whom you will beget, will be taken away; and they will become officials in the palace of the king of Babylon'"* (2 Kings 20:17-18 NASB). It's hard to imagine how such a great reformer could have fallen so far but his shocking response is as follows, *"'The word of the Lord which you have spoken is good.' For he thought, 'Is it not so, if there will be peace and truth in my days?'"* (2 Kings 20:19 NASB). It's sad to see how one so great thought solely about himself in a time when he learned his family line would bear a curse because of his foolish choice. He was actually so happy that he would enjoy blessing in his day that he lost sight of being the one leaving a legacy of evil for his descendants. He left them with a curse instead of a blessing, which is a stunning end to a great revivalist's life.

The second problem is it's difficult to have a 100-year vision for a planet you believe will soon burn because of God's judgment. It's hard to occupy, as we were commanded, and pray for His dominion to be demonstrated when our hope is based entirely on life in Heaven. This is a difficult tension for the church that exists between supposedly conflicting truths; our *blessed hope* in Christ' return, and our delight in the privilege of praying and laboring for His Kingdom (the King's Dominion) to come—now! The promise of Christ's return does not give me permission to be irresponsible with Christ's command.

SHEEP AND GOAT NATIONS

We have the honor of living at a time when our lives make a dramatic difference in the outcome of world events. We were born for this hour. Our assignment is to live as though nothing were impossible. The command to disciple nations is not figurative. It was a literal command that has the backing of Heaven for those who embrace the assignment. This is a time when "sheep" and "goat" nations are being decided. Silence by the church, or unbelief concerning divine purpose, can cost us the privilege of fulfilling that part of our commission. It will end in disaster for many nations that could have had a significant outpouring of the Spirit.

Regardless of how and when you believe we are going to be taken to Heaven, we must rid ourselves of the idea that Jesus is coming to *rescue* His church. That lie has dislocated many generations of revolutionaries from their purpose in the same way a joint is pulled out of place. It has put the Church into a defensive posture of occupation to protect what we have instead of positioning ourselves for the purpose of increase. The strategy of occupation for the purpose of advancement and increase is an absolute Kingdom principle. Ask the man who buried his talent in order to protect it (see Matt. 25:24-28). He occupied (possessed) to protect (preserve) without increasing what he was given and suffered eternal consequences for his choice.

THE ULTIMATE CHALLENGE IN STEWARDSHIP

This takes us to our final truth for this challenge. We have been given the opportunity to shape the course of world history by learning to bring into our day things that were reserved for another day. That is the subject of the last chapter.

ENDNOTES

1. We found this to be a primary truth in raising our children. Disciplining for right attitudes prevents a lot of heartbreak in wrong actions. But the parents must model this principle first.

2. Remember, Kingdom abundance is not measured in what I have, but what I've given away.

CHAPTER 10

Pulling Tomorrow Into Today

We own in the present what is not yet.

To resource the earth with Heaven's resources, our understanding of stewardship must grow. Many struggle whenever leaders teach about our simple role stewarding money, and
automatically disqualify themselves from the weightier issues—like
responsibly managing our gifts, time, relationships, and the world
we live in. But the greatest honor bestowed on us as stewards is the
responsibility to steward tomorrow, today.

Our role in shaping the world around us through creative
expression is never more at the forefront than when we joyfully learn
to pull tomorrow into today. God trains us for this role whenever He
speaks to us, for in doing so He is working to awaken and establish
our affections for His Kingdom. A people whose hearts are anchored
in His world are best qualified to serve in this one. He establishes His
eternal purpose in us whenever He speaks. His Word comes from
eternity into time, giving us a track to ride on. It connects us with
eternity, causing us to impact our world through the influence of His
world.

INHERITANCE 101

The believer's inheritance is beyond human comprehension. To put the richness of that gift into the eternal future is to sell short the power of the Cross in the present. He gave us a gift beyond comprehension because we have an assignment beyond reason. Jesus gave us all things because we would need *all things* to fulfill our call. He intends to fill the earth with His glory, and His glorious Bride will play a role.

It is interesting to note that we have already inherited tomorrow—*things to come*. That makes us stewards of tomorrow in a profound way. God reveals coming events to us, and we steward the timing of those events. This amazing privilege is exemplified in Scripture and gives insight to passages that might otherwise be hard to understand.

ISRAEL WAS BLINDED BY GOD

Many times throughout the Scriptures we are faced with statements and principles that challenge our understanding of God. It's never that He could be perceived as evil or untrustworthy; but He is often mysterious and unpredictable.

Such a case is found in the Gospel of John. At first glance it looks as though God has it in for Israel and that He hopes they don't repent because He doesn't want to heal them.

> *He has blinded their eyes and He hardened their heart, so that they would not see with their eyes and perceive with their heart, and be converted and I heal them* (John 12:40 NASB).

Yet the whole of Scripture gives us a different picture. We know God never hardens a tender heart. It's the tender heart that receives what God is saying and doing. Wherever people have truly sought God, He has welcomed them with much mercy and grace, as He is the restorer of broken lives. But a hard heart is a different story completely, as God will harden a hard heart.

Pharaoh is probably the best example of this (see Exod. 7). The Bible says that he hardened his heart against the Lord, and did so repeatedly. So God finally hardened his heart for him, making his condition permanent. If Pharaoh would not be used as an instrument of righteousness, then God would use his evil to display His wonders. God's intent was now to use him as a "chess piece" for His purposes.

Israel was similarly hardened and used for His purposes. They had watched Jesus' ministry firsthand for over three years. While Nazareth was the only city we know of to resist because of unbelief, the others still didn't repent even though they saw extraordinary miracles (see Matt. 11:21). Seeing God display His wonders has a price tag—we can no longer live (think and act) the same way we did before. Miracles display God's dominion with a clarity that is seldom seen in the rest of life. To see and not change is to bring judgment upon ourselves. Such was the case for many of the cities of Israel.

God is perfect in wisdom, and is able to use the worst that man can dish out for His glory. In His sovereignty, He chose to use this *season of rejection of the Gospel* as the time He would add the Gentiles to the faith. This is discussed more clearly in Romans 11:

> *I say then, have they stumbled that they should fall? Certainly not! But through their fall, to provoke them to jealousy, salvation has come to the Gentiles* (Romans 11:11).

Israel's rejection of Jesus provided the opportunity for the Gentiles to be grafted into the olive tree, the *Israel of God* (Gal. 6:16; Rom. 11:17-24). The entire story is a fascinating study about God's sovereign plan to save people from every tribe, tongue, and nation, but unpacking this is not the purpose of this chapter. Rather, tucked away in this wonderful story is a remarkable truth: if Israel would have seen what God had purposed for them within His Kingdom in the last days, and asked for it, God would have had to give it to them. He would have answered them even though it was not His correct time for that promise to be fulfilled. So He used their hardness of heart as the basis for blinding them to insure that His purposes would be accomplished on His timetable. Instead of just saying "No," He responded by hardening their already hard hearts so they would lose their ability to perceive Kingdom possibilities.

The implication of the story—if you see it, you can have it! Perhaps it would be better to say, if God lets you see future promises, it's because He's hoping they will hook you, and cause you to hunger for those things. It is through a desperate heart that you are able to bring the fulfillment of those promises into your day.

THE PURPOSE OF REVELATION

Revelation means "to lift the veil." It is to remove a cover over something so we can see it more clearly. It doesn't create something; it simply reveals what was already there. When God reveals coming events and promises, He is giving us access to a realm in Him. All of the promises He reveals to us will be realized in time, but the acceleration of events is largely determined by the desperation of God's people. Our passion for Him and His promises speeds up the process of growth and development, making us qualified for the stewardship of those events sooner than had been planned.

BIBLICAL PRECEDENTS

Jesus and His mother, Mary, went to a wedding in John chapter 2. After they were there for a while, Mary noticed the wedding party was out of wine. She spoke to Jesus about their problem. Jesus' responded, "*Woman, what does that have to do with us? My hour has not yet come*" (John 2:4 NASB). Since Jesus only said and did what He picked up from His Father (see John 5:19), He let her know that this was not the right time to reveal Him as the miracle worker. Mary had been *pregnant* with God's promises about her son for 30 years, and found it difficult to wait much longer. She turned to the servants and told them to do whatever Jesus said. Jesus, who got all His direction from His heavenly Father, now perceived that this had become the right time. Amazing! God's timing changed! What was reserved for another day (revealing Jesus as the miracle worker) was pulled into her day through her desperation.

Another time, Jesus ministered to a woman at the well. She was a Samaritan. Jesus so profoundly impacted her that she was able to persuade the entire city to come and hear Him speak. They believed at first because of the woman's testimony, but ended up believing out of their personal contact with Him. What is important to remember is that this was not supposed to be the time for the non-Jews to hear the Gospel. The disciples were not even allowed the chance to preach to them when they were commissioned in Matthew 10, as that new focus would come after the death and resurrection of Jesus. Yet in this story, the people of the city begged Jesus to stay two more days, which He did. They pulled a privilege into their day that was reserved for another time.

THE MOST PROFOUND STORY

King David takes the prize for having perhaps the greatest story which illustrates this principle. His situation is hard for us to imagine—he was under the law. Only the high priest could come before the actual presence of God. His presence dwelt upon the mercy seat, which was inside the Holy of Holies. He could only come bringing a basin of blood, hoping that God would indeed accept the sacrifice and postpone the penalty of sin for one more year. If anyone other than the priest ever came into God's actual presence, they would die. God would kill them. There certainly wasn't a careless attitude about going to church in those days.

David is known as the man after God's heart. He had a revelation of changes in their approach to God, confirmed by Nathan and Gad, the prophets who served in his court. This insight changed everything. He saw that the blood of bulls and goats did nothing to really touch the heart of God, and that He was really looking for the sacrifices of brokenness and contrition. Another radical change that would have been nearly unimaginable in that day was that every priest would be welcome into God's presence daily. And they didn't come with a basin of blood, but instead came offering sacrifices of thanksgiving and praise.

Preparations began. The musicians and singers were trained. Israel was getting herself ready for the presence of God to return to Jerusalem. Saul, Israel's former king, had little regard for the ark of the covenant.[1] But David wanted God's presence more than anything. While there were initial problems, due to the fact they did not follow God's instructions for carrying the Ark of the Covenant, David eventually got his wish. He pitched a tent for the Ark and with great celebration brought His presence into the city and placed it into the tent. According to David's directions, the priests ministered to God 24 hours a day for decades. There were no sacrifices of animals before His presence in this tent. It was 100 percent worship.

It's important to note two things: One, what they did was forbidden by the law they lived under. And two, they were given a sneak preview of New Testament church life. Because of the blood of Jesus, each believer has access to the presence of God to minister to Him with thanksgiving, praise, and worship.

David was primarily a worshiper. As a young man he no doubt learned much about the presence and heart of God. He tasted of a lifestyle that was reserved for New Testament believers, yet hungered for that in his day. His hunger for what he saw became so strong that God let him have something in his day that was reserved for another day.

CROSSING THE GREAT DIVIDE

We have a bad habit of taking most of the good promises of the Bible and sweeping them under the mysterious rug we call "the millennium." It is a great inconsistency to say the last days began with the day of Pentecost with Acts 2, and then take the wonderful promises of the prophets about the last days and say they refer to the millennium. For example, Micah 4:1-2 (NASB) says,*"And it will come about in the last days…Many nations will come and say, 'Come and let us go up to the mountain of the Lord and to the house of the God of Jacob, that He may teach us about His ways and that we may walk in His paths…."'* The error of our ways is clearly realized in the fact that what is believed actually requires little or no faith to get what most of the Church is waiting for—the world to get worse, and the Church to get rescued. This is an irresponsible way to respond to great promise.

Had David lived with such a mind-set, he would have had to live under the restraint of Old Testament law, and not provide us the testimony of a life of celebration and joy. He illustrated the New Testament believer before there ever was such a thing.

If ever there was a line to cross where it should have been impossible to bring something from a future era into a given time, it should have been during David's day. The barrier between the law and grace was so large that what David did would have been impossible to predict, were we on the other side of the Cross. Yet the desperation of a hungry heart brought about the impossible. It drew into their hour something that was not just for the future. Nor was it just reserved for another day; it was for another race of people.[2] Yet David brought this greatest of life's privileges across the greatest divide imaginable. He had daily access to the glory of His presence! This would be something that only the blood of Jesus could make possible.

OUR GREATEST CHALLENGE

If it's true that the promises of restored cities and healed nations are actually millennium promises…and if the promise of God's glory being manifest all over the earth is far off into the future…and if in fact the people of God will not reach a place of true maturity, living like one mature man—then I must ask these questions: Is there anyone hungry enough for what He has shown us in the Scriptures that we will pull into our day something that is reserved for another? Is there anyone willing to lay themselves down to bring more of God's promises across another great divide? Or how about the promise that says everyone will know the Lord? (See Jer. 31:34.) Isn't that one worth pursuing for our cities?

If what I have shared is true, then no one can hide behind their eschatology. No one is exempt because of the doctrinal interpretation of the last days. No one is excused. If you can see the coming future promises, and He hasn't blinded your eyes to His intent, then He is hoping to hook you into the role of calling "*into being that which does not exist*" (Rom. 4:17 NASB). It is the role of the desperate heart of faith. We have the opportunity to affect the direction and flow of history through our prayers and intercessions. This is when we take hold of the future. This is why He wants to show us, "*things to come*" (John 16:13). The future is now, and it belongs to us.

Where Did all the Seasons Go

His Kingdom only knows increase and acceleration. It is the hunger of God's people that helps accelerate the process of development and growth, and actually speeds up time. It is my conviction that God is trying to get rid of our excuse concerning "seasons." Many have lived in a spiritual winter for most of their lives and called it *God's dealings*. The metaphor of the seasons has become an excuse for moodiness, unbelief, depression, inactivity, and the like. It must end. As the technological development has increased exponentially, so the development and maturity of this generation will increase.

Trees planted by God's river bear fruit 12 months of the year. They are the prophetic prototype of the last days' generation that has experienced the acceleration prophesied. How else do you think it's possible for the *"plowman to overtake the reaper?"* (Amos 9:13). This is an amazing prophetic picture of a time when planting and harvesting are done in one motion. How else can we come into the maturity talked about in Zechariah when the weakest among us is like David and the strongest is like God? (See Zech. 12:8.) These things are reserved for the hour directly ahead of us. Let's grab hold of tomorrow, today. We don't have time to waste and then blame God for it. It is the season to apprehend, because we see!

There's a message for us in the cursed fig tree. Jesus cursed it for not bearing fruit *out of season*. It died immediately. Was He unreasonable? Did He lose His temper? Or was He showing us something about His expectations for our lives that we'd just as soon ignore? He has the right to expect the fruit of the impossible from those He has created for the impossible. The Spirit of the resurrected Christ living in me has disqualified me from the mundane and ordinary. I am qualified for the impossible, because I'm a believing believer. Faith qualifies me for the impossible.

We have a plant in our prayer house that is supposed to have blossoms for a couple months of the year. But in the presence of the Lord upon that prayer house, it blooms year-round. He is trying to get our attention with natural phenomenon that point to these truths.

ITS NEW DAY

God is using the hunger of His people to increase the momentum of the day, bringing about drastic changes in the pace of development. Brand-new believers are not waiting for the *mature* to tell them that something is possible. They've read the Book, and they know it's legal. This tattooed generation with their body piercings and little fear of death has locked into the possibility of significance. They have seen what prior generations have called impossible, and will settle for nothing less. I, for one, join myself with them in the quest for the authentic Gospel that has no walls, no impossibilities, with an absolute surrender to the King and His Kingdom.

God doesn't reveal coming events to make us strategists. He shows us the future to make us dissatisfied[3] because hungry people move the resources of Heaven like no one else possibly could. It's the real reason the rich have such a hard time entering the Kingdom—there's so little hunger for what is real, what is unseen—their desperation has been numbed by an abundance of the inferior.

The Purpose of Contending

Two years ago I sought for a breakthrough in my dad's healing. It never came, and he went home to be with Jesus—but that's a story for another day. Let's just say there are no deficiencies on God's side of the equation. It felt like I was pushing against a 1,000-pound rock that wouldn't budge. And although I pushed against that rock for months, it never moved. We celebrated his home-going and vowed to continue to push against those things which cut people's lives short.

It wasn't too long afterward that I realized that while I never moved that 1,000-pound boulder, I can now move the 500-pound rock right next to it. And I couldn't have moved this size rock before contending with the 1,000-pounder. Contending shapes us and makes us capable of carrying more than we've ever been able before, and opens up for us areas of anointing in ministry that were previously out of reach.

Often times God uses the fight to increase a person's experience in Him, far above all those around them. I call it *a spike in human experience*. In times past, people with that elevated position of experience and the extraordinary anointing and favor that goes with it used it to draw people to themselves to receive from their gift. While that is always a part of the purpose of a gift, it falls short of God's intent entirely. The elevated experience is the position to equip the Body of Christ so that what was once the high point of breakthrough for an individual has become the new norm for the Church. Contending brings a breakthrough that must be shared. All must benefit from the price we pay to labor through the heat of the day. It's just His way.

DREAMERS, LET'S GATHER

We are in a race. It's a race between what is and what could be. We are uniquely positioned with the richest inheritance of all time. It has been accumulating through several thousand years of humanity encountering God, and God encountering humanity. The righteous dead are watching. They fill the heavenly stands, and have been given the name, "*cloud of witnesses*" (Heb. 12:1). They realize that in a relay race, each runner receives a prize according to how the last runner finishes. They invested in us for this final leg of the race, and are now waiting to see what we will do with what we've been given.

We've been given the capacity to dream and, more importantly, to dream with God. His language continues to be unveiled, His heart is being imparted, and permission has been given to try to exaggerate His goodness. We have been given the right to surpass the accomplishments of previous generations using creativity through wisdom to solve the issues facing us. Their ceiling is our floor. This is our time to run.

ONLY CHILDREN ARE READY

I remember when I was a child and my parents would have guests come over to our house to visit. It was always exciting to be part of the food and the fun. But it was painful to have to go to bed while they were still there, sitting in our living room, talking and having fun. The laughter that echoed back into my room was just torture. It was impossible for me to sleep in that atmosphere. Sometimes, when I couldn't take it any longer, I would sneak quietly into the hallway, just to listen. I didn't want to miss anything. If my parents caught me they usually sent me back to bed. But there were a few times when they thought my curiosity was humorous enough to let me come out to be with them just a little longer. The risk was worth it!

I'm in the hallway again. And the thought of missing something that could have been the experience of my generation is pure torture. I can't possibly sleep in this atmosphere, because if I do, I know I'll miss the reason for which I was born.

ENDNOTES

1. A gold-covered box, with the Mercy Seat on top—this is where the Presence of God dwelt for Israel.

2. Believers are actually a new creation, a new race of people. See Second Corinthians 5:17 and First Peter 2:9.

3. One of the secrets of maintaining a revival is being thankful for what God has done, while remaining dissatisfied because there is more.

Strengthen Yourself in the Lord

How to Release the Hidden Power of God in Your Life

by

BILL JOHNSON

DEDICATION

I dedicate this book to Randy Clark: Your humility, integrity, and passion for God has affected millions of people—and I am one. Your encouragement and support has been monumental in my life. Thank you for your friendship and for the example you have been to me in stewarding the life of miracles. Thanks, Randy.

ACKNOWLEDGEMENTS

Thanks to Dann Farrelly and Pam Spinosi for your editorial help, again. Thanks to Mary Walker and Judy Franklin for your constant encouragement and help in putting this book together. Special thanks to Allison Armerding for helping me with the actual writing of this book. You are all priceless!

Endorsements

In many decades of ministry across the world, I have discovered that people, whatever their background, have two primary questions: "Who am I?" and "What is my purpose?" Bill Johnson masterfully answers these questions as he shares the tools that the Lord has taught him to use to strengthen himself. This great pastor's insights will show you how God has equipped you with all the tools necessary to fulfill your destiny. Whatever dire circumstances you have gone through, this book will help you lay hold of God's provision to finish the journey in victory as you "strengthen yourself in the Lord."

Dr. Mahesh Chavda
Author, *The Hidden Power of Prayer and Fasting*

In the midst of a world of chaos and confusion in the atmosphere around us, the enemy attempts to develop a plan to take advantage of us. One key to our lives is not allowing seeming defeats, discouragements, and robbing strategies of the enemy to overtake us and create a failure mentality in our thought process. In *Strengthen Yourself in the Lord: How to Release the Hidden Power of God in Your Life*, Bill Johnson has created a way of thinking to help you develop a victory plan for your life. This book will cause you to develop a mentality of blessing, being blessed, celebration, and praise that will unlock the BEST that the Lord has for you in the future!

Dr. Chuck D. Pierce
President, Glory of Zion International, Inc.
Vice President, Global Harvest Ministries

Bill's new book provides rich, powerful encouragement for every Christian fighting for spiritual survival, and that would include most of us at some point. But more than that, Bill points the way forward for all of us who want to press on toward our high calling in Jesus, not allowing anything to hold us back from our destiny. Bill speaks from experience, and his life, relationships and the testimonies that follow his ministry are evidence that he knows the way...

Rolland and Heidi Baker
Iris Ministries

Bill Johnson's "toolbag" is loaded with the necessary equipment to build a life of faith and blessing. I was assured that no ministry that walks in the measure of revelation that Bill does is accidental, and once again, I see the practical ways that the Father has sustained him and advanced him in a most remarkable and gifted ministry. I believe it is the basis for who he is and what he does.

Bishop Joseph L. Garlington

CONTENTS

	Introduction 13
Chapter 1	The Secret to David's Promotion 15
Chapter 2	Staying Connected to Your Destiny 31
Chapter 3	Disarming Hell Through Thanksgiving. . 49
Chapter 4	The Personal Breakthrough Moment . . 63
Chapter 5	Releasing the Hidden Things. 79
Chapter 6	Possessed by Promises 91
Chapter 7	Keeping the Testimony 105
Chapter 8	Controlling Your Environment 119
Chapter 9	The Desperate Cry 131
Chapter 10	Not On My Shift! 155

INTRODUCTION

It's time to be strong and of great courage. I don't know that there has ever been a time when courage and faith were more needed. But I don't say this because of the darkness of the hour. That is a given. I say it because of the realm of God's promises that linger over the Church, waiting for someone to see it—to believe it—to say yes to what could be!

To live in courage requires encouragement. And sometimes the only one to encourage you is you. Not knowing how to strengthen ourselves has cost the Church dearly. It is the key to promotion! It is what turned David's darkest hour into the *backdoor* to the throne room. And it will be the same for you. When you learn how to strengthen yourself, you will reach your destiny, fulfill your God-born dreams, and become a person who can accurately represent Jesus—re-presenting Jesus to the world.

Chapter 1

The Secret to David's Promotion

If you want to kill giants,

follow a giant killer!

K ing David towers above all other Old Testament figures in this sense—he is remembered not so much for the greatness of his actions, but for the greatness of his heart for God. His passionate heart set him apart in God's eyes long before he ever won great military victories, before he revolutionized the nature of worship in Israel, or even ushered in Israel's Golden Age of economic and spiritual prosperity. While David was still in obscurity, God saw that he was a man after His own heart. (See Acts 13:22.)

What was the evidence of David's heart after God? Scripture indicates two primary aspects of David's life before he was anointed king. First, when nobody was looking, when nobody was calling prayer meetings or leading a revival in Judah, David was pouring out his heart in worship and prayer to God in the fields where he tended his father's sheep. With no one around, his pursuit of God was motivated by nothing but a desire to know God for His own sake.

David's relationship with the Lord was highly unusual for his day because the entire paradigm for worship in Israel at the time was focused on the sacrifice of animals to temporarily deal with sin, and not the sacrifice of praise from the heart. His heart led him beyond the letter of the law to the heart of the Lord, Himself. Secondly, David's battles against the lion and the bear revealed his heart for God because he relied completely on God for victory. This trust indicated that David's heart for the Lord was not something that changed according to his circumstances. He had integrity of heart. (See 1 Sam. 17:37.)

GROOMED TO REIGN

God did not bring the *man after His heart* straight from the pasture to the palace. Incredibly, David did not assume the throne until 10-13 years *after* Samuel had anointed him to be king. In those interim years, David endured more difficulty, persecution, and rejection than many of us face in a lifetime. He probably didn't expect it to take so long to become king.

In contrast, Saul, the previous king, had no such difficulty; he was crowned very shortly after being anointed by Samuel. But God did not want another King Saul. While Saul was truly the best man Israel had to offer when they demanded a king (see 1 Sam. 8:6), his heart had not been groomed through testing before he assumed the throne. As king, Saul was entrusted with a measure of anointing to lead the armies of Israel to victory and shepherd the people. Yet, without the strength of character that only comes by winning private battles, these public victories exposed the previously hidden weakness of Saul's heart toward God. That weakness, combined with his growing appetite for the favor of man, led him to bring glory to himself and disobey the Lord. Saul's untested heart allowed that which was given to make him successful, to ultimately destroy him.

So David, even though he already possessed a heart for the Lord, was led into years of testing that groomed him to handle the glory and responsibility of the throne. The scriptural account of this season in David's life is filled with lessons on the kinds of character tests we all face on the road to fulfilling our destiny in God. But the real question—what is it about David that ultimately qualifies him to become king? What brings about the moment in which God says, "OK, now you're ready"? I would like to suggest that it was David's ability to do something in the face of the deepest betrayal and rejection imaginable. When he stood completely alone, that is when David "*strengthened himself in the Lord his God*" (1 Sam. 30:6).

THE ROLE OF REJECTION

Seeing the progression in the tests David faced is valuable for understanding the significance of this choice that became the tipping point for his being enthroned as king. The following is a "*Reader's Digest*" version of David's life in the years after he was anointed.

These years actually began with apparent success. David's unique intimacy with the Lord had already set him apart and given him what no other man in Israel had—great courage, fueled by a righteous indignation at the enemies who were taunting the armies of the living God. David, armor-less and alone, boldly defied the odds and ran at Goliath, winning a great victory over the giant as well as the Philistines. This exploit instantly earned him favor with the people and King Saul. As a result, He moved into the palace, became best friends with the king's son, and married the king's daughter. By all accounts, the fulfillment of Samuel's word over him seemed imminent.

But then King Saul got wind of a song that the women of the city were singing, "Saul has killed his thousands, and David his ten thousands." Consumed with jealousy, he launched a campaign to end David's life. After dodging Saul's spears, David painfully came to terms with the reality that he was going to have to leave Jerusalem to survive. He probably had no idea that this demonized madman would chase him for over a decade as far away from the throne as possible. Saul's rejection of him was the first sign that David's schooling for the kingship was based on testing his ability to believe and walk in the Word over his life, even when the circumstances seemed to completely oppose and deny his destiny.

We can see another character test he faced when, after leaving Jerusalem and hiding in several places for a while, David rescued the village of Keilah from the Philistines. He found out that Saul knew he was there, so he asked the Lord whether he would come after him, and whether the citizens he had just saved—his own Jewish brothers—were going to protect him or turn him over to Saul. God said, "He's coming for you, and they're going to turn you over." Rejected again, he headed for the wilderness.

By this time he also had some followers, but they were *"everyone who was in distress, everyone who was in debt, and everyone who was discontented..."* (1 Sam. 22:2). They were the rejects of society. David demonstrated a true king's heart by embracing these men, and spent the next ten years or so training them in life and in warfare. Under his leadership, these "rejects" became his "mighty men." (Interestingly, at least four of these men ended up killing giants, just as David had done. If you want to kill giants, follow a giant killer!) Eventually David moved his men to the land of the Philistines, whose king gave him a city, Ziklag. From Ziklag, David led nightly raids against the enemies of Israel, convincing the Philistines he was doing it for them. Then one day

> If you want
> to kill giants,
> follow a
> giant killer!

the Philistines decided to fight Israel. Many of the men wanted to take David along because of his obvious military strength and prowess. But the princes of the Philistines wouldn't let David go, saying that he would turn on them in the battle and defeat them in order to get back on Saul's good side. After this humiliation, David and his men then returned to Ziklag, only to find it burned and looted by the Amalekites. Every wife, child, and possession was gone.

David's seriously bad day would have been the last straw for most of us. He had been rejected by the king, rejected by the Israelites, and even rejected by their enemies. (You know you've had a bad day when the *devil* rejects you.) But in this moment, David faces the deepest and most betraying rejection of all. At the sight of their burned city and missing families, his mighty men—those he'd turned from disenfranchised to contributing citizens, whom he'd persevered with for years, and whose families he'd protected and provided for—talked about stoning him. Now even the rejected of society had rejected him. David was rejected, and was about to be killed. There really isn't much difference between their attitude and the common prejudice in our society today: If there's a problem, get rid of the guy at the top. But this is a deeper injustice because these men owe their lives to David.

Scripture records what David is feeling in this moment:

Now David was greatly distressed, for the people spoke of stoning him, because the soul of all the people was grieved, every man for his sons and his daughters... (1 Samuel 30:6).

Without question I would feel "greatly distressed" too if my life is threatened by my closest friends. But how does David respond? Does he run for his life? Does he become indignant and start defending his place as their leader by reminding them that they owe him their lives? He easily could have done either, but this is what he did instead:

...But David strengthened himself in the Lord his God (1 Samuel 30:6).

THE BACK DOOR TO THE THRONE ROOM

Facing a volatile group of men ready to stone him caused him not to look to himself for strength but to the Lord his God. His faith gave him the courage to essentially say, "Come on, guys! We've got wives and kids to bring back!" Amazingly, this was all it took to knock the sense back into his men. He simply called them back to the purpose and vision for their lives—demonstrating the true character of a strengthened leader. God gave him the strength to master his own distress, look past the offense of his men's rejection, and rally them together to get their families back. When he turned to the men in strength, they pulled themselves together, went after the Amalekites, and retrieved every person and possession that had been taken. But David's personal breakthrough in this moment, his ability to strengthen himself and be faithful to his purpose instead of collapsing under pressure, not only saved his life, it also enabled him to lead his men to victory. His breakthrough kept him standing in front of an unseen door that was just about to open—the door to the throne room. The very battle the Philistines had just prevented him from fighting was the battle in which Saul and Jonathan died. Only a short time later, Israel crowned David king. His darkest moment led him to the back door of the throne room.

LEAVING A LEGACY THAT LASTS

The story, of course, does not end there. The true significance of David's promotion from the field to the throne is seen in his kingly legacy. It would be stunning enough if David had only written the Psalms, established an unprecedented form of worship in Jerusalem, designed the Temple, and brought Israel into its Golden Age; but King David was so important to God that he was named *the* forerunner of the Messiah. Jesus, throughout *eternity*, will be identified as the Son of David and sit on David's throne. David was promoted to a place of such favor and influence with God that he altered the course of history forever.

David's life was not set down in Scripture merely to inspire us. We only need to read the accounts of his sins to know that he was not some kind of superhero. David's life is really a call to every believer. If one man who was a sinner who lived hundreds of years before the blood of Jesus was shed, could come into that place of favor with God, then how much more should those who are covered by that blood be able to come into an even greater destiny—to be like Christ and finish His work on the planet? John describes the destiny we've received in Jesus in Revelation 5:9-10, the destiny all of Heaven is singing about: "...*You were slain, and have redeemed us to God by Your blood out of every tribe and tongue and people and nation, and have made us **kings and priests** to our God; and we shall reign on the earth.*" As proof that our position as kings and priests is not something less than the position David held, the writer of Ephesians states that we are seated in Christ in heavenly places (see Eph. 2:6). If Jesus is currently seated on the throne of David, then so are we!

We are living in a time when the Lord is restoring this revelation to His people—that the blood of Jesus was not shed merely to save us from our sins, but to restore us to a relationship with God in which we partner with Him as kings and priests to bring the planet under His rule and reign. We have delegated authority to establish His Kingdom wherever the sole of our foot treads. But the fact is, while God calls us "kings," the degree to which we walk in that position is a matter of *potential.* And as Larry Randolph points out, God is not responsible for making us reach our potential. A lot of believers think God is not fulfilling the prophetic words over their lives because they have missed the fact that the word was pointing to their potential, which requires their participation. God won't fulfill your potential because He wants you to become a mature believer who thinks and acts like Him out of your own free will. Mature believers are those He can trust with the secrets of His heart because they will not use the favor He gives for their own purposes, but for His.

INCREASED FAVOR SECURES OUR DESTINY

Some of us who have been raised in a democratic society may struggle with the idea that God gives more favor to some people than others. God's favor is not the same as His love. You cannot do anything to change the vastness of God's love for you. But even Jesus Himself had to grow "...*in favor with God and man*" (Luke 2:52). This verse amazes me. I can understand the fact that He needed to grow in favor with man, but why did He have to grow in favor with God? He was perfect in every way. The answer lies in the fact that Jesus did everything He did *as a man,* laying His divinity aside, in order to be a model for us. Therefore, He, like David, had to be tested. At His baptism, He received His anointing as the Spirit descended on Him and remained, and He was declared by the Father to be the Son of God. But instead of launching right into His ministry, He was led by the Spirit into the wilderness. There He was tested by the enemy, specifically in the area of the Word that had just been spoken over Him. If you look at the account of Jesus' temptation in Luke, you'll notice that He goes into the wilderness "*filled with the Holy Spirit*" and He returns *"in the power of the Spirit"* (Luke 4:1,14). Because He passed the test, the expression of the word over His life, the favor to walk in His potential, was released in a greater measure.

The "favor" that Jesus grew in is the word *charis*, which refers to the divine grace and ability of God Himself that comes upon and enables a person to accomplish His purposes. As Jesus modeled, each of us must grow in favor if we are going to fulfill our destiny in God. But favor, because it is so glorious and powerful, is a weighty thing. Thus, God, in His mercy, gives you His favor in the measure your character can handle, taking you from glory to glory, faith to faith, and strength to strength.

THE PURPOSE AND PRIORITY OF MINISTERING TO YOURSELF

David's life shows us that the ability to strengthen and minister to ourselves is a vital skill that we must learn if we are going to develop the character to fulfill our potential as kings and priests. It is impossible for anyone to reach his ultimate destiny in life without learning to minister to himself. We can best appreciate the significance of this ability by understanding the nature of the role to which we are called. When Scripture says *"we shall reign on the earth"* (Rev. 5:10), the implication is that every one of us has a destiny to stand in a position where we influence people around us. Each of us will have a different size and kind of sphere of influence, but we are all called as leaders in society. We are not called to "rule over others" in the sense of domination. In God's Kingdom, the power of rule is the divine enablement to serve others more effectively. And just as kings are to provide protection and prosperity for their citizens, so those who serve well in God's Kingdom will offer safety and blessing to all who come under their influence.

Perhaps the first quality that distinguishes a leader is *initiative.* God knew David would succeed as a leader because he took the initiative to seek Him in the secret place. This is the same quality of maturity that He is looking for in us. To experience the positive peer pressure and momentum of a move of God in a corporate group is wonderful. But those who seek God's face and pursue His destiny for their lives when nobody is around, are the people who possess the initiative required to strengthen themselves. If they learn to sustain their initiative to seek God by strengthening themselves in testing, they will be the people who will experience the personal breakthroughs that release a corporate blessing to those around them.

God wants us to learn how to strengthen ourselves through Him because developing our skills will promote spiritual longevity. We need longevity because our destiny and potential cannot be attained in a few years; they extend to the end of our lifetime here on earth. For this reason, I like to tell the students in our School of Supernatural Ministry, "Anyone can burn for God for a year. Come back in twenty years, take me out to coffee, and tell me you're still burning." Then I spend much of the school year teaching them the tools I've learned for strengthening myself. It's obvious that the students possess enough initiative to pay the price to come to school; but without discovering and using tools to minister to themselves, they won't, I'm convinced, be able to sustain the desire that brought them initially. Sadly, I know too many Christian leaders who lack this ability, and as a result are suffering from burnout or moral failure.

Now, let me be clear that learning to strengthen ourselves does not mean that we develop an independent lifestyle. Our lifestyle as believers is always focused on serving, loving, and leaning on the Body of Christ. But for the sake of becoming mature and growing in favor so that we can bless those around us, God brings moments into our lives when we have to stand alone in difficulty and testing. God will even blind the eyes and deafen the ears of our closest friends in those moments so we can learn to minister to ourselves. We must recognize this because I know a lot of believers who fall into bitterness, thinking their friends are failing them in a hard time. Understanding God's priority to teach us this lesson helps us to avoid that trap.

VICTORY AS A LIFESTYLE

This book is written to share the tools that the Lord has taught me to use to strengthen myself. My purpose is not to make an exhaustive list of tools in the Scripture, but to show you the things that have brought me through tough days in the trenches. As you read about the things that God has put in your arsenal, my desire is that the *conviction* of the destiny over your life will be more deeply rooted in your heart. He has equipped you for great victory—not just merely to break through, but to release and establish the dominion of God around you. However, it's your responsibility to use these tools to bring strength to yourself so you can stand in that victory. The invitation of a lifetime is before you—an invitation to walk in a place of favor where you co-labor with God and make history as a king and priest of His choosing. Let's rise to the challenge!

Chapter 2

STAYING CONNECTED TO YOUR DESTINY

✠ *The enemy uses lies to make*
problems appear bigger
than the solutions we carry. ✠

✠ *God never sets us up*
to fail—only to grow. ✠

K eeping tabs on all the different aspects of the Christian life can be overwhelming. There is a seemingly endless list of responsibilities to attend to. There is the issue of relationships inside and outside of our immediate family, our place of employment, ministry, community involvement, and evangelism. And then there's the issue of Christian disciplines like prayer, personal Bible study, witnessing, corporate gatherings, fasting—the list goes on and on. And to make matters worse, most of us are quite capable of making simple things very complex. Yet Jesus illustrated a simple lifestyle: one that is carefree—not irresponsible, but simply without cares. Solomon seemed to recognize a key to this great Kingdom lifestyle when he said, "*Watch over your heart with all diligence, for from it flow the springs of life*" (Prov. 4:23 NASB). All the issues of our lives flow forth like rivers from one central location—the heart—and what we do in stewarding that one place determines the outcome of our lives.

We live in the crossroads daily—that place between mystery and revelation. My job is to trust my heavenly Father with the problems and situations I don't understand, and focus on stewarding my will to what I know to be true. My success in watching over my heart determines the measure of Kingdom breakthrough I will experience in life. In other words, my internal reality often defines the nature of my external reality: if I prosper in my heart, my life will prosper.

Strengthening ourselves in the Lord is an essential part of stewarding our heart. The tools that I have learned to use to strengthen myself in the Lord have become calculated responses to the warning lights of my heart. But the fact is, I can only respond correctly if I already recognize and understand the signals my heart sends. If the oil light comes on in my car, and my response is to take it to the car wash, I clearly do not understand what the light means. Worse yet, the real problem has not been dealt with and will soon manifest in a breakdown. When it comes to my heart, I have found that the only way I can correctly use the tools I've received to strengthen myself is to establish foundational truths in my thinking—truths about the nature of reality, who God is, and who He has made me to be. These truths help me identify my heart signals. I will share some of that thinking in this chapter as context for understanding the tools I use to strengthen myself. I will address those helpful tools in the remainder of the book.

BECOMING FROM BEHOLDING

Did you know that your thinking and your heart are intimately connected? The Western mind-set compartmentalizes human beings when it comes to feelings and thinking—the heart feels and the mind thinks. But Scripture says, "*For as he **thinks in his heart, so is he...**" (Prov. 23:7). In fact, the Hebrew definition of the word "heart" encompasses the entirety of your "inner man." Your heart is the seat of your mind, imagination, will, desires, emotions, affections, memory, and conscience. It is also the center of your communion with the Spirit of God and possesses the faculties that perceive spiritual reality. Scripture refers to this spiritual perception as "the eyes of your heart." Thus, your heart is what enables you to have *faith*, which is the "*evidence of things not seen*" (Heb. 11:1). Your faith grows as your heart, led by the Holy Spirit, perceives and understands the invisible realm of spiritual reality. That unseen realm governs the visible realm and brings your mind and will into agreement with the reality of the Kingdom. In essence, what I have just described is the process of renewing the mind.

Our internal *focus* on and agreement with spiritual reality—either the reality of God's Kingdom, established on the truth, or the destructive reality of the enemy's kingdom, established on lies—gives permission for that reality to flow into the "issues of life."

This power of agreement with spiritual reality through our focus adds another dimension to the principle that life flows from the heart: *you become what you behold.* As I said in the previous chapter, God has made clear what we are becoming—the potential we are all called to grow into throughout our lifetime. We are becoming kings and priests of the planet, following the lead of our Elder Brother, Jesus. This is why Hebrews tells us to *fix our eyes on Jesus* (see Heb. 12:2). Our goal is to sustain our focus on Him because we become like the One we behold. The degree to which we understand our identity and purpose—who we are becoming—is always determined by the degree of our revelation of Jesus. He is the exact representation of the Father, in whose image we were created.

Beholding Jesus cannot be reduced to reading about Him in Scripture. He died so that the same Spirit who was in and upon Him, giving Him constant access to what the Father was saying and doing, could be sent to live in us. The truth is that every believer has constant access to the manifest presence of God. We are an open heaven. But we have to take advantage of that access, and we do that by turning our focus on Him. Only in that place of communion with Him do we come to *know* Him, and consequently, gain the revelation of our identity and purpose. And as we agree with the *revelation* of who He is, the *reality* of who He is starts to flow into our lives and transform us into His likeness. All fruitfulness in our lives flows from this place of intimacy with the Lord.

AGREEING WITH THE UNSEEN

Because our communion with the Lord is the power source of our lives and connects us with our eternal purpose as kings and priests of the planet, the kingdom of darkness is generally aimed at dislodging us from it and getting us to focus on something else. The enemy knows that our job, as we walk in our position of delegated authority, is to destroy his works—to close the distance between the invisible reality of God's Kingdom and the unredeemed reality of our circumstances. The inferior reality of our physical circumstances always yields to the superior reality of the Kingdom—but we can only release that Kingdom to the degree to which our heart and mind are in agreement with it. So the enemy uses lies of accusation and intimidation to make the problems and conflicts in our lives, which result from the incongruence between the heavenly reality and earthly reality, appear bigger than the solutions we carry.

> The enemy uses lies to make problems appear bigger than the solutions we carry.

In the moments when we are confronted by the clash between the seen and the unseen realms, God has an agenda and the enemy has an agenda. We always choose to partner with one or the other. In doing so, we decide whether the situation is a test that proves and strengthens our character and faith to walk in our purpose, showing God that He can entrust us with more of Himself, or whether the situation is a temptation away from God into bitterness, doubt, anxiety, and disappointment. This choice really should be a no-brainer for us. I mean, who cares what the devil's agenda is? God's agenda is so glorious, and His love and purposes for our lives are so great, that everything else pales in comparison. We should all be like Nehemiah, who, when the enemies of Israel tried to get him to come out of the city and talk with them on the Plain of Ono, said, "*...I am doing a great work and I cannot come down. Why should the work cease while I leave it and go down to you?*" (Neh. 6:3).

But the truth is that we can only ignore the enemy when we are firmly convinced that we are doing a great work for God, a work that He has commissioned us to do. Our *co-mission* comes from our *sub-mission* to His primary mission: "*on earth as it is in Heaven.*" Only a passionate devotion to God and an unwavering conviction about the identity and purpose He has given us will be stronger than the enemy's resolve to distract us. If we are not convinced of our purpose, then we will entertain the enemy's lies and invite his destruction into our lives. The key to gaining this conviction and passion is, once again, a sustained focus on the Lord and His Word over us. One of the most poignant explanations in Scripture for why Israel failed to walk in their covenant with God is in Lamentations 1:9: "*...She did not consider her destiny; therefore her collapse was awesome.*" Jerusalem had an awesome destiny. But her failure to consider it led to an awesome collapse. Her destruction was equal in proportion to her potential for greatness. The reason we see human beings capable of great destruction and evil—we are the ones in God's creation who have the greatest potential for greatness. The key to either great purpose or great destruction lies in where we choose to sustain our focus. Knowing this fact should move us to jealously guard our intimacy with the Lord.

PERSONAL VICTORY—CORPORATE BLESSING

You probably noticed this, but the tests that David endured were tests that specifically addressed his ability to keep his focus on his identity and purpose. He was tested by coming into circumstances that directly contradicted God's Word over his life. His job was to ignore the enemy's agenda and develop the strength of character that God was after. It was like God was saying, "OK David, I've called you as a man after my own heart and anointed you to be king of Israel. That is your destiny. Will you be a king with my heart when the man currently in your position is attacking you, chasing you, and doing everything to keep you from your destiny? Will you be that king when the Jews you are supposed to rule intend to turn you over to the enemy? Will you be that king when your army consists of a bunch of losers? Will you be that king when your palace is a cave in the wilderness? And will you be that king when your closest friends disown you and threaten your life? If you can strengthen yourself in

Me, then you can be trusted to be that king when all the circumstances line up."

David's actions prove that He believed God's promises over his life. Likewise, the difficulties in our lives expose the degree to which we really believe that God is for us and that His words about our destiny are true. This is the essence of faith—not intellectual assent to truths; but the practical trust we express in God based on who we know Him to be through our relationship with Him. We express that trust when we choose to listen to Him in the midst of our circumstances more than any other voice and then respond to our circumstances in light of what He has said. The tools that David used to strengthen himself in his tests had to be activities that kept him connected to God and to what God had said, because what he did in these tests was consistent with the word over his life, and released purpose to those around him.

I would venture to say that the things David did to strengthen himself were some of the very same things that he did to connect with the Lord *before* he was brought into the time of testing. He did not go into the wilderness without tools to face the tests he would meet there. God took him there because he was ready—not yet ready for the kingship, but for a series of tests that increased in difficulty as he proved strong enough to handle them. This reveals a truth about the nature of God that should give us good reason to trust Him when we experience challenges in life. That truth—always be prepared for the moment in which you're standing, because God never fails to give you the tools you need beforehand. You can see this aspect of His nature in this episode of the Exodus story:

> *Then it came to pass, when Pharaoh had let the people go, that God did not lead them by way of the land of the Philistines, although that was near; for God said, "Lest perhaps the people change their minds when they see war, and return to Egypt"* (Exodus 13:17).

God kept the Israelites away from a challenge they were not prepared to face. The corollary truth is that the battles and tests He led them into were ones for which He had prepared them. God is a good Father. He never sets us up to fail, but only to grow. Just as I would never send my own children against a challenge they were unprepared to handle, neither does He. God nevers sets us up to fail—only to grow!

> God never set us up to fail—only to grow.

THE CORNERSTONE OF REVELATION—GOD IS GOOD

I believe that the reason many believers fall into the trap of fear and anxiety in the midst of crisis is because they allow the enemy to successfully distract them from the fact that they are prepared with tools they already have in their arsenal. It's easy for us to feel blindsided by events that we did not expect; but nothing surprises God, which is why He prepares us for what's ahead. Remembering that He has seen ahead and has prepared us is simple, but it makes a huge difference in our response to difficulty. When we have our hearts anchored in this truth about His nature, we will be oriented to take inventory of our tools and start using them when we come up against a challenge. The bedrock of an automatic response from us is the burning conviction that God is good, always good! Doubting His goodness, making up explanations for things we don't understand (the source of a lot of bad theology), or falling into anxiety and disappointment won't be options for us. It's like knowing exactly what to do when the oil light goes on in our car. When the truth of God's goodness is *not* firmly anchored in our hearts, we are not only dislodged from our purpose in conflict, but we don't possess the sensitivity of heart, the faith, to perceive the tools God gives us to prepare us before we encounter a challenge. We learn this lesson from Jesus' disciples. Shortly after they witnessed the miracle of the loaves and fishes, the disciples were in a boat in the middle of a storm on the lake. In the midst of the storm, Jesus walked out on the water to them and stilled the storm. The disciples were overwhelmed by His demonstration of power, their unbelief, and probably their own lack of readiness to face another obstacle with their own authority. Mark gave the following explanation for their reaction: *"For they had not understood about the loaves, because their heart was hardened"* (Mark 6:52). In this season of His ministry, Jesus was training His disciples to do what He did. Every miracle He did in their presence was a lesson about the nature of God and an invitation for them to live from that revelation. In calming the storm He was demonstrating a dimension of God's power and authority that logically connected to the power and authority He had demonstrated earlier in the miracle of the loaves. It's like He had taught them multiplication and was moving on to algebra; but they couldn't move on, because they didn't understand the first lesson.

Why didn't they get the lesson of the loaves? Their hearts were hard. They lacked the basic faith in who God is and they lacked an understanding of the way He works to orient them to learn the lessons He was teaching to prepare them for life and ministry—in this case, facing another storm. What a sobering lesson it is to see that it is possible to be perfectly obedient to the Lord's commands (in obtaining the available food, and in handing it out to the multitudes), be used in bringing forth a miracle, and still not get the tools that God made available because of a hard heart. Jesus' rebuke gave them a chance to repent that they might recover what they had missed in the miracle.

Our ability to connect with what God is doing in the midst of difficult circumstances depends on our ability to remember who He is and what He has done in our lives—our relational history with Him. I guarantee that if you are currently facing a situation that seems beyond your strength or understanding, and you take some time to rehearse your history with the Lord over the last 12 months or so, you will always find a tool—a prophetic word, a Scripture verse that has leapt out at you, a testimony, or a prayer strategy, for example—that God has put in your arsenal, something that provides a key to overcome the present situation. You also might need to repent for any hardness of heart that has kept you from getting what He has made available to you.

As you become more and more convinced that you are a person with a great identity and purpose, that you are prepared for the moment you're standing in, and that all of Heaven is waiting to back you up as you choose to be faithful to your purpose, your perception of which forces are the most operative in your life will shift. That perception will open you up to the lessons about the unseen realities all around you. Such a shift makes learning natural.

Joseph discovered this. As he came into his destiny, he saw that God's plans and purposes had a momentum and power that outweighed the evil plans of his brothers. He said, "*But as for you, you meant evil against me; but God meant it for good, in order to bring it about as it is this day, to save many people alive*" (Gen. 50:20). His statement doesn't deny the reality that his

STAYING CONNECTED TO YOUR DESTINY

brothers made choices that affected his life, but focuses on the superior reality that their plans couldn't cancel out God's purpose for him. In fact, those evil intentions became the very tools that God used to bring Joseph into his promotion and the ultimate fulfillment of God's promise. While God doesn't create evil, evil does not limit His ability to bring about the fulfillment of all that He has purposed to do in us.

THE BENEFITS OF CONFLICT

This is another reason never to be concerned about what the enemy might be planning. (I'm not denying our need for discernment; but our discernment is never to give undue attention to the devil. It's mainly designed to recognize which channel the enemy's voice is speaking on so we can push the "mute" button.) The devil has never been a threat to God. God could easily wipe out the whole kingdom of darkness in a moment. God decided it would be more beneficial and more glorious to share His victory with sons and daughters made in His image who can put on display what He's like. And He's not above using the devil as a pawn to accomplish His purposes, just as He used Pharaoh as an enemy of Israel. Psalm 105, in recounting the history of Israel's journey to Egypt and their triumphal Exodus, says:

He increased His people greatly, and made them stronger than their enemies. He turned their heart to hate His people, to deal craftily with His servants. He sent Moses His servant, and Aaron whom He

*had chosen. They performed His signs among them,
and wonders in the land of Ham…He also brought
them out with silver and gold, and there was none
feeble among His tribes. Egypt was glad when they
departed, for the fear of them had fallen upon them*
(Psalm 105:24-38).

This verse is basically saying that God sent Israel to
Egypt so He could pick a fight. He blessed and multi-
plied His people until they were a threat to the enemy,
then went to the enemy, hardened their hearts, and
provoked them. This divine setup justified His rising
up on behalf of His people, displaying His wonders,
pouring out plagues on the Egyptians, and bringing
the Israelites out loaded with spoils. What a strategy!

So God not only prepares us for conflict, He leads
us right into it. I'm not saying He is the cause of difficulty in our lives. He is not, nor has He ever been, the
sort of Father who brings torment, sickness, or persecution into the lives of His children to teach them how
to be more Christ-like. The point is that when we are
pursuing our God-given purpose, every situation in
our lives works together to accomplish it. We never
have to live in a moment of conflict without divine
purpose because God can win with any hand, even a
pair of twos.

In reality, He already *has* won. Our job is to align
our hearts with the reality of the victory of the Cross so
that we can see His purposes and redemption at work
around us. Then we can recognize how to partner with

Heaven in our circumstances. People who have this perspective stand out because they get happy when they encounter a problem. They know it is their assignment, privilege, and joy to see impossibilities and problems bend their knees to the name of Jesus.

THE FRONTLINES OF BATTLE— THE PLACE OF GREATEST SAFETY

While each believer has a different assignment corresponding to his or her unique gifts and talents, these assignments work to accomplish one purpose— the establishment of the Kingdom "*on earth as it is in Heaven.*" This Kingdom, as Scripture says, "*forcefully advances*" (see Matt. 11:12)—first to displace the attitudes of the carnal man in our own lives and then to destroy the works of the devil around us. The violence of this process may seem overwhelming at times, but it is safer to stay in the midst of this conflict than to adopt a defensive, conservative approach to the Christian life. The safest place for us to be at any point in our lives is passionately pursing God and the purposes to which He has called us. Passionate pursuit positions us for advancement. To live in the defensive posture protecting what we have is quite dangerous. Just ask the man who buried his one talent (see Matt. 25:18-28).

Our assignment and destiny is to advance the Kingdom, and comes with an umbrella of grace and favor that works to preserve our lives, no matter what's going on around us. The moment we take a back seat in our pursuit of the Kingdom is the moment we become exposed to fiery darts of deception.

The more we establish these truths about reality in our thinking, the more we will understand the priority of stewarding our hearts. Your destiny begins in your heart. The more you gaze on the face of Jesus with the eyes of your heart, the more you see who you are becoming. The more your energies and thoughts are focused on your destiny, the more your passion and conviction grow: "I am alive to burn for God. I'm alive to make Him known." Your passion and conviction give you a momentum to pursue this one thing, from which all other passions and purposes flow. Your pursuit is the thing that attracts Heaven to bring you into that destiny.

So as I navigate the various challenges and obstacles on the highway to my destiny, I'm watching the warning lights of my heart. I must sustain my connection with the Source of life. Really, there's only one light—the oil light. It's the oil of His presence that gives me everything I need and anoints me to fulfill my purpose. But He only gives me the measure of His presence that I'm willing to jealously guard. So I have to build the strength of will and character to focus all my energies on carrying His presence with excellence. I can't afford to have a moment in my life when the circumstances distract me from tending that fire in my heart—even a situation when I must tend the fire by myself.

Chapter 3

DISARMING HELL
THROUGH THANKSGIVING

Thanksgiving keeps us

sane and alive.

When you were born again, the desire to please God and do His will became part of your nature. You don't have to work it up; it comes naturally. What many believers don't know is that God did not put that desire in us and then make His will something so obscure that we couldn't discover and accomplish it. The will of God instinctively becomes the will of believers through intimate relationship with Jesus Christ.

The will of God is not complicated. Many young people ask me to pray for them saying, "I just want to know what God's will is for my life." I often tell them that I already know what God's will is. It is found in the Lord's Prayer: "*Your will be done on earth as it is in heaven*" (Matt. 6:10). God's will is simply for Heaven's reality to become earth's reality.

OUR ROLE IN FULFILLING "*AS IT IS IN HEAVEN*"

We are God's delegated authority. As such, our obedience plays an important role in seeing the will of

God accomplished on the earth. In First Thessalonians 5:16-18, Paul instructs us to: "*Rejoice always, pray without ceasing, in everything give thanks; **for this is the will of God** in Christ Jesus for you.*" Two things in this statement stand out. First of all, the will of God is not merely focused on whether we become a doctor or a teacher or whether we're supposed to have tuna or peanut butter for lunch. It is focused on what we do to position our heart in relationship to God at all times, in all circumstances. Secondly, rejoicing, praying and thanksgiving are all acts of *our* will that, particularly in times of difficulty, weakness and uncertainty, require faith. They are activities that draw our focus to Heaven so we can agree with what is true, no matter what we feel or perceive with our physical senses and emotions. And since our agreement is what attracts the strength and reality of Heaven into our lives and circumstances, it makes sense that these activities fulfill the will of God expressed in the Lord's Prayer—*on earth as it is in Heaven.* The transformation of the heart is the first step in bringing heaven to earth.

Because rejoicing, prayer, and thanksgiving attract heaven; they are vital tools for strengthening ourselves in the Lord. You'll notice that all of them are meant to be continuously ongoing in our lives. They're not reserved for crises or holidays. They're a lifestyle—as are all the tools that we use to minister to ourselves. A big reason for this is that in the midst of crisis and difficulty, it is usually hard if not impossible to sit down and reason out how we should respond. Difficulty has a way of exposing the degree to which our lives and minds have been truly transformed by a heavenly perspective for certain responses to be habitual. The things we practice as a lifestyle equip us for difficulties.

In the next two chapters I share some of the ways that the Lord has taught me to *rejoice* and *pray*, as well as the insights I've gained about how and why these things bring strength. But here I'm going to talk about *thanksgiving*.

Thanksgiving agrees with Heaven by acknowledging the truth that our lives are a gift from God, and that He is sovereign over all. God is extravagantly generous, and the life He has given us to experience on this planet is not a life of survival, but of abundance and blessing. But unless we properly recognize what we've been given, we won't be able to experience that life. That's the reality of receiving a gift. If we don't understand what we've been given, we won't understand its purpose and be able to experience its benefit.

Imagine Christmas morning. You've spent the last few months shopping and picking out unique gifts for each of your family members that show your intimate knowledge of their interests and desires. You have spared no expense to get gifts of the highest quality that will be both enjoyable and beneficial to each person. But when your family comes to the Christmas tree, one person completely ignores the presents. Another person opens your gift, but starts using it for something other than what it was made for. Still another just holds the gift, and refuses to unwrap it.

And to make matters worse, none of them even acknowledge that their gifts are from you. Can you see how these responses are not only foolish, but are deeply harmful to the relationship?

Sadly, this is how many Christians respond to God's gifts, particularly the gifts of the Spirit. So many people fail to receive what the Lord has offered them because they don't understand what the gifts are or how to use them. They say ridiculous things like, "Well, tongues is the least of the gifts, so I don't need to pursue it." If my children said this about one of the presents I had put under the tree for them, I'd be very upset. I'd say, "This is yours! I don't care how small you think it is. I bought it with you in mind, and I don't give cheap gifts. If you'll just open it, I'll show you what it is and how to use it." Such a rejection of gifts is absolute arrogance.

Thankfulness carries an attitude of humility. Thanksgiving is the only proper way to receive what God has given us because it honors our relationship with Him by expressing trust in His goodness, even if we don't yet understand what we've received. God gives us "every good and perfect gift" for two primary reasons. He gives to make us prosper so we can succeed in life, and He gives to demonstrate His love as an invitation to relationship. When we practice thanksgiving as a lifestyle, we recognize that the gifts we have received from the Lord came with these purposes. Thanksgiving sets us on a course to know God in relationship and discover the reasons for which He made us.

THE GREAT PRICE OF LITTLE THANKS

When God tells us to give Him thanks, He's not insinuating that He gives in order to get something from us. He doesn't manipulate us with His gifts. He wants us to thank Him because thankfulness acknowledges the truth about our lives. And when we agree with the truth, then the truth sets us free to see and manifest the greatness that He has put in us as the ones He has made in His image. When we withhold thanks from God, we actually cut ourselves off from who we are. This is what Paul explains in Romans 1:18-21.

> *For the wrath of God is revealed from heaven against all ungodliness and unrighteousness of men, who suppress the truth in unrighteousness…so that they are without excuse, because, although they knew God, they did not glorify Him as God, **nor were thankful**, but became futile in their thoughts, and their foolish hearts were darkened.*

Paul is basically saying that God has not kept who He is a secret. Knowing God is not hard. It's actually the most obvious thing in the world. All you have to do is glorify Him as God and be thankful. This response, because it agrees with the truth, gives you open access to the vast treasures of the knowledge of God. But without that response, your thoughts become *futile* and your heart is *darkened*. Futile means "purposeless." When we fail to sustain the response of thanksgiving for everything in our lives, our thinking is cut off from our purpose in God. When we lose sight of our purpose, we will inevitably make choices that are outside of God's intentions for our lives, and this can only be destructive because it works against His design for us. A dark heart is a heart that is unable to perceive spiritual reality. It is unmoved by the desires and affections of the Lord, and therefore cannot respond to His invitation to relationship, which is the source of life. As Paul goes on to explain in Romans chapter 1, a dark heart perverts our desires and leads us into all kinds of sin that degrades our identity and relationships. The most perverted sins known to mankind came about through a door left open because of the absence of thankfulness.

THE PURIFYING NATURE OF THANKFULNESS

Since thanksgiving keeps us sane and alive by connecting us to the source of our life and purpose, it makes sense that Paul instructs us to give thanks "*in everything.*" Thanksgiving keeps us sane and alive. But there is a specific dimension of thanksgiving that is particularly powerful in times of difficulty and adversity. We find this principle in Paul's first letter to Timothy.

> Thanksgiving keeps us sane and alive.

Now the Spirit expressly says that in latter times some will depart from the faith, giving heed to

> *deceiving spirits and doctrines of demons...com-*
> *manding to abstain from foods which God created to*
> *be received with thanksgiving by those who believe*
> *and know the truth. For every creature of God is*
> *good, and nothing is to be refused if it is received*
> *with thanksgiving; for it is sanctified by the word of*
> *God and prayer* (1 Timothy 4:1-5).

Food was one of the biggest "disputable matters" that the early Church struggled with, particularly regarding the issue of eating food offered to idols. Jewish and Gentile believers alike feared that this food was defiled by having been dedicated to demonic spirits. False teachers of the time preyed upon this superstition and caused all kinds of bondage and division. Interestingly, in this passage Paul doesn't debunk the superstition and say that dedicating food to idols is powerless. He simply says that combining thanksgiving with the Word and prayer is powerful enough to de-authorize that dedication and create a stronger one—a dedication to the Lord. He is saying thanksgiving *sanctifies* whatever it touches.

Sanctification is a significant subject throughout Scripture. In the Old Testament it was primarily associated with the specific rituals God prescribed for setting aside various instruments, vessels, and pieces of furniture for priestly use in the Tabernacle of Moses, and later the Temple of Solomon. After a goldsmith had finished fashioning a bowl for use in the sacrifices, for example, it would be sprinkled with blood from the altar. From that point on, it would never be used for anything but priestly service in the Temple. It was completely set apart for God—sanctified. In the New Testament, believers are sanctified by the Blood of Jesus and set apart for God. This sanctification is even more powerful, because we do not merely become vessels that He can use to accomplish His purposes. The very process by which His life, power and love flow through us is the process that transforms us into His likeness. We become *like* the One with whom we are set apart.

When Paul says that thanksgiving sanctifies unclean food, he is saying that it sets it apart for God and His purposes. Thanksgiving actually changes the very nature of the food into something holy. This truth extends beyond unclean food. It extends to every situation in your life in which you find other powers at work besides the power of God. It's vital to remember that not everything that happens in life is His will. He didn't cause the crisis a nation or individual may be facing. He actually *can't* give things that are not good because He doesn't have them. Someone can only give what he has. God only gives good gifts, because He is good, and has only good gifts to give. So giving thanks in everything does not mean saying that the adversity came from God. But giving thanks in the midst of an adverse situation, a difficulty intended to undermine your faith and destroy you, enables you to take hold of that situation and set it apart to God and His purposes. When you give thanks, the weapon the enemy meant to use to dislodge you from your divine purpose is put into your hands and becomes the very thing that brings you more fully into that purpose. Jesus declared that He sends us out with the same assignment the Father gave to Him—to destroy the works of the devil (see 1 John 3:8). Thanksgiving accomplishes the divine justice of the Kingdom, where the enemy is destroyed by the very thing he intended to use for our destruction. Just knowing that we can participate in destroying the enemy's purposes should alone move us to give thanks!

RELEASING JUSTICE

One of the clearest examples of divine justice in Scripture is found in the Book of Esther: the story of Haman, who was hung on the very gallows he built to destroy Mordecai. Later, this justice was made even more complete when Mordecai assumed Haman's position in the king's court. The wonderful thing about this story is that Mordecai didn't have to bring justice himself. He simply kept his focus on his duty to the heathen king and to his people. This is the nature of warfare in the Kingdom. We don't battle by focusing on the devil. We keep our focus on the King and His Kingdom, and the devil cannot help but be unseated by God's ever-increasing government released through our lives, which illustrates another reason why thanksgiving is powerful in times of adversity. Psalm 100:4 says that we "*enter into His gates with thanksgiving.*" Thanksgiving brings us into the manifest presence of

God and connects us with what He is doing and saying in the midst of our circumstances. Thanksgiving helps to establish our focus on Him so that our awareness shifts from earthly reality to heavenly reality—which we must do in order to release the strength of Heaven into our circumstances.

KEEPING MY AWARENESS OF GOD

I have purposed to try to live in such a way that nothing ever gets bigger than my consciousness of God's presence. Sometimes conflict can be as simple as bad news on TV. If it starts to weigh on my heart and grow bigger than my awareness of God, I consciously turn my affection toward Him to become more aware of His presence. If that doesn't work, I turn off the TV or leave the room to redirect my focus until my awareness of Him is bigger than that which weighs heavily on my heart. I can't just know in my head that He's bigger; I have to have my entire being in a position where I am aware of His presence and expect His world to invade my life and circumstances. If I don't sustain this expectation, I will expect other forces to be the prime movers in my life and will begin to live defensively instead of offensively.

When I stay close to the presence of God through thanksgiving, I not only become aware of His absolute ability to invade the impossible, I sense His radical love and delight in me! As I give thanks for the good gifts He's put in my life, I present convincing evidence that He is my Father, He is for me, and His opinion pretty much cancels out all the others. The wonderful thing is that when we simply begin to give thanks, even when it seems difficult to remember one answered prayer, it isn't too long before our *focus* on the good in our lives creates an opening for the Lord's joy. And it's the joy of the Lord that is our strength. I believe that James was talking about giving thanks when he said to *count* it all joy in trial, because giving thanks usually includes taking an inventory of God's gifts in your life. Do the math! If you want to discover the ability of thankfulness to bring you strength in difficulty, you need to keep *counting* these things *until* you come to the conclusion—it's time to rejoice! It becomes really hard to stay depressed about your circumstances when you're filled with the awareness of the love and goodness of God that surrounds and infuses your life.

There is a level of life we can reach where we practice thanksgiving as a lifestyle—a place where we remember our answered prayers. When difficulty comes along, we have a huge inventory of blessings instantly accessible to bring us into His presence as well as the joy and delight He has over us. That is a reality far greater than any accusation, crisis, or conflict that could come our way. When we learn to live in this realm, nothing can deflect us from our purpose. We even make the enemy help us get it done. From Heaven's perspective, it is reasonable to give thanks "in everything"!

Chapter 4

THE PERSONAL
BREAKTHROUGH MOMENT

*Physical obedience brings
spiritual breakthrough.*

As a young pastor in Weaverville I had more than my share of "Blue Mondays." No matter what wonderful things had happened on Sunday, sometimes all I could remember was what had been lacking in the services. My slides into discouragement were fueled by the comparisons I made between my spiritual heroes and myself. I've always loved reading about revivalists and great men and women of faith—people like John G. Lake, Charles Finney, or Rees Howells. But when I started comparing myself to them, I found that my faith always came up short, and it wouldn't be long before I went into an emotional tailspin over the obvious differences between me and them. Reading the amazing book by Rees Howells, *Intercessor*, made me wonder if I was even breathing, let alone saved. The focus on my limitations didn't help me feel better especially when there were real problems to deal with as a pastor.

Betrayal, abandonment, rejection, and accusation all seemed to come with the position. I often felt like there was a huge black cloud over me. I had enough sense to know that discouragement and depression were not good things. Although I managed to get victory before the next Sunday, because I did carry the conviction that our time together in the house of the Lord was to be a day of celebration, I didn't know how to live that way. Yet.

THE ULTIMATE PRIORITY

One of the priorities that had already been established in my heart as a young man was the priority of worship. My father trained our family and his congregation that our identity as believers is first as worshipers. This meant that our main job was ministering to the Lord, and that everything we did in ministry to people should be an overflow and outgrowth of that primary ministry. Not only that, but he taught and demonstrated that we are to model our praise and worship according to the definition and description in the Psalms, which includes physical expression, like dancing, shouting, clapping, leaping, and making a joyful noise. Emphasizing biblical patterns of worship constituted a big paradigm shift in normal church at the time. At the beginning of this shift many people were resistant to such displays. They were entrenched in the idea that weeping and looking serious were the only genuine manifestations of true spirituality. I agreed with my dad that we should do the stuff in the

Book, but my problem was stepping out of my "reserved personality" box—that is until I realized that God commands us to do it, and that He wouldn't command us to do something that He didn't put in our new nature. That means my real personality in Christ includes the capacity to demonstrate my love for God through biblically mandated expressions. It's who I am. To allow my self-image of being reserved and quiet to rob me of experiencing my new nature that is free to outwardly express my joy in God is a spiritual injustice. I am not willing to come into an agreement with that lie. As a result, I began to dance before the Lord with joy in private long before I had seen anyone do it in a service.

As I discovered, praise isn't pleasing to the flesh, which may be one reason why it's so powerful in removing that cloud of oppression. The enemy is empowered by human agreement. To agree with anything he says gives him a place to kill, steal, and destroy. We fuel the cloud of oppression by agreeing with our enemy. Praise, with rejoicing, cancels that agreement.

INTROSPECTION KILLS THE LIFE OF PRAISE

Praise was one of the primary tools that God had equipped me with as a young man to strengthen myself in the discouragement of my early years as a pastor. I could be questioning a million things about my life, but I never had to question whether I was in the right place when I was giving God praise. It became my default when I slid into the fog of confusion and depression. In Weaverville, our home was behind the church so I often went to the sanctuary late at night, put worship music on the sound system, and spent time praising and worshiping God. Sometimes I remained until early in the morning. I danced, shouted, and basically required myself to do whatever I didn't *feel* like doing. The Psalmist David wrote, "*Bless the Lord, O my soul.*" He commands his own soul to come into order and give God glory. It's important that we learn how to bring our soul, and even our bodies into submission to the purposes of God. Back then I would make sure that the intensity of my praise was in equal proportion to the size of the cloud over my head. Every time, there would come a point when something inside of me would shift, and I was no longer making an effort. My mind, will, emotions, and body were completely filled with conviction of what I was declaring to the Lord. I also noticed that the cloud over my head had disappeared and I was alive in God!

I came to understand that the cloud wasn't just *over* my head; it was *inside* it. I mistakenly thought that focusing on my lack and comparing myself to others was a posture of humility. In fact, it was the opposite. Instead of focusing on God's greatness in my life, I was focusing on myself. I was actually agreeing with the enemy by making my own problems bigger than God's promises. And my agreement invited that cloud of oppression to hover over me.

The only way to break an agreement with a lie is *repentance*, which means to change the way you think. In that place of praise, I fed my mind on the truth of God's nature *until* it created a new agreement with heavenly reality. When that agreement was established, the reality started to manifest in my emotions, mind, and body. But I also came to understand more deeply why my dad taught us to *do* what the Scripture said regarding praise. Making an agreement with Heaven actually requires more than repentance of the mind. You need physical proof to make repentance a legally binding reality. By lining my physical body up with what the Word said, I brought my whole being into agreement with the truth. In doing so, I experienced the principle

> Physical obedience brings spiritual breakgthrough.

that physical obedience brings spiritual breakthrough. This may seem a little backward to those of us who hate the idea of going through religious motions and desire to be "authentic" in our worship. Physical obedience bring spiritual breakthrough. But the measure of authenticity is not what you're feeling or thinking. Those things either line up with authentic reality or they don't. And if they don't, Scripture tells us that we get there by *moving*. Some say it's hypocritical to do something you don't feel like doing. I think it's hypocritical to do only what I feel like doing and call myself a believing believer. Right actions release right emotions and right thinking.

But why is it right to sing, shout, dance and leap? Why does God seem to want these radical expressions more than silent, awed reverence? While there is certainly a time for the latter, acts of *celebration* get way more press in the psalmist's descriptions of how we approach God. The reason—God is a God to celebrate. His every action and thought toward us are extravagant expressions of His love, kindness, goodness, and delight in us; and He gives it all not only to bless us for a moment, but to invite us into the deeper blessing of knowing Him. He delights in us, so He wants us to delight in Him. He rejoices over us with singing (see Zeph. 3:17), so He wants us to rejoice in Him with singing. When we give to Him what He gives to us, we step further into relationship with Him, deepening our heart-connection with the source of life.

Not only that, but when we do what He is doing, aligning our bodies as well as our spirits and souls with what He has said, there is a release of His nature that flows to us in that place of intimacy. The Holy Spirit is the most joyful person in existence, and joy is one of the primary expressions of His Kingdom in our lives (see Rom. 14:17). His command to "rejoice always" is really an expression of His desire for us to have joy! He is simply telling us how to receive it. We not only rejoice *because* we have joy—we rejoice in our *pursuit* of joy.

THE IMPORTANCE OF MINISTERING TO GOD

In the previous chapter, I explained that thanksgiving should naturally lead to rejoicing when we follow James' instruction to "*count it all joy.*" As we count up all that God has done, we shouldn't stop at merely thanking God. In every one of the acts of God is a revelation of His nature. And as we see God's nature—His extravagance, joy, love, faithfulness, goodness, and power—the only sensible response is to praise Him. Praise and rejoicing are two sides of the same coin, as we see in Psalm 9:2: "*I will be glad and rejoice in You; I will sing praise to Your name, O Most High.*" It's hard to praise effectively without rejoicing, without bringing our body, soul, and spirit into an expression of celebration. We can't rejoice without having a reason, and that reason is God's nature, revealed in His relationship with us, that we declare in our praises. When God says to "rejoice always," the implication is that we are to establish praise as a lifestyle.

The praise that flows from thanksgiving is described in Hebrews 13:15 as a "sacrifice." This verse gives us a guideline for what kind of activities genuinely qualify as praise. First of all, praise should cost us something. Only then is it a proper response to the God who has given us the costly gift of His own Son. When I forced myself to rejoice in those nights alone in the sanctuary, I was offering God my time, my focus, and my comfort. I was stepping beyond what was convenient and beyond all the pressures of my circumstances. That is what made the act of praise a costly expression. Secondly, a sacrifice of praise should always require faith because it's impossible to please Him apart from faith. Hebrews 11:4 explains that it was "*By faith Abel offered to God a more excellent sacrifice than Cain....*"

It certainly requires faith to rejoice when that's the last thing you feel like doing or seems to make sense in the face of your present circumstances. It doesn't take much faith to hang your head and sing "Thou Art Worthy" when you're really just thinking, "I am worthless!" Truly rejoicing in Him requires that you stand on the truth that you are already accepted by Him where you are. Rejoicing requires you to acknowledge that His goodness and faithfulness are more real than your present difficulty. It especially requires you to agree that your life is not really about you!

Only the rejoicing that requires you to agree with God's perspective on your situation is the sacrifice of praise that pleases Him and has the power to transform you. It is the expression of faith. Sometimes that rejoicing is what David describes in Psalm 2:11: "*rejoice with trembling.*" In other words, you don't have to feel full of faith to rejoice—you just have to do it.

While the nature of praise and thanksgiving is different, they should always go together, because they are sequential steps toward strengthening ourselves in His manifest presence. Psalm 100:4 says we *"enter into His gates with thanksgiving, and into His courts with praise."* This verse is a road map into the presence of God. Thus, our goal should be to sustain thanks and praise until our whole being is alive to His presence. But we also have to remember in that moment that the focus doesn't change from ministering to God to our getting what we need.

Thanksgiving and praise are tools to strengthen ourselves not because they help us get something from the Lord, but because they reconnect us to our primary purpose—to minister to Him in worship. They bring us into His presence; and true worship is something that only happens in that place of communion with His presence. In worship, the sacrifice is no longer physical expression or verbal declarations. We *are* the sacrifice. Fire always falls on sacrifice. And when we are the sacrifice, we cannot help but be changed.

THE SACRIFICE THAT MAKES YOU RICH

Remember the woman with the alabaster vial of perfume who ministered to Jesus? Scripture tells us two things about this vial: it was worth a year's wages (probably this woman's only financial security), and it could only be used on one occasion—because it was in a container that had to be broken to be opened. Not only did she pour the entire contents on Jesus, she did it in a very public display of affection, weeping over His feet and wiping them with her hair. This extreme act provoked extreme offense in all who were present, including His disciples. They were embarrassed by her emotion and disgusted by the waste of money. But Jesus had a different perspective and response. He explained that she had anointed Him for His burial, crediting her with more insight into His true identity than anyone else. She had given Him exactly the kind of worship He deserved, thereby demonstrating faith. And not only that, when everyone left the house, Jesus wasn't the only one drenched in the beautiful fragrance—the aroma encircled the woman as well.

This is what happens when we worship. We don't come to worship saying, "I'm giving this to you so we can share it." Like the woman, we worship to say, "Everything is yours, God." But we can't come from that place of communion with Him without having who He is rub off on us. David said that He is our glory and the lifter of our heads (see Ps. 3:3). We can't be with Him without having our heads lifted to see Him. And you can't look at Him and then look back at your circumstances with the same perspective. Also, you can't experience the realm of His glory, which is His realm of supernatural provision, without receiving a measure of His grace and strength.

One of the primary ways that many believers need to be renewed in their perspective is by getting rid of the idea that intentionally ignoring the problems around them, and even within them, in order to give God praise and thanks, is irresponsible. Believers often fall into the trap of thinking they can find a solution by looking at a problem from every angle and letting it consume their world. But what happens is that the affections of their hearts get drawn away from the Lord, to the point that they care more about the problem than about giving Him what He deserves. They are letting other voices speak louder than His, and that is always irresponsible!

I am responsible to Him first, and for this reason, I have decided to live in a healthy state of denial. When the devil puts a request for attention across my desk, I say, "REQUEST DENIED!" I am aware that there are situations constantly around me that, if I'm not careful, can bring me into discouragement. Most of the time I'm living about 15 minutes away from discouragement if I make a series of wrong choices. But I also know that I never again have to live with discouragement like I used to. I have learned to ignore problems just enough so they don't become a threat to the affections of my heart. I know I'm not being irresponsible because God has promised me over and over that if I'm faithful to be who He has called me to be, especially as a worshiper, He is more than happy to bring the solutions. This does not mean we are not to give attention to problems—but we need to address them from God's perspective.

Praise Brings a Divine Encounter

Here are a just a couple of the promises in Scriptures regarding the benefits we receive when we're faithful to give Him praise and worship. Psalm 22:3 declares, *"You are holy, enthroned in the praises of Israel."* Our praises actually create a platform in our circumstances for the King to sit on His throne and release the reality of His Kingdom. And when the Kingdom comes, it always destroys the kingdom of darkness. This is how Isaiah describes it:

> *Sing to the Lord a new song, and His praise from the ends of the earth, you who go down to the sea, and all that is in it, you coastlands and you inhabitants of them! Let the wilderness and its cities lift up their voice, the villages that Kedar inhabits. Let the inhabitants of Sela sing, let them shout from the top of the mountains. Let them give glory to the Lord, and declare His praise in the coastlands. The Lord shall go forth like a mighty man; He shall stir up His zeal like a man of war. He shall cry out, yes, shout aloud; He shall prevail against His enemies* (Isaiah 42:10-13).

He's basically saying that while Israel is celebrating and praising God, God is taking it upon Himself to go out and destroy their enemies. What a deal! This is what happens when God is enthroned in our praises. For example, I can't keep count of all the testimonies I've heard of people who were lost in the presence of God in worship, and only afterward realized that they had been healed. After one service, two individuals, unrelated to each other, came and told me that they had been healed of the lingering effects of a broken neck they had suffered many years earlier. They were both sitting in the same section of the sanctuary, and both were healed during worship!

If those people happened to be rejoicing "with trembling," God certainly gave them yet another good reason to rejoice in Him with real joy. He is more than ready to convince us that He is worthy of our praise. But more than that, He is hoping we'll respond to His invitation to walk in a mature relationship with Him, one in which our primary focus, like His, is not on *getting* but *giving*. Times of difficulty give us an opportunity we don't have otherwise, and that is the opportunity to demonstrate sacrificial love to Him by ministering to Him instead of attending to our pressing needs. In those times we give Him praise solely because we are convinced that knowing Him is the reason to rejoice. When He sees that singleness of heart for Him, that total abandonment, He can't stay away. This kind of relationship is what makes strengthening yourself in the Lord completely opposed to self-sufficiency. It works according to the logic of the Kingdom, which says that you must lose your life to save it. You must give in order to receive. If you need strength, you give yourself so totally to the Lord and His purposes that the Lord becomes the only One who can give you the supernatural strength you need.

So I challenge you to take the time each day to look past the problems and needs around you long enough to give God an extravagant expression of praise and rejoicing. I promise you'll discover that while His blessings are awesome, *He* is the greatest blessing of all. You might also happen to realize that you're becoming a joyful person. After all, God is in a good mood. If you hang around Him, His joy is bound to rub off!

Chapter 5

RELEASING THE HIDDEN THINGS

He is transforming a decent
little cottage into a
palace He can live in!

One of the most powerful metaphors for the people of God throughout the Scriptures is that we are the *house of God*. The reality that the blood of Jesus made a way for the Spirit of God Himself to dwell inside us is absolutely mind-boggling. But, God moved into a house that needs to be gutted and remodeled, so to speak. Thus, the moment we choose to follow Christ, we sign up for an ongoing process of transformation in our lives that works to change us into a house that can truly express the glory and nature of God in the world. Peter puts it like this: "*You also, as living stones, are being built up a spiritual house, a holy priesthood, to offer up spiritual sacrifices acceptable to God through Jesus Christ*" (1 Peter 2:5). Paul explains in Romans 12:1-2 that this ongoing transformation is taking place primarily in the dimensions of our mind, which must be renewed, and our body, which must be given as a "living sacrifice." The reason—without a yielded heart, a renewed mind, and surrendered body, we can't fully cooperate with the Holy Spirit, who is the Architect and Builder at work in our lives. C.S. Lewis describes this building process in *Mere Christianity*:

> Imagine yourself as a living house. God comes in to rebuild that house. At first, perhaps, you can understand what He is doing. He is getting the drains right and stopping the leaks in the roof and so on: you knew that those jobs needed doing and so you are not surprised. But presently He starts knocking the house about in a way that hurts abominably and does not seem to make sense. What on earth is He up to? The explanation is that He is building quite a different house from the one you thought of—throwing out a new wing here, putting on an extra floor here, running up towers, making courtyards. You thought you were going to be made into a decent little cottage: but He is building a palace. He intends to come and live in it himself.[1]

> He is transforming a decent little cottage into a palace.

The key in this illustration is that we must come to understand the "explanation" of what God is doing—His purposes in transforming us. If our minds are not renewed to cooperate with His purposes, we will still be using the "stinking thinking" of our carnal man, which, as Paul tells us, is *"enmity against God"* (Rom. 8:7). It is a sobering thing, but we either have our minds renewed, and become co-laborers with the Lord, or our minds are set against Him! There is no neutral ground. Rejecting the mind of Christ quenches the Holy Spirit and sabotages the building He is doing in our lives. He is transforming a decent little cottage into a palace He can live in!

BUILDING THE BUILDING OF DIVINE PURPOSE

As we've already seen, strengthening ourselves in the Lord is focused on bringing our hearts, minds, and bodies in line with the purposes of God, which results in our having the strength to be true to that purpose in the face of difficulty and opposition. The very word "strengthening" is part of the language of building that is going on our lives. Interestingly, for the most part in the New Testament, we are not doing the building. God is doing the building, as are the men and women He has commissioned to disciple His body. For example, Paul describes himself as a "masterbuilder" who laid the spiritual foundations of the house of God, the community of the redeemed, in Corinth (see 1 Cor. 3:10). However, there are two specific verses that describe something that we do to build ourselves. Jude writes, *"But you, beloved, building yourselves up on your most holy faith, praying in the Holy Spirit"* (Jude 1:20). I believe that "praying in the Holy

Spirit" here specifically refers to praying in tongues, and that Jude is associating this particular activity with building ourselves up in our faith. The reason I believe this is because the same idea is expressed in First Corinthians 14:4: "*He who speaks in a tongue edifies himself....*" The word "edify" means to *build up*. We get the word "edifice" from the same root. As Lance Wallnau teaches, when we pray in tongues, we are constructing an internal edifice of faith from which the purposes of God become manifest.

How does praying in tongues build us up in our faith? To answer this we must first understand what we are doing when we pray in tongues. Paul explains, "*For he who speaks in a tongue does not speak to men but to God, for no one understands him; however, in the spirit he speaks mysteries*" (1 Cor. 14:2). When we speak in tongues, we are using our voices to give utterance to the expressions of our spirits as they commune with the Holy Spirit. This is powerful because our spirits pray in perfect agreement with God because they speak from the new nature we received when we were born again. By engaging our soul, along with our physical body in what our spirits are saying, we come more completely into agreement with the Holy Spirit. As we sustain this prayer, it leads to the same breakthrough we experience when we physically express praise—we become aware of the manifest presence of God. Or, you could say that our bodies and minds begin to experience an increased measure of the reality that our spirits already experience in the Lord's presence.

UNVEILING SECRETS THROUGH PRAYER

In particular, praying in the Spirit gives us access to the reality that the Holy Spirit is teaching us how to think and pray. Jesus explained to His disciples that after He ascended, the Father would send the Spirit for this specific purpose:

> *However, when He, the Spirit of truth, has come, He will guide you into all truth; for He will not speak on His own authority, but whatever He hears He will speak; and He will tell you things to come. He will glorify Me, for He will take of what is Mine and declare it to you* (John 16:13-14).

This is a glorious promise, but we have to understand that the Holy Spirit is not speaking on a megaphone, nor is His the only voice vying for our attention. In order to connect our minds to the frequency on which He is speaking, we have to take a posture of listening by dialing down the voice of our own thoughts and waiting to hear Him. I call it *leaning into His voice*. Praying in tongues is a powerful tool that can turn our focus from the things that distract us, while at the same time help us to us become aware of His presence and lean into His voice.

This posture invites the Spirit of revelation to enlighten the *"eyes of our understanding"* (see Eph. 1:18). Understanding is something every person naturally desires to have. We especially want to understand the reasons for things that happen in life, particularly in times of tragedy and crisis. It is never legal to make up our own reasons when we can't seem to reconcile our understanding of Scripture with what we see around us. Sometimes pastors and others in ministry fall to this pressure by trying to give an explanation to something that God is not explaining. Much bad theology is created in such times of pressure—it pleases man by bringing an artificial peace, but is not found in the nature of God.

Scripture first gives us the comfort that when we don't know how to pray, the Holy Spirit Himself prays for us (Rom. 8:26). But then He also gives us the wonderful gift of tongues, which allows us to pray in agreement with the Lord when we lack understanding. Moreover, by drawing us into an awareness of the Lord's presence where our minds perceive what the Spirit is saying, praying in the Spirit actually gives us access to the understanding we need.

When we move into praying with understanding as well as praying with the Spirit, as Paul instructed (1 Cor. 14:14), we further increase the level of our agreement with God in prayer. The fact that praying in the Spirit increases our ability to agree with God in prayer is the key to understanding how praying in the Spirit builds our faith. Praying in tongues bypasses the human intellect and immediately activates our Spirit born faith: for faith does not come from the mind. The link between our level of agreement with Heaven and the level of faith we demonstrate is seen most clearly in Jesus' ministry and in His explanation for how He did what He did. He simply said that He only did what He saw His Father do and said what He heard His Father say (see John 5:19; 12:49). Because everything He did and said was in complete agreement with His Father, everything He did and said was done with faith that released the reality of His Father's Kingdom into the circumstances around Him. That kind of constant connection to the presence of God, which sustains an increasing understanding of who God is and the way He moves, is the heart of faith for the believer. The end result is that we can actually start to think and act like Him.

PRAYING WITH GOD

For this reason, the most effective life of prayer to which God has called us is not a life of throwing up prayer requests and hoping that one will bring an answer. The prayer of faith that always gets results is the kind we can pray because we have drawn close to His heart and heard Him talk about what He wants to do. Then we can stand in the place of delegated authority as a co-laborer and declare what He had said over our circumstances. Asking God to swoop down and fix the problems in our lives does not take the kind of faith God is looking for. The disciples discovered this when they woke up Jesus to do something about a life-threatening storm they were in. First, they asked the Savior of the world a pretty dumb question: "...*Do you not care that we are perishing?*" (Mark 4:38). Then they watched in awe as He fixed their problem.

What caught them even more off guard was that, after answering their prayer, He turned and rebuked them for their lack of faith. The reality is that most anyone cries out to God for help when he's desperate. But desperation is not always an expression of faith. What God was looking for was the kind of faith that would enable them to enforce the will of God through declaration. It is mountain-moving faith, or in this case, storm-canceling faith.

Remember that Scripture is very clear about the plan the Holy Spirit is following as He builds us into His house. If we'll cooperate with Him, we'll start to look just like Jesus. For this reason, I believe God desires every believer to mature to the place where we increasingly see what the Father is doing, hear what He's saying, and step out in faith to agree with Him, just as Christ did. And one of the first gifts the Spirit gives to believers to release the hidden things is the ability to pray in tongues because He knows we need this tool to train our hearts, minds, and bodies to perceive and agree with what He's doing. As you learn how to "build yourself up on your most holy faith" using this tool, a sign of growth will be that God will gradually wean you away from expecting Him to bring quick fixes. Instead, you'll find yourself in situations that simply *will not* shift until you lean into His voice, hear what He's saying, and stand in faith to make that declaration over your life. And as we learn to do this, we find that while getting answers to prayer is wonderful and important, hearing His voice in the intimacy of prayer is the true source of our strength and life.

ENDNOTE

1. C.S. Lewis, *Mere Christianity* (New York: Touchstone, 1996), 176.

Chapter 6

POSSESSED
BY PROMISES

*Meditating on the promises
of God will strengthen you.*

Throughout this book I have been showing how the tools we use to strengthen ourselves in the Lord are designed to keep us connected with our identity and purpose. Perhaps this is obvious, but we only know our identity and purpose because God *tells* us what they are. Renewing our minds requires us to learn how to let His words over our lives completely cancel out our old beliefs about who we are—even before we see His word manifesting fully in us. This is how we demonstrate faith.

David's destiny to be king did not begin with his ascent to the throne but with God's declaration of that destiny through the prophet Samuel. There were probably days in the wilderness when the only evidence he could present as proof that the Word was true was his memory of what Samuel said and the oil dripping from his head. But the fact that David pursued his destiny to its fulfillment, without quitting and without taking shortcuts, is clear evidence that he believed what God had said. His faith was not based on circumstances, but on who he knew God to be from his history with Him. Like Sarah, he *"judged Him faithful who had promised"* (Heb. 11:11).

UNLOCKING THE POTENTIAL OF THE PROMISE

When you are born again, you inherit every promise of God for the believer. Peter tells us that these *"great and precious promises"* are the things that make us *"partakers of the divine nature"* (see 2 Peter 1:4)—they unlock our potential to become like Christ. But we don't truly possess these promises until three things happen. We first begin to possess a promise when it is spoken into our hearts by the Holy Spirit. As we read in the previous chapter, the Holy Spirit takes what is Christ's and declares it to us, telling us things to come (see John 16:13-14). The declaration of the Spirit is what places the promises of the Kingdom into our account. Whenever God speaks to us, His prophetic anointing is released in what He says. That word may come to you through another person, or an anointed prayer that is being prayed over you, a passage of Scripture that leapt out at you as you read, a dream or vision, or by the still, small voice of the Spirit in your inner man. That anointing does not just tell you what will be; it is *creating* what will be. It's as if a railroad track is being laid down before you that leads directly to the fulfillment of the Word.

It is impossible for God to lie. His Word is always in complete agreement with His nature and character, and therefore His very words release His power to accomplish what He has said. This is what the angel declared to Mary: "*For with God nothing will be impossible*" (Luke 1:37). The word for "word" is *rhema,* which is the freshly spoken Word of God. The word "impossible" means without ability. An expanded literal translation of this verse could be, "No freshly spoken word from God will ever come to you that does not contain its own ability to perform itself!"

This latent power in the promises of God increases our understanding of why we can trust the faithfulness of the One who promises. And a practical demonstration of trust is precisely the next thing that needs to happen for you to possess your promises. Thankfully, you don't need to understand the Word in order to show the Lord that you trust His Word as truth. You start moving down that railroad track to your destiny by simply *receiving* the Word. That's what Mary did after hearing the amazing promise that she would bear the Christ-child. She responded to the angel, "*Let it be to me according to your Word*" (Luke 1:38). There was no way she could comprehend what the angel had said to her or see how it could possibly happen. All she needed to know was that the Lord had spoken and that she could trust Him. As a result of her faith, she will be called "blessed" for eternity. What a destiny!

The third thing that must happen for you to possess your promises is that your faith in the promise must be tested and proven. Paul gave this instruction to Timothy: "*This charge I commit to you, son Timothy, according to the prophecies made concerning you, that by them you may wage a good warfare*" (1 Tim. 1:18). When the Holy Spirit declares a promise into your account, He has also put a weapon into your arsenal. This tells us two things. First, you will often have to contend for that Word against someone who will try to steal it from you. Secondly, if you contend for the promise by using the promise, you will be victorious. We can see this in the life of Christ. At His baptism, the Father made a declaration over him—"*This is my beloved Son in whom I am well pleased.*" Then Jesus was led into the desert to be tempted by the devil, who said, "If you are the Son of God…." The enemy was directly challenging the Word God had spoken. Jesus replied with Scripture: "*Man…*[lives] *by every word that proceeds from the mouth of God*" (Matt. 4:4). He stood on the promise of the Father on the basis of the fact that God was the One who had made the promise, and God's Words are the source of life. He refused to engage in pointlessly trying to determine His life outside of that Word. He had enough proof that the Father's Word over His life was true, not because He could point to evidence of its manifestation, but because He had *heard* the Word and *received* it.

POSITIONED FOR FULFILLMENT

Jesus' response teaches us that the only way we can position ourselves to see our promises fulfilled is by refusing to define ourselves according to anything but what God has said about us. Jesus rebuked the Pharisees in Mark 7:13, for "*making the Word of God of no effect through your tradition which you have handed down....*" In other words, the Pharisees insisted on defining themselves and their world according to human interpretation and practice rather than the Word of God. The words "of no effect" mean to *render powerless*, giving the picture of pulling the plug on the most powerful thing in the universe—the Word of God. Nothing can diminish the fact that His Word comes fully equipped. But we can shut off our access to that power by choosing to define our lives outside of what God has said.

Defining ourselves by the Word of God requires that we constantly train our minds to think in agreement with that Word. This means we have to remind ourselves of His promises often. But don't stop there! Learn to *meditate* on them. Like Mary, we must treasure them up and ponder them in our hearts (see Luke 2:19). While Eastern meditation tries to get people to empty their minds, biblical meditation focuses on our filling our minds—and our mouths—with the truth. Joshua 1:8 says, "*This Book of the Law shall not depart from your **mouth**, but you shall meditate in it day and night, that you may observe to do according to all that is written in it. For then you will make your way prosperous, and then you will have good success.*" One of the definitions for the Hebrew word "meditate" is "to mutter." Meditating involves repeating the words God has said *out loud.* As

Joshua was told, this regular repetition of what God had said is the key to our ability to *do* the Word. When we declare the Word over our own life and prophesy our own destiny in agreement with Him, we release the anointing of the Spirit in a greater measure to bring the Word to pass. The verse says that when we do this, we are actually *making* our way prosperous. Meditating on the promises of God is something we can do and are responsible to do in order to determine where we're going in life; it is a vital tool for strengthening ourselves in the Lord so we can walk in our identity and purpose. Meditating on the promises of God will strengthen you.

> Meditating on the promises of God will strengthen you.

MANNING THE RUDDER OF MY SHIP

I write down the promises and prophecies that are spoken over me. Like the rudder of a ship, they determine the direction for my thoughts and desires, and eventually my life. I put the shorter ones on 3x5 cards, and the longer ones I keep in a file on my computer. They are in my briefcase and go wherever I go—and I read them often. Since I spend about half the year on the road, I take them with me so I can meditate on them while I'm flying. I often look around and see various businessmen and women who represent companies like Apple Computer or Ford Motor Company. Usually they are looking over their business plans and the notes for their strategic meetings. I, in turn, am examining the mind of Christ about me. Those little 3x5 cards remind me that I represent the Kingdom of God, and that my mind and body must stay current with my role and responsibilities as a delegated authority in this world. I can't afford to have thoughts in my head about me that God doesn't have in His. It's impossible to be consistently effective in fulfilling His purposes unless I am continually training my mind to think of myself according to what God says about me.

I also regularly read portions of Scripture that have been quickened in my heart by the Holy Spirit as words for my life. He has given me personal ownership of the promises through His declaration. I liken these promises as rooms in a mansion that are specifically designed for me; they are realms in God that are great *abiding places*. Romans 8:23 says that we "*groan within ourselves*" in our desire to see our destiny fulfilled. I believe that this is what the psalmist describes when he says, "*Deep calls unto deep*" (Psalm 42:7). The deep cry of my heart calls to the deep desire of the Lord to see me fulfill my potential as His son—the potential that is prophesied in these portions of Scriptures that He has declared over me. If I'm feeling heavy or discouraged, I'll read these passages until I sense the reality of that dwelling place, and can feel that promise burning in my heart once again. Joshua 1:5-9 has been one of my "rooms" for 35 years. It's not just a verse I've memorized;

it's the Word of the Lord for my life, so I go there often and find rest and refreshing, and I renew my perspective on my divine purpose.

But perhaps the most important part of this practice has to do with my experience in the book of Psalms. If I am being bombarded mentally or emotionally, or am just spiritually drained and struggling with my faith, I go to the Psalms. I read and continue to read until I *hear my voice.* Every human condition known to mankind is found in those songs: and I know there will be something there that will address my situation. There are times when I've read 20 or more psalms before finding my heart's cry on the pages of that Book. And when I do, I know I have found a resting place. I stay there and feed my soul by reading it over and over again. Sometimes I'll sing the words to a spontaneous melody. Other times, I use the things discussed in the psalm like "weapons" in praise—except I'm not focused on the devil. I use this "abiding place" to "faith my way" out of any hole I find myself in.

INHERITING PROMISES

It's so important to "treasure up and ponder" the promises of the Lord over your life. Your demonstrated value for the voice of the Lord is what determines the degree to which you attract more promises into your life. Romans 10:17 says that "*faith comes by hearing.*" And Hebrews 11:33 says that it was through faith that the saints of old "*obtained promises.*" The link between "hearing" and "obtaining promises" is faith. When we treasure His promises by holding them close to our heart and anchoring our soul in them through prayerful meditation, we are demonstrating that we believe they are true, and we are showing practical trust in the One who has given them to us. That trust shows Him that He can trust us with more.

The fact that the Holy Spirit is assigned to us to transfer our inherited promises into our account makes it clear that we need to have an ongoing relationship of hearing Him. Life does not come from every word that has already been spoken, but by every word that "*proceeds from the mouth of God*" (Matt. 4:4). Notice "proceeds" is present tense. It is the Holy Spirit's breath on the pages of Scripture that brings us into the place of life and purpose. When we take what we hear and meditate on it, allowing it to train our thinking, our affections, and our behavior, it becomes an abiding word in us. The abiding Word creates a reality in our lives that resonates with the voice of the Spirit, enabling us to perceive it when it comes. Jesus rebuked the Pharisees on this point:

> *And the Father Himself, who sent Me, has testified of Me. You have neither heard His voice at any time, nor seen His form. But you do not have His Word abiding in you, because whom He sent, Him you do not believe. You search the Scriptures, for in them you think you have eternal life; and these are they which testify of Me. But you are not willing to come to Me that you may have life* (John 5:37-40).

In other words, the sign that the Word is abiding in you is that you recognize the presence of God and have faith for what He wants to do! His rebuke also implies that the Scriptures can only help in establishing that abiding Word in us if we respond to them by turning to the *Person* of Christ for life. Revelation is to bring us into a divine encounter, or else it will only make us religious (satisfied with form without power.) When we've been given a promise from the Scripture, it should provoke us to seek the One who both gives and fulfills His Word. On the other hand, when we don't have His Word abiding in us, the implication is serious. The Pharisees made the greatest error of all. They prayed the prayers for the Messiah to come, but never recognized Him for who He was, even when He was right in front of them. It was all because the Word was not abiding in them, as stated in John 5:38, "*But you do not have His Word abiding in you, because whom He sent, Him you do not believe.*"

We live by every word that proceeds from His mouth. Likewise, when we fail to listen to and live by that Word, we cut ourselves off from life. With stakes so high, I would strongly urge you to collect and record the prophetic words and promises over your life. Take a risk! Even write down the ones you're not sure of, and see if God will breathe on them in such a way that they become life to you. And equally important, review them often.

I would also urge you to read the Scriptures from the posture of "leaning into His voice." Expectation has everything to do with what you receive from God. Rather than expecting to gain mere information, answers to your questions, or "proof texts" to make a point, listen for the voice of the Spirit to take the words on the page and deposit them into your heart as a personal word for *you*. When you hear it, it will create that distinctive resonating in your spirit that makes you say, "Wow! I really have no idea what that means yet, but that's so right!" Receive it, write it down, meditate on it, declare it over your life, and let it draw you down the track into your eternal purpose.

Chapter 7

KEEPING
THE TESTIMONY

*Testimonies of God connect
generations to His promises.*

As kings and priests of the planet, we have a dual responsibility: first to act as representatives of man to God through intercession, and secondly to act as representatives of God to man by proclaiming and demonstrating the Gospel of the Kingdom. Christ is our model in both of these roles. In His death, He represented sinful humanity to God and took our judgment. Now, "...*He always lives to make intercession for* [us]" (Heb. 7:25). And as a representative from God to man, Colossians tells us that Christ is "*the image of the invisible God*" and that "*it pleased the Father that in Him all the fullness should dwell*" (Col. 1:15,19). That means that Jesus is perfect theology. If we are tempted to believe something about God that we can't see revealed in Christ, then we'd better reject it. In His life and ministry, Jesus perfectly *re-presented* the Father by doing what His Father did and saying what His Father said.

One of the primary truths that Jesus proved is that it is simply impossible to represent God accurately without demonstrations of power. Miracles are not something that only Jesus and a small number of highly anointed ministers are expected to produce. The anointing that was on Christ is the same Holy Spirit who has been given to *every* believer. He is the One who qualifies us as members of the royal priesthood of God and calls us to continue the ministry of Christ by demonstrating what God is like through the miraculous.

TESTIMONIES REVEAL GOD'S NATURE

A doctrine of demons has been at work for many years to deny the people of God legal access to the realm of the miraculous as an essential element of their identity and purpose as believers. Thankfully, this revelation is currently being restored on a widespread basis. With it comes the revelation of one of the most profound treasures and tools we have inherited— the testimony. A testimony is the written or spoken record of anything that God has done, and every part of that record becomes your family history the moment you are born again. David declared *"I have inherited Your testimonies forever, for they are the joy of my heart"* (Ps. 119:111 NASB). This means that every story of every miracle or sign that God has ever performed is your story because you have become related to the God who made them happen.

The testimonies of God are the tools that equip us to walk in our purpose to demonstrate what He is like through the miraculous. First, they reveal the nature of God and how He does things—His ways. Secondly, this awareness of who God is creates an expectation in our hearts for God's ways to be manifested in our lives. The Hebrew root word for "testimony" means "do again." Every record of what God has done in generations past is a promise of what He will do again in our lives, because He is the same yesterday, today and forever, and is no respecter of persons (see Heb. 13:8; Acts 10:34). Not only that, Revelation 19:10 says, "*the testimony of Jesus is the spirit of prophecy*." As you read in the previous chapter, the prophetic anointing does not just declare what God wants do to, but also carries creative power to bring what is declared into being. The testimony releases this anointing. When we declare what God has done, power is released to make that testimony happen again in the lives of those who hear it.

The testimonies of God are what connect each succeeding generation of believers to His covenant promises. For this reason, God put specific instructions in the Law of Moses for the people of Israel to rehearse the testimony on a daily basis and teach it to their children. Their entire social and family life was to be built on the repetition of the testimony (see Deut. 6). They also had to build memorial stones, such as the ones they were commanded to set up after crossing the Jordan River into the Promised Land, representing what God had done. Testimonies of God connect generations to His promises. When the children of the next generation passed by these stones and asked about them, their parents were to give the testimony (see Joshua 4:5-7) of that crossing, with the implication that, "This is your God too! You inherit this land and the promises that He gave us, and He is ready to keep those promises in your generation." David explains it like this:

> Testimonies of God connect generations to His promises.

For He established a testimony in Jacob, And appointed a law in Israel, Which He commanded our fathers, That they should make them known to their children; That the generation to come might know them, The children who would be born, That they may arise and declare them to their children, That they may set their hope in God, And not forget the works of God, But keep His commandments (Psalm 78:5-7).

CREATING EXPECTATION

Keeping the testimony caused Israel to "set their hope in God"—that is, to sustain their expectation for God to keep His promises through His miraculous invasions of power. Our expectation of God is what determines our level of faith. And we have to have faith in order to "keep His commandments." All of Christ's commands, from "heal the sick" to "love your neighbor" are only possible to fulfill through the supernatural empowerment of His Spirit that comes through faith. Likewise, the Israelites were given a mission from God to take the Promised Land from their enemies and establish themselves as a nation, a mission that entirely depended on their ability to position themselves for the invasion of God's power through faith. He was the one who gave them the strategies and the strength to do the impossible. As long as they remembered what God had said and done and stepped out in faith with His strategies, they won supernatural victories. But when the people stopped keeping the testimony, their faith for the miraculous diminished, and so did their obedience to His commands. If you study the history of Israel in the Old Testament, you'll find that every generation that stopped walking in their covenant with God did so because they forgot His works. David goes on in Psalm 78 to describe such a generation:

> *The children of Ephraim, being armed and carrying bows, Turned back in the day of battle. They did not keep the covenant of God, They refused to walk in His law, And forgot His works And His wonders that He had shown them* (Psalm 78:9-11).

You'll notice that these people were equipped for battle: *being armed and carrying bows.* The problem was not that God had sent them into battle without preparation.

They possessed the testimonies of what God had done for their fathers that, if declared, would not only give them the courage to step out in faith but would release a prophetic anointing to repeat those acts. The problem was that they had forgotten them. Thus they lacked the strength and faith needed to face the battle.

THE COST OF NEGLECT

I'm amazed at the human capacity to forget the most extraordinary, mind-boggling things, particularly the miraculous—but it usually doesn't happen overnight. Forgetting is a downward spiral that begins with the very natural tendency to gradually talk less about the cancer that was instantly healed, for example. Other things start to occupy our minds. But then, the less we keep the testimony in our conversation and our minds, the lower goes our expectation to see the miraculous. Our lowered expectation keeps us from recognizing and stepping into opportunities to see the miraculous. And the less we experience the miraculous, the less we have to talk about. We talk less, expect less, and experience less until we end up in the place where we meet someone with cancer and we go, "God! Help!" Our expectation and faith are small, even though we've seen God fix this problem before. We are armed and carrying bows, but we've forgotten that fact; and unless we remember what God has done and rise up in the faith provided in the testimony, we will turn back from the divine opportunities for victory right in front of us.

If you've studied the Old Testament, you know that the failure of Israel to keep the testimony and defeat the enemies in their land had serious consequences. By choosing instead to coexist with their enemies in the same territory, they became vulnerable to idolatry, which led them to break their covenant with God and invite all kinds of curses and problems into their lives. They lost their identity as the people of God and became just like the people around them. Failing to keep the testimony not only makes us forget who God is, but who we are. Like Israel, the only thing that distinguishes believers from the rest of the world is the reality that God is active among us. When we lose sight of that, we are no different than anyone else—with one exception, we will experience more serious consequences because we are accountable for the revelation of God we've received in the testimonies. We rob people of their encounters with Him when we forget that the testimony matters to God.

KEEPING AWARE OF THE GOD WHO INVADES THE IMPOSSIBLE

What does it take to keep the testimony so we can stay out of the downward spiral and carry out our responsibility to represent God with power? It simply takes following the prescriptions that God gave His people in the first place. We are to establish a culture of the testimony in our personal lives, in our homes, and in our churches. We're to talk about it when we get up, when we eat a meal, when we go to work, and when we go to bed. We're to build memorials that remind us of what God has done and consider them regularly.

I started keeping a journal a number of years ago for the sole purpose of recording the miracles I've witnessed. I'm not the best at journaling, but I am deeply convinced of the power I've seen and my own human ability to forget what I've witnessed. I believe in the weightiness of the consequences if I should forget His miracles, so I journal. I owe my children, grandchildren, and future generations a record of the interventions of God in my generation. The testimony itself is their inheritance.

As a pastor, I have emphasized this principle to my staff and our congregation. Our team begins every staff and board meeting with an hour or two of sharing testimonies of what God has done in the previous weeks and months. We know that we can't afford to make plans for the direction of the church without an overwhelming awareness of the God who invades the impossible. If we lack that awareness, we will lack faith and courage, and our plans will fall short of the mission God has given us. When we have that awareness, however, we not only leave our meetings feeling incredibly encouraged by the goodness and power of God, we leave full of faith that God intends to do it all again this week. We also walk out carrying a full arsenal of testimonies that contain the potential to multiply themselves as we declare them over the lives of people we have the opportunity to touch.

If I don't stay aware of the God who invades the impossible, I will reduce ministry to my ministry gifts. All of our gifts are like the sails on a boat. We can sit in the harbor (church) and admire one another's sails; but without wind they are worthless! Our gifts are designed to catch the wind of God so we can accomplish what is humanly impossible. The testimony keeps our sails hoisted.

As for our congregation and our School of Ministry, they have equally embraced the value of the testimony. Many of the testimonies we share at our staff and board meetings are their stories, which means that the people are not just out there ministering in the power of God, they're talking about it and it's getting back to us. One of the most significant fruits of this testimony culture is that more and more of the stories we're hearing are related to the sharing of testimonies.

One Sunday when I taught on the power of the testimony, we showed a video in our service of a little boy running around after his club feet had been healed. After seeing this video, some students from the School of Ministry were so excited that they went down to the mall the next day to pray for anyone they could find. They saw a woman walking with a leg brace and a cane, so they naturally assumed she was a target for a miracle. They began talking to her and shared the testimony about the boy whose feet had been healed. Moved by the story, she allowed them to pray for her knee, which had a tumor on it. The tumor disappeared, so she took off her brace. Then one of the young men who was praying for her said, "The fire of God is hitting your back right here," and pointed to a particular spot. In surprise she felt the spot and found that another tumor, which she had kept to herself, had also disappeared! She walked out of the mall carrying her brace and cane on one arm, and her grandchild on the other, to whom the students heard her explain, "I don't need these anymore."

This woman experienced the prophetic power of the testimony. Declaring the testimony created a divine moment for God to do it again! And the miracles that occur when testimonies are shared continue to multiply—not only in our community, but all over the world. There is perhaps no other revelation that I've seen so dramatically change how people "do church" in the places where I travel and teach than the power of the testimony because it is calling them back to their true identity and purpose in God.

LEAVING AN INHERITANCE THROUGH TESTIMONY

Keeping the testimony is a responsibility that God gave to every man and woman in Israel, not merely their leaders. The fact that each individual is accountable for keeping the testimony as a lifestyle defines this as one of the primary tools we must use to strengthen ourselves. We can't expect others to keep the testimony for us. Beyond keeping testimonies in our conversation, we are also to meditate on them. Meditation is powerful because it involves our imagination, which actually can lead us into a significant level of experience, and experience is a vital part of renewing the mind. The writer of Psalm 66 says, "*Come and see the works of God...He turned the sea into dry land; they went through the river on foot.*" This writer could not have possibly seen God part the Red Sea and the Jordan River. But through inspired imagination, he was able to come into a level of experiencing these miracles that enabled him to own these events as his own history. If you are someone who feels like you haven't seen very many miracles, you first need to remember that you possess every story of God's as your own. Then, because they're yours, you should study the testimonies of Scripture and collect the testimonies of both historical saints and the saints around you so you can meditate on them. Meditation on the testimonies trains your mind to think from the realm of faith.

David made it clear that it was his study of the testimonies that enabled him to access such a powerful revelation of God: "*I have more understanding than all my teachers, for Your testimonies are my meditation*" (Ps. 119:99). And because of his level of revelation, David became the only man in the Old Testament to walk the dual role of king and priest. If the testimonies brought David into that destiny before he could experience unbroken communion with God through the

Holy Spirit, how much more will they bring us into our destiny now that we have the Spirit of Revelation within us? As kings and priests, our entire identity stands on the foundation of our family history in God. If we don't know where we came from, we won't know where we're going or how to get there. We must learn to keep the testimony.

Chapter 8

CONTROLLING YOUR ENVIRONMENT

Jesus was moved to action,
not by human need,
but by His Father's heart.

As I have developed a lifestyle of feeding on the promises and prophecies of God over my life and meditating on His testimonies, something interesting has happened. People with testimonies now constantly find me, like heat-seeking missiles. Because the nature of the testimony carries a prophetic anointing, it's as though I am prophesied over on a continual basis. As a result, I have a steady supply of encouragement and strength that shows up wherever I am, all over the world. It's amazing. When we value what God values, His blessings will hunt us down.

Jesus made a statement that explains how our value for the testimonies and promises of the Lord draws more of them into our lives. He said, "*Take heed what you hear. With the same measure you use, it will be measured to you; and to you who hear, more will be given*" (Mark 4:24). Clearly Jesus is not referring merely to the physical act of perceiving sound. He's talking about hearing that involves listening. When we listen, we allow what we are hearing to gain our attention and focus, which in turn influences our beliefs and values. These beliefs and values set a standard for our ears that ultimately determines the voices that we pick up in our environment. This standard is also what draws us to certain people more than others.

Because I've set a standard for my ears by valuing the testimony, I attract people with the same standard. On the other hand, people with an ungodly standard are attracted to people with that same standard. If we were to take someone with a reputation for loving gossip and put that person into a new job with 50 other employees they'd never met, within seven days every other gossip-lover in the place would be drawn to that person. Our values communicate something in the spiritual realm that alerts others with the same values to our presence.

SETTING A STANDARD FOR OUR EARS

The standard we set for our ears also determines our ability to strengthen ourselves because strengthening ourselves begins with our choice to listen to God's voice more than any other. By the way, I hope it's obvious that learning to strengthen ourselves does not imply that we are the source of our strength. Rather, "*I can do all things **through Christ** who strengthens me*" (Phil. 4:13). And Christ "[upholds] *all things by the word of His power*"—*including us* (Heb. 1:3). Thus, every tool in our arsenal is designed to help us draw from the strength made available to us by hearing His voice. Listening is what enables us to establish agreement with Him through obeying His voice, and our agreement is what releases heavenly strength and resources into our lives and circumstances. However, as I just described, the standard we set for our ears can attract heavenly strength that comes through interactions with other people who speak and live from a heavenly perspective. Therefore, by purposefully associating with people who share our values and controlling our interactions with people who don't, we strengthen ourselves.

I strongly believe that we are all called to minister to anyone and everyone to whom the Holy Spirit would lead us. We're to accept them unconditionally and show them the love and power of God. Certainly there will also be individuals who God calls us to do business with, to befriend over a period of time in order to introduce them to Jesus, or to disciple in the faith. But these kinds of relationships are a completely different ballgame from friendships in which we open ourselves to the influence of our friend's perspective and values. We need to be careful about who is close to us and gives input into our lives.

STRENGTH COMES FROM COVENANT PEOPLE

Our close friendships, especially with our spouses, are powerful, because they are built on covenant.

Covenant establishes an agreement that allows the spiritual reality that governs your life to flow to the other person, and vice versa. This is why it is so vital to develop friendships with people whose lives consistently display the fruit of the Kingdom. When we steward covenant friendships with people of faith, we stay connected to a growing source of strength that often greatly determines our ability to persevere through difficult times.

I am blessed to have close friendships with people of genuine faith. Time and time again I have been uplifted and strengthened simply by being with them. Often I was not even able to mention the difficult situation I was facing at the time, yet I left encouraged. There are several reasons for this. First, our love and honor for one another creates an exchange of life whenever we interact. Because my friends are people of faith, they naturally exude hope, promise, and joy. It doesn't take long when I'm with them for their attitude and spirit to be infectious. But even more, covenant friendships, when they're built on knowing each other after the Spirit, have the effect of calling us back to who we truly are in Christ. They refresh our connection to our purpose and identity, and when our vision for those things is renewed, usually our strength is too. For this reason, I know that one of the best ways to strengthen myself when I'm tired or discouraged is to grab hold of a friend and spend some time with him.

KEEP THE WEEDS OUT OF THE GARDEN

On the other hand, I have found that when I am in an emotionally vulnerable place, or even if I'm just physically tired, I have to be careful to make sure I am not around people who like to complain or be critical. I have always had strong personal boundaries in place for discerning and interacting with people who speak from a place of negativity or unbelief. Normally I will minister to them, but I will not give them access to my life. When I'm lacking strength, however, I will intentionally avoid them. It may not sound very compassionate, but I am the only one who is responsible for keeping my heart free from doubt and judgment, and I alone can recognize when I am vulnerable to the influence of people who agree with those spirits. The powerful effect of people's personalities and values are given as a warning by Solomon when he says, *"Do not associate with a man given to anger; or go with a hot-tempered man, or you will learn his ways and find a snare for yourself"* (Prov. 22:24-25 NASB).

Not all ungodly counsel comes from the ungodly. While many mean well, they lack the faith perspective that I strive for, and tend to work to make me more like them than they do to actually try to help me to become stronger in my trust in God. My job is to protect myself from such an influence, especially when I am vulnerable. My heart is a garden. Some people are good at planting weeds, while others plant the Kingdom. My job, and yours, is to know the difference.

THE PLACE OF SOLITUDE

The gospels specifically mention occasions in which Jesus took His disciples away from the crowds to rest and be together. The testimony of revival history teaches us that very few men and women of God really learn how and when to do this. In case after case, the same person who carried a marvelous anointing that brought salvation, healing, and deliverance to thousands of people lacked the wisdom to see that he wouldn't be able to sustain that ministry if he didn't learn to get away from the crowds long enough to get physical rest and cultivate life-giving relationships with family and friends who would reaffirm his or her focus on the Kingdom. As a result, many of these revivalists died young, and many of their family members suffered physically and spiritually.

We can't afford to miss the lesson these stories teach us. If we are going to become people who God can entrust with greater measures of favor and anointing to fulfill our purpose as a royal priesthood, we have to be people who are prepared for the reality that we are going to attract needy people. People's needs can exert tremendous pressure on us, and that pressure will expose the places in our heart that care more about meeting the expectations of others than doing only what Jesus is doing. In His ministry, Jesus met the needs of many people, but He also walked past a lot of other needy people. He understood that as one man, the only way He could succeed at what He was doing was to keep Himself in a place where what moved Him to action was not merely human need, but the actual heart of His Father. Jesus was moved to action not by human need but by His Father's heart.

The strength of our intimacy with the Father and with the close covenant relationships in our lives is what will largely determine our ability to minister from a place of faith and obedience to God rather than a place of striving to please or help people. The people who are most vulnerable to over-extending themselves on behalf of ministry relationships are people who struggle with intimacy—both with God and others. Ministry can be a great place for them to feel connected and loved, but the truth is, without the accountability that only comes from covenant friendships, they are just being set up for burnout or compromise. This is why God will pull many ministers out of ministry for a time just to learn how to be friends with Him apart from working for Him. All true fruitfulness flows from that intimacy with Him.

> Jesus was moved to action not by by human need but by His Father's heart.

I have found that there are three main sources of distractions that we must learn to overcome in order to stay on track with our destiny.

First, there are the distractions from the devil. He plays on our old fears and addictions to get us to sin.

Gradually, as our minds are transformed and our senses are trained to hunger and thirst for God, those temptations don't really hold much interest anymore.

Secondly, in that transformation process, we deal more with distractions from ourselves—places where our old, limited ways of thinking keep us from perceiving and responding to what God is trying to teach us.

But in the end, some of the most difficult distractions to avoid are not the ones that come from the devil or ourselves. They're from God. They're the blessings, the favor, the prosperity, the miracles, and all the amazing gifts that He pours out in our lives. Obviously He gave them to us for our enjoyment and success. But they also have a way of revealing whether we will choose the benefits of friendship above the Friend Himself.

Every time we start to coast on the benefits of our covenant relationships with God and those closest to us, we are going to violate love. It must be settled in our hearts that we maintain a posture of intentionally pursuing these relationships for their own sakes, and for what we can bring to them. We also have to purpose never to let the needs of people we are not in covenant with dictate what we have to give to our close relationships. In our commitment to use the strength we have for their blessing, we actually sow into the moment when we will need strength for ourselves. That's the nature of our Father's Kingdom.

HEALTHY HUMOR

One final note: most of the people of faith who consistently make a contribution to my life in times of need are also people with a great sense of humor. I tend to take myself too seriously and resist laughter in difficult times. Joy in trial takes faith; but being with people I trust enough to relax around helps to foster the atmosphere where laughter comes easily and often. Sometimes just being together, telling funny stories, sharing joyful experiences, and even laughing at myself, is just what the doctor ordered. Laughter really is good medicine.

Chapter 9

THE
DESPERATE CRY

Focus on God's answers—
not your problems.

God wants us to succeed!

The Holy Spirit will give
you water to sustain you through
the dry and barren times.

The tools presented in this book are not meant to be an exhaustive list of the ways we can strengthen ourselves in the Lord. I have only addressed the things with which I have the most experience. My goal is to convince you that God has equipped you with everything you need to fulfill your destiny. It's not complicated. What is most important to me is for the Body of Christ to be *absolutely possessed* by the revelation of the greatness of our destiny. Without this understanding, we will probably not be willing to pay the price of learning to strengthen ourselves.

SURPRISED BY JOY

The Holy Spirit is the only One who can reveal who we're called to be. This is why the conviction of the Holy Spirit is one of the most precious gifts we receive throughout our lifetimes. Sadly, for years this gift has been confused with its very antithesis: the condemnation of the enemy. One of the clearest pictures of the difference between conviction and condemnation is found in the Book of Nehemiah. As you may know, Nehemiah led the Jewish exiles in the task of rebuilding the walls of Jerusalem and restoring the city following their Babylonian captivity. At one point the people set aside a day to renew their covenant with God by listening to the elders read and explain the Book of the Law, which they had not heard for years. As they understood the words that were read, they saw how high God's standard for their lives was and how far below it they actually lived. They naturally started weeping and mourning. But Nehemiah and the other leaders corrected them for this response to the Holy Spirit's conviction:

> *And Nehemiah, who was the governor, Ezra the priest and scribe, and the Levites who taught the people said to all the people, "This day is holy to the Lord your God; do not mourn nor weep." For all the people wept, when they heard the words of the Law.*
>
> *Then he said to them, "Go your way, eat the fat, drink the sweet, and send portions to those for whom nothing is prepared; for this day is holy to our Lord. Do not sorrow, for the joy of the Lord is your strength."*
>
> *So the Levites quieted all the people, saying, "Be still, for the day is holy; do not be grieved." And all the people went their way to eat and drink, to send portions and rejoice greatly, because they understood*

the words that were declared to them (Nehemiah 8:9-12)

For many who were raised in church, weeping over the fact that we don't measure up to God's standard for life as taught in the Scriptures is considered the one *legitimate* sign of conviction and repentance. And *holiness* is something generally associated with somberness and tears and not with joy. That *bent* in our value system has caused us to mislabel many things in life, such as the frequent mistake of referring to depressed individuals as "prophets" or at least as "intercessors." But in Nehemiah's story of rebuilding the fallen city of Jerusalem, we discover that holiness is more connected to joy and rejoicing. Israel was forbidden to weep when the priest publicly read God's Word, even though they fell far short of what God required from them. They were given a warning not to weep, and instead rejoice and celebrate with a feast. Absolutely shocking! Sinners were to celebrate with joy because they *understood* God's call to holiness!

The idea that the best response to conviction is getting depressed derives from wrong beliefs that blind us to the Holy Spirit's purpose in exposing the places where we fall short of our high calling in Christ. There is a place for tears in this process as we're told that it is godly sorrow that leads us to repentance. But when we have a wrong view of God as a legalistic father who is unhappy with our every move, we distort what was supposed to lead us to an encounter with Him that brings transformation. Instead, many develop attitudes of somberness in a fleshly attempt to be holy. Consequently, we've misunderstood and misappropriated the fullness of His grace, which does not merely forgive our sin, but empowers us to live like Him. These beliefs create an opportunity for the *accuser of the brethren* to speak up in the moments when we see areas of sin or weakness in our lives, and convince us that we're hopeless cases. We are deceived into thinking that his accusations are godly conviction because we can't deny the fact that we need to change.

THE NEEDED SHIFT IN FOCUS

The real problem is not in what we lack, but how we respond to what God has said. Focusing on our problems more than God's answers should be a dead giveaway that we're really dealing with condemnation, not the Holy Spirit's conviction. Focus on God's answers—not your problems. When the Holy Spirit shows us where we are falling short, the bigger reality is not the areas where we're not yet walking in our destiny, but the destiny itself. So many of us read the verse that "*all have sinned and fall short of the glory of God*" (Rom. 3:23) and focus more on the fact that all have fallen short than the fact that we are destined for glory! The conviction

> Focus on God's answers— not your problems.

THE DESPERATE CRY

of the Holy Spirit is actually a call to turn our focus away from our sin and our limitations. He's saying, "You're made for more than this. Lift your head and set your sights higher." Such a renewed perspective is supposed to seem overwhelmingly impossible. That way we're more likely to draw near to Him and allow His grace to bring us into our destiny.

When we recognize the purpose for the Holy Spirit's conviction, we start to understand how we need to interpret the kinds of tests He allows us to face in our lives. It's obvious that the real tests are not the situations that challenge our strengths, but the ones that expose our weaknesses. David's biggest test was not facing Goliath; it was overcoming his own vulnerability to distress by strengthening himself. In fact, most of the warfare we deal with in the Christian life is really internal. As we realign our wrong thinking and transform our old behavior patterns, it is amazing how we find that the devil and the world pose less and less of a threat to the flow of the life of God through us.

But, as previously mentioned, the thing we forget is that God prepares us for *all* of our battles. We have to remember that when our weaknesses are exposed, it is because God has already given us the tools we need to overcome them. This is why the Israelites were commanded to rejoice in the face of their shortcomings. The Holy Spirit not only convicted them of their destiny; He equipped them with a promise: "*The joy of the Lord is your strength.*" In other words, it's the Lord's joy over our lives that contains the strength needed to

step toward our destiny. And how do we get that joy? We rejoice. We align our bodies and souls with the promise because that posture is what invites the manifestation of the promise. That this response to conviction is what God is looking for should make sense because it requires faith. To rejoice when you win the *Reader's Digest* Sweepstakes is easy, but to rejoice before you get your desired breakthrough takes faith.

POSITIONED TO RECEIVE

Receiving the promises of our destiny, as mentioned in Chapter 6, requires that we position ourselves in a certain way. Jesus gave His disciples a command: *"Behold, I send the Promise of My Father upon you; but tarry in the city of Jerusalem until you are endued with power from on high"* (Luke 24:49). I want to point out that this promise was not about their salvation. Jesus had already breathed on them and said, *"...Receive the Holy Spirit"* (John 20:22). He did this in direct parallel to the Father's first breathing life into Adam. It was an act of creation that fulfilled the promise of Psalm 102:18, that *"...a people yet to be created* [would] *praise the Lord."* Since the salvation encounter is specifically what brings this new creation reality into our lives, I believe that this moment was when the disciples were born again. Pentecost was another event, a second touch. If their salvation had brought them *out of the red*, so to speak, Pentecost was about getting them into the black so they could minister in power more consistently and have something to give away to others.

So what had to happen between salvation and Pentecost? "*These all continued with one accord in prayer and supplication...*" (Acts 1:14). The word *continued* means "to be steadfastly attentive to; to persevere and not to faint; to be in constant readiness for." The disciples didn't assume the promise Jesus gave them would just happen, nor did they assume that "*tarrying in Jerusalem*" meant hanging out and doing business as usual. They stayed in one place and contended in prayer. When Heaven invaded earth on the Day of Pentecost, it was because earth had invaded Heaven for ten days. Their contending in faith for the promise both prepared them to receive it and enabled them to draw it to them.

CREATED FOR GLORY

The disciples were strengthening themselves in that upper room. Strengthening ourselves in the Lord is all about being prepared to receive and steward the fulfillment of our promises. Think of "invading Heaven" in the physical sense. In order for an astronaut to venture beyond the earth's atmosphere, he must be covered in a pressurized suit that can resist the vacuum of outer space. Without it, his body would instantly explode. If you and I are going to touch the realm of God's *glory*—and the word "glory" literally means "weight"—we are going to have to exert some internal pressure in order to build enough strength to live in that atmosphere and be carriers of that glory on earth.

And to carry His glory is exactly what we are made to do—the Christian life is not only about getting saved so we go to Heaven when we die. Rather, it's about learning to live in Heaven's reality now so that we can co-labor with Christ to establish His Kingdom on earth. The reason the Church has "dumbed down" the Great Commission of discipling nations and seeing the knowledge of the glory of the Lord cover the earth has everything to do with our failure to pick up the baton of the early church by contending for the authentic ongoing baptism of the Holy Spirit. As the Book of Acts testifies, this baptism was never meant as a one-time event but as an ongoing series of encounters that enable us to walk in increasing levels of power, fulfilling the assignment Jesus gave to His Body. Please note that some of the same people mentioned in the upper room in Acts 2 are also in the outpouring in Acts 4:29-31.

The indwelling Spirit we receive at salvation is the Spirit of adoption who calls out "Abba Father," and gives us unbroken access to His heart. The revelation of His Kingdom and knowledge of His will that is to come to earth pours forth in these encounters. But as we truly come to know the Father and what He wants to do, we should be convinced that knowing is not enough. His whole plan centers on the unveiling of His sons and daughters, who will walk in the authority

Jesus received at His death and bring liberty to all of creation (see Rom. 8:19-21). For this reason, the Holy Spirit did not come only to dwell within us, but to rest upon us with the same Christ-anointing Jesus had in order to release Heaven's answers to earth's dilemmas. In other words, He came to manifest the Kingdom. This is the *ongoing* baptism we need.

I am so grateful that in the last century the Holy Spirit has brought much of the Body of Christ world-wide back to the pursuit and experience of this baptism. What baffles me is that there are so many believers who taste of this glorious anointing and stop short of undertaking a lifelong pursuit of more. Every man and woman I know who has been launched into a ministry of signs and wonders through his or her experience with the Holy Spirit understands that he/she must never stop contending for and experiencing further encounters. However, they also understand that their journey of contending is a journey of stewardship. Too many people in revival don't know how to steward what they received when they were baptized in the Holy Ghost, so they keep coming back to the same place, asking God to fill them again. This mind-set lacks a fundamental understanding of how God establishes His Kingdom.

HOW THE KINGDOM COMES

At one point, Jesus picked up on His disciples' misunderstanding of how the Kingdom would come. After witnessing thousands of miracles, and signs and wonders confirming His message that "*the kingdom of heaven is at hand*," the disciples expected that "*the kingdom of God would appear immediately*" (Luke 19:11). So Jesus told them a parable about a nobleman who left the country and entrusted his servants with various sums of money to invest while he was gone. When the nobleman returned, he had each person give an account of what he had done with what he was given. In response he gave each person authority over cities in his realm in direct correlation to his ability to invest and manage what he had been given to steward. For example, the one who managed to use ten units of money well and gain ten more, he made the governor over ten cities. He then condemned the servant who had hidden the money rather than investing it (Luke 19:12-27). This is how the Kingdom of God comes— not all at once, but little by little as the people of God steward the anointing they received in their last encounter. We can't take cities and nations for God because He already possesses them. That's why in the second Psalm it says to ask God for the nations, and He'll give them to us as our inheritance. Our job is to become ones to whom He can entrust His authority until entire cities and nations come under the righteous influence of those who serve well, carrying God's agenda. This kind of increase comes to those who are faithful with what they've been given.

So how do we steward what's been given to us? We use the tools we've been given to contend for the promises and desires that God has birthed in our hearts through the Holy Spirit. We also take other specific steps of faith and obedience in order to line up our thinking and behavior with what we've heard. If you have a longing to preach the Gospel, a first step might be preaching to yourself in the car. It may be a small beginning, but we can't despise it because faith says that it's not where you are, but where you're going that is important. And faith understands that spiritual release comes through physical obedience.

Faith must conquer our fear of failure if we are going to fully embrace a journey of transformation. As the lesson from Nehemiah teaches, our promises and desires are usually connected to the places where we need to grow in our character and in our capacity to think and live like God. If there were no power to change, it would be cruel for God to give us promises that we could never qualify to receive. But because the Spirit of the resurrected Christ lives in our bodies, His promises and desires are the keys to our breakthrough. We have to come to see the places of lack in our lives as the very places where God intends to bring us into our greatest victories—if we will take the risk to step out on our promises.

FROM DESPERATION TO FAITH

For years I was bothered by the fact that even though I preached that God was a God of miracles, I wasn't seeing the miraculous. I couldn't be satisfied with just having good theology because my experience denied what my theology said. I went from being bothered to being consumed with godly jealousy when I heard reports of healings breaking out in The Vineyard Movement through John Wimber and others. In the midst of this season, I received a prophetic word from my friend Mario Murillo saying that God was going to anoint me to walk in a ministry of healing and miracles. I took that word, wrote it down, and began to declare it over my life on a regular basis. Over ten years ago, the Lord began to fulfill His word, and I have consistently and increasingly seen the miraculous as I minister the Gospel.

Recently I had an opportunity to reconnect with Mario, and I pulled out the worn 3x5 card with his prophetic word on it. Knowing how I had contended for the word, he began to explain to me that I was like Hannah. Hannah wanted the very thing that her barrenness prevented her from having—a child. But instead of succumbing to bitterness and disappointment, she cried out to the Lord. Hers had to be a cry of faith, because in that cry, she developed a resolve to set apart her desire completely to the Lord. She was so consumed by her desire that she lost all consciousness about what others thought of her. Mario explained that the Lord used my barrenness in the realm of miracles to develop that same desperate cry in me that Hannah had—to the point where I didn't care if I was misunderstood. In contending for the promise, I strengthened my resolve to guard the anointing jealously when it was finally given, and use it completely for the Lord's purposes. This resolve is essential in becoming trustworthy to experience the fulfillment of the promise.

As Jesus' parable on the talents indicates, the length of time between the day in which we are entrusted with a "talent" and the day in which God calls us to account for our stewardship is undetermined. I didn't know how long I would need to keep praying and laying hands on people in expectation for my prophetic word to be fulfilled. But my heart was set on pilgrimage. There was no "plan B." Because I lived in pursuit of the promise, each day brought me closer to my breakthrough. The very fact that I had a promise from God guaranteed that there would be a day in which the Lord would assess what I had done and judge whether my stewardship of the promise had adequately prepared me to steward the realm of anointing spoken of in the promise.

If we don't set our hearts on the end goal, we will despise the day of small beginnings. We also won't be able to recognize how far we've come from those beginnings. We have to learn to sustain deep gratitude for what God has done in the past while keeping our eyes fixed on the possibilities that are ever before us until the Kingdom comes in its fullness. With this perspective, we also need to sustain the awareness that we've already received whatever will be necessary for the next phase of our journey. God wants us to succeed!

> God wants us to succeed!

God has set us up to succeed. Yes, He commanded us to disciple the nations. It looks like an impossible task. But Jesus is the Desire of the Nations, and He dwells inside us. He lives in us to make it possible for us to succeed in the impossible assignment to disciple nations. Our job is learning to let Him out, and we only do that to the degree that we are like Him. This is why the desire to become like Him is the driving passion of the Christian life. When we truly see who He is and what He's done for us, when we've tasted His love and power, a desperate conviction is born in us—we simply cannot live any longer with the areas in our lives that are inconsistent with who Jesus is. This conviction must grip our hearts so completely that we resolve never to quit until we are completely conformed to His image. In becoming like Christ, we become the very thing the world longs for.

PERSONAL TRANSFORMATION— THE ULTIMATE AMBITION

To be transformed into His image is the passion that drives our priority to learn how to strengthen ourselves. No one else can fulfill my destiny for me. No one else can possess my promises. Complacency will not draw the baptism of the Holy Spirit into my life. There's something about exercising my will and faith to step beyond convenience that matters to God. On one occasion, Jesus saw that His disciples were struggling in the midst of a storm, so He walked out on the lake. But He didn't walk to them. The Bible says,

"*He...would have passed them by*" (Mark 6:48). The *cry* of His disciples is what turned Him their way. He was showing them that God is available to us—He is always within reach.

God has already pursued us with a love so totally overwhelming that it will take all of eternity to plumb its depths. But He protects the opportunities that we have to use our will to pursue Him. That's how faith works. If He says He will catch us, we jump because only when we jump, can He do what He promised. Only as we step out to do the supernatural things He has asked of us can we appropriate the supernatural power He's already given us to achieve these impossible tasks.

The Sons of Korah give us a wonderful description of how this process of maturing in strength and character takes place in our lives:

Blessed is the man whose strength is in You, whose heart is set on pilgrimage.

As they pass through the Valley of Baca, they make it a spring; the rain also covers it with pools. They go from strength to strength; each one appears before God in Zion (Psalm 84:5-7).

Baca means "weeping." The Valley of Weeping is a prophetic picture of any difficulty in our lives, every kind of loss, crisis, need, or pain. Those whose strength is in the Lord and whose hearts are set on His pilgrimage—on running the race to the end and fulfilling the destiny God has given them—can take those places of disappointment and turn them into a spring.

When we refuse to let circumstances and areas of personal weakness determine our level of faith and passion, we will discover the secret of victory in every situation. Instead of being bound by the limitations set by our natural environment, we choose to lift up our heart's cry to the Lord in the dry and barren place and actually draw "water" to the surface that the Holy Spirit has already poured out in our lives. It's much like digging in dry and cracked soil until you find water. But this water is actually a spring of great refreshing. It lies just beneath the surface of our driest set of circumstances. Remember, Jesus promised that rivers of living water would flow from our hearts (see John 7:38). The Holy Spirit will give you water to sustain you through the dry and barren times.

> The Holy Spirit will give you water to sustain you through the dry and barren times.

It is very important to believe this is true. For then we are conscious of the fact that we are NEVER far from water! And when we stir up the passion of our hearts for the promises of God in a place of weakness, we not only create a spring, we attract the outpouring of the Spirit that covers that place with pools—new realms of anointing. When we discover springs beneath our dry moments, we attract rain. Water attracts water. Correctly stewarding the Holy Spirit's work in our past (digging in dry places) attracts the water of outpouring (that which is to come). This is Kingdom stewardship: taking the barren areas of our lives, the places of unfulfilled dreams and great disappointment, and drawing the springs of life from our own hearts, knowing that the Holy Spirit lives within us and is never without life to give. He who has promised is faithful. Fulfilling the demands of this principle of stewardship is how we *"go from strength to strength,"* and ultimately reach our destination, appearing *"before God in Zion"*—a picture that not only speaks of going to Heaven when we die, but of becoming people who live from Heaven toward earth, right now.

MY VALLEY OF WEEPING

In 2003, while on a ministry trip to Brazil with Randy Clark and his Global Awakening team, I received the news that during a simple surgical procedure, the doctors discovered pancreatic cancer in my dad. I left Brazil early to be with him and join my family in the battle for his life.

My dad has always been the greatest encouragement in my life. But he was that way to most everyone who knew him. He was a true Barnabas—*a son of encouragement.* In addition to all the obvious reasons to want my dad to live, I knew that I needed his continual help in what God was doing here in Redding, California. I also wanted him to see the fruit of his own labor—he was the pastor who had set the original course of direction for our church well over 20 years before I became the pastor.

I felt moved to ask God to repeat Hezekiah's miracle for my dad. While facing death, Hezekiah cried out to God and was given an additional 15 years of life on earth. Since God is no respecter of persons, and is the same yesterday, today, and forever, it seemed like an appropriate prayer for this situation. Great numbers of people started praying the same prayer, asking for the additional years given to Hezekiah to be given to my dad. In fact, one woman whom I had never met told me that God had spoken the same "Hezekiah miracle" to her to give me as a promise for my dad; I received it gladly.

Ironically, cancer has been a prayer target of ours for quite a few years. Cancer has become the Goliath that taunts the armies of the living God and I have a righteous anger over the violation of the name of the Lord. We refuse to show any respect for the name cancer, as it is inferior to the name of Jesus. Through the years, we have seen a great number of cancer cases healed in and through our church. In fact, someone in our town actually started a rumor after their own healing: "Go to Bethel; they don't tolerate cancer!" While we have not seen everyone healed who comes to us, we are in pursuit, believing that God will give us that kind of breakthrough and ultimately release to us a "cancer free zone."

In spite of our many breakthroughs with others, I arrived at my own *Valley of Baca* when my dad died of cancer following a six-month battle. It was as though I pushed against a thousand-pound rock for six months; it never budged. Spiritual disease can set in when any of us has disappointment that is not brought into the open for God's healing touch. *"Hope deferred makes the heart sick..."* (Prov. 13:12). I knew that allowing disappointment to dominate my heart would cause a blinding of my eyes to the hand of God working in me.

Strengthening myself in the Lord helped me to stay away from anxiety long enough to make an important discovery: next to the thousand-pound rock is a five hundred-pound rock that I couldn't have moved before the battle for my dad's life. Pushing against the rock that never moved actually strengthened me by reinforcing my resolve to live in divine purpose and to establish the backbone of perseverance. By refusing to change my focus, I discovered that I can now move the five hundred-pound rock that I couldn't have moved before the battle. To keep myself from the sickness of heart warned about in Proverbs 13:12, I monitored the *attitude* of my heart. This was one way of turning my valley of weeping into springs of refreshing, for it is from the heart that all the issues of life flow. (See Proverbs 4:23.)

I can't afford to have thoughts in my head that aren't in God's. It's a great misconception to think that God gives cancer—He doesn't have it to give. I refuse to blame God for my dad's cancer, or any other calamity in life, for that matter. We simply live in a world of conflict and sin. Bad stuff happens. While I may not understand "why," I do understand that neither God nor His covenant is deficient.

While God is big enough to use every situation for His glory, it doesn't mean that the given problem was His will. Not everything that happens in life is God's will. We must stop blaming Him. The cornerstone of our theology is the fact that *God is always good and is the giver of only good gifts.* He is always faithful, and always keeps His promises. There is no evil or darkness in Him.

His goodness and faithfulness become the focus of my praise. I celebrate those aspects of His nature during what sometimes appear to be *contradictory circumstances.* After my dad's death, I discovered the privilege of giving God a sacrificial offering of praise that I will never be able to give Him in eternity. My offering was given in the midst of sadness, disappointment, and confusion—none of which will I ever experience in Heaven. Only in this life will we be able to give an offering with that kind of "fragrance."

If we fall short in our pursuit of a miracle, the lack is never on God's side of the equation. When the disciples were tempted to think in that way, Jesus gave them insight into the real issue, saying, "*This kind can come out by nothing but prayer and fasting*" (Mark 9:29). Most of us who fast and pray tend to do so in pursuit of a specific miracle instead of pursuing a miracle lifestyle. Jesus neither fasted nor prayed in this situation because His life was filled with prayer and fasting, which gave Him access to the desired supernatural way of living. We must think in terms of gaining access to a *lifestyle* instead of only obtaining a one-time breakthrough in a specific circumstance. We owe the world around us that kind of a heavenly demonstration.

Learning to face the possibility of lack on our end, without succumbing to guilt and shame, is key to maintaining focus in the pursuit of the Christ-like life of miracles. I refuse to sacrifice the revelation that *God is always good* on the altar of human reason because of my need to make sense of my seemingly unanswered prayer. I much prefer the discomfort caused by realizing an area of immaturity in my life if it will provoke me to pursue God until I get a breakthrough. Many who discover and admit to their need for personal growth in the midst of tragic loss fall into regret and self-criticism. Regret is a common killer in the church and must be dealt with—get it covered by the blood of Jesus and leave it there!

Use your loss as the foundation for another person's gain by calling for divine justice! That means I must continue pursuing the same breakthrough I was seeking for my dad, but now change my focus to others who have the same need. God's system of justice requires a thief to pay back seven times what he stole. I am asking God for a seven times greater anointing against cancer than I had before. (Interestingly, right after I wrote this part of the chapter, I received a testimony of another case of cancer healed through our ministry—*pancreatic cancer! That* is divine justice!)

You Have Been Summoned

An invitation is before us. We are living in days of revival in which God is bringing wonderful times of refreshing to His Church and drawing the lost to taste His salvation through mighty acts of power. But through this extravagant outpouring of grace, the Father is hoping to woo a generation of His sons and daughters to embrace the call to maturity, the call to contend in His strength for the personal breakthroughs we need to carry greater measures of His Kingdom power and love to the world around us. This is the race set before us. May we be those who learn to bring strength to ourselves, that we might run with perseverance!

Chapter 10

NOT ON
MY SHIFT!

*Through Him, we have
authority over every storm.*

Our call to disciple nations begins with the understanding of what it means to be a disciple. Jesus made the requirements to follow Him very clear: "*He who does not take his cross and follow after Me is not worthy of Me*" (Matt. 10:38). Jesus is not saying that we have to experience punishment for our sins. That alone was His cross to bear. Taking up your cross means embracing the truth that your life is not about you. Romans 14:7 puts it this way, "*For none of us lives to himself, and no one dies to himself.*" Jesus' cross was not about Him. His cross was about pleasing His Father and redeeming us. Likewise, our cross is not about us, but about living our lives for Christ and doing our part to make His mission succeed on earth.

The life of David shows us that personal break-through releases a corporate blessing to those around us. The Cross of Christ did the same thing, as it was Jesus' personal breakthrough. He had a destiny to fulfill that demanded great strength to be able to resist any temptation, distraction, or opposition that would turn Him from His course. His obedience released the greatest corporate blessing in history—salvation made available for the entire human race. Likewise, the cross we embrace will release a blessing, not only to the people around us who experience the benefits of Jesus' salvation, but to the Lord, who through our stewardship takes possession of His inheritance on earth.

Paul tells us that we are "*...heirs of God and joint heirs with Christ, if indeed we suffer with Him, that we may also be glorified together*" (Rom. 8:17). Jesus suffered by resisting the very things He would overcome through His death and resurrection—the kingdom of darkness and its reign of sin and death over the human race. Likewise, the cross we take up and the suffering that we endure as believers is the resistance of the enemy forces that we have been delegated to displace from the land that we have inherited with Christ. Exercising the power and authority we've been given to take our territory from the enemy is what strengthens our character to stand in a place of influence in that territory to establish the Kingdom. We're not merely to bind the strongman, kick him out of the house, and take back what he has stolen from us. We're supposed to become Kingdom strongmen who can release the blessings of Heaven to fill the house.

This is what Jesus was trying to teach His disciples in Mark 4. He told them it was time to pack up their ministry on one side of the lake and cross over to the other side, a region where they had not yet heard the message of the Kingdom. On the way they encountered a storm that attempted to destroy them. Jesus calmed the storm with a word and they were able to complete their journey. When they reached the shore, a demon-possessed madman came out of the hills and started worshiping Jesus. When Jesus cast the demons out, they begged not to be sent away from that geographical location. This indicated that the demons possessing the man were in control of the principality over the region. He had been their strongman to legislate an atmosphere of chaos in the area, and the storm that tried to prevent Jesus and His disciples from entering the region was a manifestation of their power. But their power was insufficient to keep the man from worshiping Jesus (no number of demons can stop anyone from worshiping Jesus!) The man's worship brought him under the superior authority of the Kingdom, and the principality over the region was displaced.

This disturbance to the atmosphere was so violent that the people in the region became fearful and demanded that Jesus and His disciples leave. Yet Jesus wouldn't let His new convert follow Him away from his own town even though it was an extremely hostile environment for a young believer. Instead, He commissioned him to lead His evangelistic outreach to the region: "...*Go home to your friends, and tell them what great things the Lord has done for you, and how He has had compassion on you*" (Mark 5:19). Some time later when Jesus returned to the area, every person in every city showed up to hear Him. One man's encounter with Jesus shifted the perspective of an entire multitude from rejecting God to hungering for Him.

WHEN UNBELIEF GETS AN ANSWERED PRAYER

It's a marvelous story, but we often miss the implication of a certain moment. After Jesus calmed the storm, He turned to His disciples and said, "*Why are you so fearful? How is it that you have no faith?*" (Mark 4:40). To many of us, His response seems a little extreme. We think it's our job to ask God to fix our problems, and it is His job to answer. But Jesus was saying, "I just had to do the job that I've trained you to do."

Jesus told His disciples that it was better for Him to go away because then His Father could send the Holy Spirit to dwell within us. This means that in the storms of our lives, we're better off than the disciples, who merely had Jesus sleeping in the boat with them. We have His very Spirit dwelling inside us. If we follow His lead, we will always have authority over the storm. But when we try to save our lives rather than leaning into the assignment and destiny that the Father has given us, we are not only costing ourselves an opportunity for a personal breakthrough in our faith; we are costing the people in the sphere of influence to which God has called us the opportunity to experience the blessing that is released when our faith displaces an oppressive atmosphere with a heavenly one. So many Christians look at the storms in their lives and the corruption in the world and conclude that their job is just to try to hang on until they die or until the Rapture. But people of faith have a different perspective—they look into the storm and see the opportunity of a lifetime. Through Him, we have authority over every storm.

> Through Him, we have authority over every storm.

Spiritual giants have the habit of rising up during history's darkest moments to meet the challenge. People like Jonathan Edwards, William Booth, John G. Lake, and Aimee Semple McPherson were true disciples of Christ who captured the understanding that everything Jesus did was a model for their personal assignment. They looked into the storms of their day—the manifestations of the kingdom of darkness in the territory they were convicted was the rightful inheritance of the Lord—and rose up with faith to displace those storms, declaring, "Not on my shift!" Knowing their assignment was to shape the course of world history, they refused to give in to the sheer volume of darkness that surrounded them. They saw that all of Heaven backed them in their *humanly impossible* assignment.

Now is the time to allow the stories of these men and women of God to do more than awe us. Jesus never intended that only a few special believers would walk in a great anointing like His to change the spiritual climate over regions. He had trained every one of His disciples in that boat to do what He did. It is time for a whole generation of believers to embrace the opportunity before them—to take up their cross and contend for the breakthroughs that will allow God to entrust them with measures of anointing great enough to take back the inheritance we are invited to share with Him.

To do this, we will need great courage because we will be required to take risks when we step out in faith into what we've seen and heard from the Lord. We will never take that step if our hope rests on experiencing another great event, like waiting for the next wave of revival to sweep in or a prophet to call us out and give us a word. We must take personal responsibility to strengthen every weak place and break our agreement with fear. We must become the ongoing manifestation of revival and stop waiting for outside circumstances to line up with our dreams. We do this by giving thanks and rejoicing, praying as He prays, meditating on promises and testimonies, and associating with people of faith—not just when others around us are doing so, but continuously, as a lifestyle.

Utilizing these tools is the only way we can access the strength and courage we need in the midst of the storm because they remind us of who we are and what God has commissioned us to do. Most of all, they remind us that we are fully equipped for victory, not because we have a formula that always works, but because *God is with us and within us.*

This is His promise for every son and daughter who hears the call to contend for their promised land:

> *Have I not commanded you? Be strong and of good courage; do not be afraid, nor be dismayed, for the LORD your God is with you wherever you go* (Joshua 1:9).